Caroline Dakers is Professor ⸢   ⸥story at Central Saint Martins (University of the Arts L   ⸥n). Her previous books include *Clouds: The Biography of a Country House*; *The Holland Park Circle*; and *A Genius for Money: Business, Art* and *the Morrisons*.

FOREVER ENGLAND

The Countryside at War
1914–1918

CAROLINE DAKERS

LONDON · NEW YORK

New edition published in 2016 by
I.B.Tauris & Co. Ltd
London • New York
www.ibtauris.com

First published in hardback in 1987 by Constable and Company Limited

ISBN: 978 1 78453 484 4

A full CIP record for this book is available from the British Library
A full CIP record is available from the Library of Congress

Library of Congress Catalog Card Number: available

Printed and bound by CPI Group (UK) Ltd, Croydon, CR0 4YY

Contents

	Illustrations	vii
	Preface to Paperback Edition	1
	Acknowledgements	9
	Introduction	11
1.	Over by Christmas	21
2.	Writers and Artists in the Countryside	47
3.	In the Manor House	76
4.	In the Village	105
5.	On the Farm: The Fight for Food	130
6.	In Foreign Fields	158
7.	Aftermath: The Countryside at Peace	183
	References	211
	Bibliography	223
	Index	229

Illustrations

'A Wish' by George Clausen (*Imperial War Museum*)
The Old Nailshop
Little Iddens
Weirleigh
'Going Home' by 'a Subaltern, R.F.A.'
More sketches by 'a Subaltern, R.F.A.'
The Artists Rifles (*Copyright Horace W. Nicholls*)
Stanway House (*Earl of Wemyss*)
Stanway House (*Earl of Wemyss*)
Amisfield (*Earl of Wemyss*)
Mells Manor House (by kind permission of *Country Life*)
Sir John Horner (*Earl of Oxford and Asquith*)
Frances Horner (*Earl of Oxford and Asquith*)
Mells Village Post Office 1912 (*Millicent Holmes*)
Mells Village Post Office 1915 (*Millicent Holmes*)
Mells Park House (*Millicent Holmes*)
Open letter from Sir John and Frances Horner (*Millicent Holmes*)
Designs for Mells Park House by Sir Edwin Lutyens (*RIBA*)
Mells Park House (*Millicent Holmes*)
Clouds (by kind permission of *Country Life*)
Clouds drawing room (*Earl of Wemyss*)
Clouds (*Earl of Wemyss*)
Rt. Hon. George Wyndham and his son Perf (*Earl of Wemyss*)
Lieutenant Percy Wyndham (*Copyright Bassano*)
Babraham Hall (*Earl of Wemyss*)
Charles Adeane (*Royal Agricultural Society of England*)
St Mary's Fletching
'The Cottager's Roll of Honour'
Woman-Power (*Punch*)
'Deserving the Medaille Militaire' (*Copyright Emil Frechon*)
Dexter-Angus bulls at Sandringham

Sketch by Ms C. M. M. Prunell, land girl (*Imperial War Museum*)
'A Land Girl Ploughing' by Cecil Aldin (*Imperial War Museum*)
'Hoeing' by Randolph Schwabe (*Imperial War Museum*)
'The Women's Land Army and German Prisoners' by Randolph
    Schwabe (*Imperial War Museum*)
'Binks's Patent Futurist Scarecrow' (*Punch*)
Frank Cook's paint box
Neuf Moulin, near Abbeville by Frank Cook (*Lt. Col. Frank Palmer
    Cook, OBE, TD*)
Vauchelles, Somme by Frank Cook (*Lt. Col. Frank Palmer Cook, OBE, TD*)
Zouave Wood, Ypres Salient by Frank Cook (*Lt. Col. Frank Palmer
    Cook, OBE, TD*)
Yvo Charteris's grave (*Earl of Wemyss*)
Edward Thomas's grave
Raymond Asquith's grave
Firing line in front of Ypres 1915 by Frank Cook (*Lt. Col. Frank
    Palmer Cook, OBE, TD*)
Trenches, Beaumont Hamel
View of the Somme and Lutyens's Memorial to the Missing at Thiepval
Mary Wemyss at Longniddry (*Earl of Wemyss*)
Mary Wemyss as a young girl by Val Prinsep (*Earl of Wemyss*)
Mary Wemyss as a young woman by Edward Poynter (*Earl of Wemyss*)
Wemyss Terrace Longniddry
Frontispiece to Village Centres Council pamphlet (*Imperial War Museum*)
Stanway House *c.* 1923 (*Copyright W.J. Butt, Earl of Wemyss*)
Stanway grounds July 1929 (*Earl of Wemyss*)
David Charteris at Stanway (*Earl of Oxford and Asquith*)
Julian Asquith (*Earl of Oxford and Asquith*)
Aberlady War Memorial
Mells Village War Memorial
Statue of Edward Horner (*Earl of Oxford and Asquith*)
Design for Edward Horner Memorial by Sir Edwin Lutyens (*RIBA*)
Broad Chalk War Memorial

Preface to Paperback Edition

Even if historians write forwards, telling a sequential narrative, they *think* backwards from the present into the past.[1]

The life of the country and city is moving and present.[2]

Forever England: The Countryside at War 1914–1918 was first published in 1987, almost seventy years after the end of the First World War. The idea behind the book was new, to make connections and examine the contradictions between the physical effects of war on the countryside of England and France and the response of writers and artists. While farmers, deprived of their horses and labourers, struggled to meet government demands for more wheat, writers expressed the often-repeated sentiment that it was worth dying in defence of an imagined, predominantly rural England. The poet Edward Thomas's response when asked why he was enlisting is typical: 'He stopped, and picked up a pinch of earth. "Literally, for this." He crumbled it between finger and thumb, and let it fall.'[3] The idea was not confined to writers, but commonly expressed in popular culture and, during the war, by soldiers: 'I always feel that I am fighting for England, English fields, lanes, trees, English atmospheres, and good days in England.'[4]

During the war, an unchanging pastoral landscape was perceived to be under attack from invading rapacious Germans. But the results of victory were not always welcome. The poet Edmund Blunden, before the war 'in love with every rural thing', found his soul 'grown strange in France'.

> I have seen a green country, useful to the race,
> Knocked silly with guns and mines, its villages vanished,

Even the last rat and the last kestrel banished –
God bless us all, this was peculiar grace.[5]

The young architect Clough Williams-Ellis was horrified at the post-war building of council-houses he could only see as blots on the landscape: 'we were invited to preserve England. We believed, we fought . . . we saved our country that we might ourselves destroy it.'[6] But with no heirs to inherit, many large estates were broken up and villagers were left to erect memorials to the dead, whose bodies remained in 'foreign fields'.

In *The Long Shadow*, one of the more recent books marking the centenary of the First World War, David Reynolds notes the power of this rural ideal: 'for many during the Great War, both in Britain and at the front, the "civilization" for which they fought . . . boiled down to a profound if nebulous love of home, often expressed in pastoral idiom . . . man and nature ravaged in Flanders fields; man and nature in harmony in an idealized England.'[7] The linking of such an idea to the actual impact of the war on the land and the effects of government policy – 'the turnip is just as important as the shell and the Army'[8] – remains unique to *Forever England: The Countryside at War 1914–1918*.

In this preface I shall take advantage of the historian's ability to 'think backwards', to consider the context in which my original research was carried out, and then to note some of the changes that have occurred, the losses and the gains, not just in the interpretations of the war but also in approaches to research.

My own research began in the mid-1970s, for my PhD examining the response of English writers to the countryside from 1900 to 1930. Two of the most significant books informing this work were Raymond Williams, *The Country and the City* (1973) and Paul Fussell, *The Great War and Modern Memory* (1975); both became not just bestsellers but exerted a profound influence on the development of cultural studies (even though regularly repudiated by historians). Williams's analysis of the continuing pull of the country provided a convincing context for my analysis of the romantic and sentimental attitudes that prevailed, certainly in the early years of the war. 'English attitudes to the country, and to ideas of rural life, persisted with extraordinary power, so that even after the society was predominantly urban its literature, for a generation, was still predominantly rural; and even in the twentieth century, in an urban and industrial land, forms of the older ideas and experiences still remarkably persist.'[9] Fussell's exploration of the literary means by which 'the British experience on the Western Front . . . has been remembered, conventionalized, and mythologized' offered a very different approach to war studies.[10] The chapters 'Oh What a Literary War' and 'Arcadian Recourses' contextualised both my PhD and, later, *Forever England: The Countryside at War 1914–1918*.

There was no anniversary deemed significant enough to produce major commemorative events in either 1978 (sixty years after the end of the war) or 1988 (seventy years). More immediate events engulfed Britain, including the election of Margaret Thatcher in 1979, another war, in the Falklands (1982) and two years later the miners' strike. However a number of books were published that used important archives for the first time. Meirion and Susie Harries, *The War Artists: British Official War Art of the Twentieth Century* (1983) stands out. It was, as its blurb says, 'the first comprehensive account of the British official war art schemes beginning in 1916'. The Harries used the archives of both the Imperial War Museum and the Tate Gallery and although their book contained only a brief section on the home front, it opened up these extensive collections of visual material. Andrew Causey's study of Paul Nash (1980) and Frances Spalding's study of Vanessa Bell (1983) also used the Tate and the Imperial War Museum and remain the major monographs on these artists.

David Reynolds claims the 'Great War poets became iconic'[11] in the 1960s, naming key moments such as the fuller edition of Wilfred Owen's *Collected Poems* (1963) and Benjamin Britten's use of Owen in his *War Requiem* (1962). Much more followed: Jon Stallworthy's biography of Owen (1973), two biographies of Isaac Rosenberg in 1975; Edna Longley's edition of Edward Thomas's poetry (1973) and Jan Marsh's biography (1978). And, in the 1980s, Ivor Gurney's *War Letters*, edited by R.K.R. Thornton (1984) and Siegfried Sassoon's revelatory *Diaries 1915–1918*, edited by Rupert Hart-Davis (1983). There were many more. War poetry has never gone out of fashion.

A key book, Philip Longworth's *The Unending Vigil*, was revised and republished in 1985. Longworth had used, for the first time, the papers of the Commonwealth War Graves Commission and the unique contribution of Fabian Ware or 'Lord Wargraves'. Ware had taken a British Red Cross Unit out to France in September 1914 to locate and record the graves of the dead and by May 1917 his efforts resulted in 150,000 marked graves in Belgium and France. He also approached the architects Edwin Lutyens and Herbert Baker to design the permanent cemeteries to be built when the war was over. Unremarked in 1967, the new edition arrived just as the concept of public memory, of the memorialisation of conflict, emerged in academia. Reynolds is critical, referring to the phenomenon as the 'memory boom'. The war was reduced to a saga of personal tragedies, poetry not history, remembrance rather than understanding.[12] Edmund Blunden had written the original introduction for Longworth, recalling his own experiences in 'far-stretching battlefields . . . scattered with the remains of apparently for ever forgotten soldiers'.[13] When the poet died in 1974, Flanders poppies were placed on his coffin.

The 1980s also saw the arrival of personal testimony as a new academic approach. The Federation of British Family History Societies had been founded in 1974, three years after Paul Thompson, at the University of Essex, founded the Oral History Society. Thompson's work was pioneering, leading in 1987 to the creation of the National Life Story Collection, now re-branded the British Library's National Sound Archive, with the aim to 'record firsthand experiences of as wide a cross-section of present-day society as possible'.

Of course it was still possible in the 1980s (and even the 1990s) to speak to men and women – possibly one's own parents and grandparents – who had been young adults during the First World War, who might have seen active service abroad, or worked in armaments factories or on the land. Children who lived through the war years, who had perhaps lost fathers in France, at Gallipoli, in North Africa, were able to describe their own experiences 'on the home front'; some had become the keepers of family albums and scrapbooks dedicated by grieving mothers and grandmothers to their own fallen heroes. For the cultural (and oral) historian these oral testimonies were unique, offering a direct link with the past.

Frank Cook, artist, soldier and architect, was a friend of my parents, living in Cheltenham. When he enlisted in 1914, he was a young trainee architect from Devon with a fondness for the English countryside (his father ploughed with oxen). He survived the Somme and a gas attack (he lost an eye) and returned with his paint box and sketchbooks. In 1987 he was still painting the English countryside. His extensive collection of sketchbooks included one from the Second World War which he had later titled 'Out of Battle' (he had again joined up and been promoted to Lt. Colonel). His Nash-like drawings from the First World War triggered moving stories of the hospitality of the French peasants behind the lines and of friends blown up around him.

But Frank was one of a diminishing number and I never recorded his recollections. On 11 November 2009, a 'Service to Mark the Passing of the World War I Generation' was held in Westminster Abbey following the death of the last three soldiers who had served in the Great War, including Harry Patch. Lt. Colonel Frank Cook had died in 1994 aged 100.

Such personal contact is no longer possible, instead we have the internet and access to information from around the world, much of it digitised. Frank Cook's sketches will eventually be given to the Imperial War Museum to join the 18,000 individual collections of private papers as well as art, film and photographs, 'the reactions, memories and stories of the whole of society'. The museum celebrates the 'everyday' as well as the 'exceptional'; digitised and freely searchable online. One click provides images of the Women's Land Army, another brings up an essay on the fight for food; diaries of land girls I read thirty years ago are now digitised.

Writing the 'Afterword' for the 2000 edition of *The Great War and Modern Memory,* Paul Fussell described his experience researching at the Imperial War Museum a quarter of a century before. 'Every day for three months I presented myself with my researcher's pass to be conducted by a warder past the tanks and cannons installed on the ground floor, up stairways and elevators to the very top of the building. There, I was assigned a room containing nothing but a long table and a chair ... The stuff I read was in beat-up cartons, mostly, and its authenticity and variety took my breath away.'[14]

For the individual in search of family history and the war the access to information has been revolutionary. Longworth's history of the Commonwealth War Graves Commission cannot be compared to the Commission's new website with its searchable list of the fallen in both world wars, or the searchable service records of veterans in the National Archives. And Google Earth can provide a virtual tour of the cemeteries and battlefields. There is more, much more, online, including newspapers, the census, wills, birth and death certificates. TV programmes such as *Who do you think you are?,* first aired by the BBC in 2004, provide examples and inspiration.

This active localism and personal empowerment has been taken up for the centenary events, with the offer of funding from the Heritage Lottery Fund for community projects on 'The First World War: then and now'. Grants are also available from the War Memorials Trust, founded in 1997 to preserve some 100,000 war memorials across Britain. These grants are predictably being taken up by small- and medium-sized rural communities: the 'countryside at war' has become the memories of the war unlocked in the countryside. In Somerset, for example, a group has been formed with a grant of £66,500 from the HLF 'to explore the impact and long-term effect of the conflict on the county'. 'Somerset Remembers' is engaged in a range of tasks including 'reading the minutes of the Somerset War Agricultural Executive Committee from 1917'.

I have also been absorbed, at least part of the time, by the new localism. My journey since 1987 has brought me to a village in south

Wiltshire of just 200 men, women and children, still firmly linked to the land and to farming. It is surrounded by the sort of 'English soil' Edward Thomas, Siegfried Sassoon and Rupert Brooke thought they were fighting for; similar to the chalk landscapes in France, the lovely valley of the Somme.

One of the major impacts of the war on the countryside was the sale of land by landowners without heirs or fearful of the future of farming. *The Times* published an article in May 1920 noting 'England is changing hands' and by the following year some 6-8 million acres, a quarter of England, had indeed changed hands, including the Wiltshire estate of the 13th Duke of Hamilton. My cottage was part of the Duke's estate, and was sold to its tenant in 1920 for £50. From my window I can see land farmed by the same family who acquired it from the Duke after the war.

Here, we have been marking the centenary of the war by using the new digital resources to unlock the history of the young men listed on the modest war memorial inside the parish church. As David Reynolds observed, these names 'exert their own power over the living, stirring our imagination to call back the men from the shadows'.[15] Cupboards are being opened, albums dusted down. A lecture I gave in the village hall was illustrated by surviving photographs of one of the first Overtime tractors to be sent from the USA at the end of the war. Some of the audience recognised the men proudly posing beside the brand-new machine.

Berwick St John is just a few miles from the church and war memorial at Broad Chalk, the final illustration in *Forever England: The Countryside at War 1914–1918*. The memorial has changed little since 1987 when I took the photograph (and never thought I would live nearby). And the lines by Maurice Hewlett written to mark its dedication still resonate here, in 2015, in deepest England.

Eighteen out of ninety of our young men did not come back; and now we have their names as nearly imperishable as may be, and much more so than the poor faithful dust strewn in

France, or the gentle memories which will last no longer than ourselves.[16]

As Raymond Williams wrote forty years ago 'the life of country and city is moving and present'.[17]

Caroline Dakers
Berwick St John, 2015

1 David Reynolds, *The Long Shadow: The Great War and the Twentieth Century* (London, 2013), p.418.
2 Raymond Williams, *The Country and the City* (Oxford, 1973), p.17.
3 Eleanor Farjeon, *Edward Thomas The Last Four Years* (Oxford, 1979), p.154.
4 Lieutenant Carver, Royal Field Artillery, writing home from France, included in Laurence Housman (ed.), *War Letters of Fallen Englishmen* (London, 1930), p.68.
5 From Edmund Blunden, 'Report on Experience', in Max Egremont (ed.), *Some Desperate Glory: The First World War the Poets Knew* (New York, 2014), p.292.
6 Clough Williams-Ellis, *England and the Octopus* (London, 1928), p.20.
7 Reynolds, *The Long Shadow*, p.194.
8 Lord Selbourne, President of the Board of Agriculture, reported in *Country Life*, 1 July 1916.
9 Williams, *The Country and the City*, pp.10-11.
10 Paul Fussell, *The Great War and Modern Memory* (New York, 2009), p. ix, 1st published 1975.
11 Reynolds, *The Country and the City*, p.342.
12 Reynolds, *The Country and the City*, p.387.
13 Edmund Blunden, introduction to Philip Longworth, *The Unending Vigil* (London, 1985), p.xvii, 1st published 1967.
14 Fussell, *The Great War and Modern Memory*, p.425.
15 Reynolds, *The Country and the City*, p.434.
16 Maurice Hewlett, 'We Commend Our Dead', *Wiltshire Essays* (Oxford, 1921), p.210.
17 Williams, *The Country and the City*, p.17.

Acknowledgements

I owe especial thanks to the Earl of Oxford and Asquith, the Earl of Wemyss, Lord Neidpath, Lady Helen Asquith and Lt. Colonel Frank Palmer Cook. They read chapters of the book in draft and gave valuable critical opinions as well as correcting errors of fact. Frank Palmer Cook remembers vividly his experiences in the trenches and has kindly allowed me to use some of his sketches for illustrations; Lord Oxford and Lord Neidpath have lent many family photographs from Mells and Stanway.

My thanks also to the many who have allowed me to read family papers and answered endless questions, particularly James and Olinda Adeane, Alan Copps, Letitia Fowler, Pansy Helps, Millicent Holmes, Nora Osborne and Joan Wyndham.

And also to those who have answered letters and telephone queries and offered help in libraries and archives: Jeremy Alexander of *The Field*; Donald Anderle, New York Public Library; Squadron Leader Baker of the Scottish Veterans Garden City Association; Dr Isabel Barnes, National Register of Archives (Scotland); the staff of the Bath Newspaper Library; Nicola Beauman; Beryl Bradley, Uckfield Library; John Burt, University of Sussex Library; Paula Chesterman, *Punch*; Camilla Costello, *Country Life*; Dr Barry Cross, Director of the Institute of Animal Physiology and Genetics, Babraham Hall; Jane Cunningham-Reid; Charlotte Gere; Nigel Harvey, Honorary Librarian and Angela Small, Royal Agricultural Society of England; Gwyneth Hodge, Tonbridge Library; Hon. John Jolliffe; Michael McGarvie; the Drs McMann, Clouds Life Anew Trust; Dr Jan Marsh;

D. S. Porter, Bodleian Library; the staff of the RIBA Library and Drawings Collection; Mr and Mrs Norman Sneesby; Roderick Suddaby, Keeper of the Department of Documents, Imperial War Museum; the local history librarian, Taunton Library; Lance Thirkell; Mr and Mrs C. Wheeler; Jennifer Wood, Department of Art, Imperial War Museum; Francis Wyndham; Mrs Wynniatt, Stanway village.

Lastly, my gratitude to Nigel Cross for reading and re-reading the manuscript, for offering much pertinent advice, for accompanying me to the valley of the Somme and to numerous English villages and for minding our daughter who was born during the completion of the final draft.

For permission to quote from copyright material I would like to thank Valerie Corden, daughter of Edith Airey; Crane and Walton, solicitors, for extracts from Captain Bartlett's papers; Charles Dent, descendant of Geoffrey and Arthur Dent; Faber and Faber Ltd for extracts from *Memoirs of an Infantry Officer*, *The Weald of Youth*, *Siegfried's Journey* and *Diaries 1915–1918*, edited by Rupert Hart-Davis; John Freedman and Brian Cooper, executors of Mrs Rosa Freedman; for extracts from the diary of the Rev. Andrew Clark, © James Munson 1985 reprinted from *Echoes of the Great War* by Andrew Clark edited by James Munson (1985) by permission of Oxford University Press; Alison Rendle, the National Trust, for extracts from the papers of Rudyard Kipling; George Sassoon for extracts from the poetry of Siegfried Sassoon; Myfanwy Thomas (poetry, prose and letters of Edward Thomas; extracts from *Time and Again* by Helen Thomas); Elizabeth Wilson, agent for the heirs of Robert Saunders; A. P. Watt Ltd on behalf of the executors of the estate of Robert Graves (extract from a letter from Robert Graves to Siegfried Sassoon in the Berg Collection, New York Public Library).

Introduction

SIEGFRIED SASSOON was cycling through the sunny Kent countryside on the last Friday in July, 1914. It was just before the August Bank Holiday, but he was not in a holiday mood. Mrs Anley, mother of two colonels on the active list, had been visiting his mother at Paddock Wood. The rumours she brought from the War Office left Sassoon in no doubt that Britain was on the brink of war.

Sassoon had lived almost all of his twenty-eight years in the Weald of Kent. The gently-rolling countryside with its carefully tended orchards and hop-fields had provided him with support, inspiration and a sense of permanence. Now, as he pedalled towards Weirleigh, his family's Victorian country home, the familiar landscape had somehow changed. The Weald seemed content enough, the weather was perfect, the sky cloudless. However, Sassoon's awareness of impending doom affected the way he looked at his rural surroundings. Two hop-kilns, passed many times before with barely a glance, suddenly appeared 'half-tragic in their homely simplicity . . . their kindly cowls were like sign-posts pointing towards the ominous continent of Europe.'[1]

Sassoon felt the approaching war to be a direct threat to his countryside. 'The Weald had been the world of my youngness, and while I gazed across it now I felt prepared to do what I could to defend it. And after all, dying for one's native land was believed to be the most glorious thing one could possibly do!'[2] The next day he volunteered and was passed fit for active service. On Monday, the day before England declared war on Germany, he was in khaki, a private in the Sussex Yeomanry.

Rupert Brooke went on a tour of the English countryside over the Bank Holiday weekend, staying with family and friends in Herefordshire, Warwickshire and Norfolk. His response to the declaration of war appeared in 'An Unusual Young Man', published in the *New Statesman* in August. 'With a sudden tightening of his heart, he realized that there might be a raid on the English coast. He didn't imagine any possibility of it *succeeding*, but only of enemies and warfare on English soil. The idea sickened him.'[3] Sassoon imagined himself dodging about the hop-fields and orchards of Kent shooting at Germans massing in his English fields. Brooke is vaguer: 'English soil' is about to be desecrated. But it is very special soil to which he attaches mystical importance. He tries hesitantly to define its quality – which only the threat of invasion has made apparent to him – a quality which 'if he'd ever been sentimental enough to use the word, he'd have called "holiness"'.[4] Brooke's response is intensely nationalistic: 'It seemed to him the most desirable thing in the world to mingle and talk with a great many English people'. And to preserve qualities he defines as 'gentleness' and 'holiness' he is prepared to fight and to die: 'Well, if Armageddon's *on*, I suppose one should be there.'[5]

When he was in Herefordshire, Brooke stayed with a fellow Georgian poet, Wilfrid Gibson. Gibson rented 'The Old Nailshop', a half-timbered cottage situated in a small village a few miles from Ledbury. The Old Nailshop was the meeting-place for several country-loving writers throughout 1914: Robert Frost and Lascelles Abercrombie rented cottages near by, W. H. Davies and Eleanor Farjeon came from London, John Drinkwater came from Birmingham and Edward Thomas from Kent.

Thomas arrived on Bank Holiday Monday with his son; his wife and daughters followed the next day. The approach of a world war was not going to alter their plans to spend all of August in good company in the English countryside. However, Helen Thomas's journey across England on the last day of peace was made through a country already stirred up by war-excitement. 'Families on holiday were hurrying home, reservists were being called up and soldiers recalled from leave, and everywhere the stations were thronged with trunks, kitbags and other luggage and with restless and anxious people.'[6] The last stage of the journey involved a night-drive over the Malvern Hills under a full harvest moon.

Edward Thomas, walking through the countryside of orchards and meadows, experienced the same response to the declaration of war as Sassoon and Brooke.

> All I can tell is, it seemed to me that either I had never loved England, or had loved it foolishly, aesthetically, like a slave, not having realized that it was not mine unless I were willing and prepared to die rather than leave it as Belgian women and old men and children had left their country. Something I had omitted. Something, I felt, had to be done before I could look again composedly at English landscape, at the elms and poplars about the houses, at the purple-headed wood-betony with two pairs of dark leaves on a stiff stem, who stood sentinel among the grasses or bracken by hedge-side or wood's edge. What he stood sentinel for I did not know, any more than what I had got to do.[7]

What Thomas finally decided he had to do in order 'to look again composedly at English landscape' was enlist, at the age of thirty-six, the father of three young children. He joined the Artists' Rifles on 14 July 1915. After he enlisted, he was asked by Eleanor Farjeon what he was fighting for. 'He stopped, and picked up a pinch of earth. "literally, for this". He crumbled it between finger and thumb, and let it fall.'[8]

These three writers, Siegfried Sassoon, Rupert Brooke and Edward Thomas, exemplify the patriotic feelings about the English countryside which surfaced with the declaration of war. They were obviously more articulate than most of the thousands of young and not so young men who offered their lives for their country in August 1914. However, the desire to defend the English countryside was not confined to writers. There was a genuine feeling at the outbreak of war that rapacious Germans physically threatened English fields, woods, villages, streams and maidens. Lieutenant Carver of the Royal Field Artillery wrote home from France: 'I always feel that I am fighting for England, English fields, lanes, trees, English atmospheres, and good days in

England – and all that is synonymous for liberty'.[9] And a captain in the Cambridgeshire Regiment serving in France looked forwar to defeating Germany so that he could return home when 'the true business of life will begin – to teach men the beauty of the hillsides'.[10]

This romantic and idealistic view of England was voiced by the upper classes: public schoolboys raised on the highest standards of chivalry and valour. However, it must have been a view that was shared by many common soldiers. Less articulate than the officer class which included the writers Sassoon, Brooke and Thomas, they have left little written evidence of why they were prepared to die for their country. An exception is the farm labourer veteran who revealed to Ronald Blythe 'we were all so patriotic then and had been taught to love England in a fierce kind of way. The village wasn't England; England was something better than the village.'[11] In 'August 1914' John Masefield describes what he thought was the response of the men who farmed the land around his Berkshire cottage: throughout the war poets were quick to jump to conclusions on behalf of the silent majority. Masefield's labourers have defended their part of England generation after generation. They love the Berkshire loam 'dumbly', 'as breaks the hearts of the English kind',

> Then sadly rose and left the well-loved Downs,
> And so by ship to sea, and knew no more
> The fields of home, the byres, the market towns,
> Nor the dear outline of the English shore.[12]

At the end of August Edward Thomas was sent on a tour of England by the *English Review* to discover the attitudes towards the war of as wide a cross-section of the population as possible. To his surprise, although he encountered little opposition or criticism of the war, he could find few citizens willing or able to define their patriotic feelings. Conversations with new recruits and old soldiers, labourers and employers, wives and mothers, touched on any subject but the war. He thought that this avoidance of war and concentration on everyday matters, on the minutiae of village life, of local concerns, was itself part of the patriotic response. The familiar, the known, the loved were the things worth fighting for. In time of war 'the whole land is suddenly home'; England becomes 'she',[13] and threats to her become the concern of every English man and woman.

In trying to define patriotism and the English responses in time of war, Thomas found himself returning again and again to literature.

> I took up the *Compleat Angler* the other day, and felt it there. Since the war began I have not met so English a book, a book that filled me so with a sense of England, as this ... I touched the antiquity and sweetness of England – English fields, English people, English poetry, all together.[14]

This was to be the most literary of wars. And all ranks who fought, as well as those who stayed at home, appreciated and indulged in an unparalleled literariness, from the private who, on going up to the front, quoted Shakespeare,[15] to the lieutenant who reminded his father of Wordsworth's 'Happy Warrior' in the last letter he wrote home before being killed in the Battle of Loos.[16]

Throughout the war the popular press published poems and stories which reached all sections of the population. Anthologies were specially printed on India paper to be sent to the front. Quiller-Couch's *Oxford Book of English Verse* and Robert Bridges' *The Spirit of Man* were two of the most popular anthologies in the trenches. *The Spirit of Man* was first published in January 1916, offering comfort in the midst of 'the insensate and interminable slaughter, the hate and filth'.[17] By the end of the war eight further editions had appeared. Edward Marsh's anthology *Georgian Poetry* was specially selected to be sent to the front and hospitals and a less well-known Georgian anthology, *New Numbers*, found unexpected popularity with the death of Rupert Brooke: it had been the first to publish his 'war' sonnets.

All this popular literature was overwhelmingly concerned with ideas and scenes of rural England, even though only 20% of the population of England and Wales lived in the countryside. However, a high proportion of the population was only one or two generations away from the land and, more important, the culture of the nation, its sense of identity, was inextricably linked to its rural past. George Sturt was a member of a family of wheelwrights who had pursued their ancient craft in Surrey generation after generation. At the outbreak of war he defined the England he thought the 'Prussian armies' were 'outraging': 'England in her comely village customs . . . the pleasant cornfields and country lanes'. He listed the poets who exemplified rural traditions, Milton, Wordsworth, Thomas Gray and William Morris, adding 'adventures and Romance', 'kindliness' and 'tea-time'.[18]

Sturt's England is like the paintings of Helen Allingham. And who but the English would include tea-time in a list of things worth defending from the Prussian armies? Behind Sturt's musings is Rupert Brooke's poem 'The Old Vicarage, Grantchester', a vision of an ideal England dreamed up in a German café, with its unforgettable final lines: 'Stands the Church clock at ten to three? / And is there honey still for tea?' Brooke's poem echoes Thomas's discovery that ideas of England develop out of 'minute neighbouring points of home'. The patriotic feeling about home could, however, come from an imagined home as much as the real thing, a country cottage with roses round the door as much as a back-to-back in a mining village. Going out to France as a war artist, William Rothenstein wrote to Edward Marsh: 'I hope we are fighting for Grantchester: for Grantchester I am willing to squat in a trench or trudge in the desert'.[19]

Throughout the war propagandists used images of rural England to inspire men to enlist. John Galsworthy gave a public speech entitled 'The Islands of the Blessed' in August 1916. Describing the love of country for which men were willing to die, Galsworthy suffused the whole of England in a romantic glow.

> A stealing love has us fast bound; a web of who knows what memories of misty fields, and scents of clover and turned earth; of summer evenings, when sounds are far and clear; of long streets half-lighted, and town sights, not beautiful but homely; of the skies we were born beneath, and the roads we have trodden all our lives.[20]

The stress is on a village home: industrial England is omitted. Two years later, John Masefield made a public speech in America and located the idea of England 'for which men are dying, as I speak, along 5,000 miles of war . . . in the little villages of the land, in the old homes, in the churches, in countless old carvings, in old bridges, in old tunes, and in the old acts of the English'.[21]

By the end of 1914, 1,186,000 men had volunteered to fight for their King and Country. But the countryside whose constancy and permanence had inspired many of them to fight in its defence was to prove only too vulnerable to change. Britain was the only European belligerent to increase her supplies of home-produced food but to do this three million acres of grassland were ploughed up. Thousands of acres were requisitioned for army and prison camps, munitions factories and airfields; extensive areas of woodland were devastated to provide extra timber for use at home and abroad; some country towns and villages were filled to overflowing with officers, soldiers and the machinery of war; country houses were turned into hospitals and their parks were churned up by gun-carriages and tanks; in the fields labourers were replaced by truant schoolchildren, land girls in breeches, able-bodied pacifists, Belgian refugees and German prisoners.

Sassoon, in the front line with 'soaked feet, trench mouth, and feeling short of sleep', sustained his patriotism with memories of an unchanging Sussex and Kent countryside, 'dark green woodlands with pigeons circling above the tree-tops'.[22] But the huntsman he visualises walking out with the hounds is a figment of his imagination. Traditional hunts were disbanded, their huntsmen pursuing Germans instead of foxes. Farmers took the opportunity to erect wire around their fields and shoot the vermin fox. Gamekeepers and poachers were to prove some of the finest trench-soldiers; pheasants and grouse were left to grow old, undisturbed by organised mass slaughter or the surreptitious trap.

Many of the men who fought for the defence of the English countryside did not survive to witness the changes at home. Rupert Brooke died of blood poisoning in the Mediterranean and Edward Thomas was killed at the Battle of Arras. Francis Ledwidge, the Irish poet who took up arms 'for the fields along the Boyne, and the birds and the blue sky over them'[23] was killed in Flanders. Lieutenant Carver who had fought for the fields, lanes and hedges of England also died in France. The English countryside became a memorial to the dead as war memorials were erected in every village and church. Farmers lost sons and their ablest, strongest labourers. Country estates were left without heirs.

The survivors were themselves altered by the experience of war.

[17]

Sassoon had enlisted to defend his beloved Weald of Kent, only to find he was to assist in the destruction of the countryside of northern France, some of it as beautiful as the Weald. Edmund Blunden, 'in love with every rural thing', also left the Weald of Kent for service in France. Returning home after the Armistice he found

> Oaks, once my friends, with ugly murmurings
> Madden me, and ivy whirs like condor wings.
> The very bat that stoops and whips askance
> Shrills malice at the soul grown strange in France.

And then there were the permanently crippled, the blind and the limbless who would never be able to walk, to ride across or to work again in English fields, or even to see the beauty of the countryside. Robert Saunders, headmaster of a village school in Sussex, described the return of the young soldiers on whom he had urged 'the duty of patriotism'. 'Going to school the other day I met Wally Tester in a bath chair . . . you can imagine what he is like with one eye gone, a little piece of nose near the mouth, then a gap, then a little more nose joining the forehead, the face and hands a bluish grey colour.'[25]

Ironically some of the fit survivors, particularly those who managed to avoid the trenches altogether, were able to benefit from the death of others. Landowners, crippled by death duties, or without sons to inherit, sold their estates to the survivors, in some cases enabling their own tenant farmers to own land for the first time. Amesbury Abbey estate, for example, which included Stonehenge, was put on the market in 1915 after the death of its owner, Sir Edmund Antrobus, closely followed by the death in battle of his only son. The farms were bought by Antrobus's tenants. By the end of 1919 over a million acres of land had changed hands in England and Wales.

Even the government bought up land on which to settle ex-soldiers. It was thought that the open-air life digging in no-man's-land was the perfect training for more digging on English smallholdings. County councils acquired land on which to build rows of council houses. Farm labourers might appreciate the replacements for their often insanitary and cramped tied cottages but the architect and ex-soldier Clough Williams-Ellis was scathing about the eyesores which began to surround English villages. 'We were invited to fight to preserve England. We believed, we fought . . . we saved our country that we might ourselves destroy it'.[26]

The war changed farming practices. The teams of plough horses which were once a familiar feature of the landscape had been taken for service in France. Many were blown up along with the gun-carriages they pulled through the Flanders mud. Instead, in the wake of the newly invented tank, tractors and steam ploughs belched and rumbled across English fields. Farming had become more mechanised and more scientific. Attacks on British shipping and the loss of some trading partners led to the development of artificial manures and fertilisers to supplement home supplies. New types of grain were developed, better breeding stock were produced and after the war agricultural research received greater funding from government and industry. All this was a long way from the vision of an unchanging pastoral landscape under attack from invading rapacious Germans.

1

Over by Christmas

THROUGHOUT the weekend just before the August Bank Holiday there were many and varied sights and sounds of the preparations for war. Mary, Countess of Wemyss, entertaining family and friends at Stanway, her Jacobean manor house in Gloucestershire, heard the unfamiliar rumble of trains in the night 'which brought home facts!'[1] The government had taken over the railways and for the next four years troops and the machinery of war would have priority. The guests at Stanway talked endlessly of war and on Sunday Duff Cooper was summoned by his superiors to the Foreign Office. Looking back across the years of war which killed two of her sons, Mary Wemyss recalled 'this sudden summons was the first pebble that fell into the pool of the age-long peace of Stanway, Didbrook and Toddington. They were still drowsy, still scarcely alarmed.'

The Stanway estate was about five thousand acres in size. It was once owned by Tewkesbury Abbey and passed, by marriage, to the Earls of Wemyss at the beginning of the nineteenth century. At the outbreak of the First World War it was predominantly pasture and woodland: a typical Cotswold agricultural estate with neat stone walling on the high ground, its farm buildings, cottages and manor house all built of warm golden Cotswold stone. It also remained, as did most rural estates, under a paternalist rule: the Wemyss family wielded power and influence in local and national politics, in local justice, education and religious worship. The war was to have a considerable impact on a pattern of life which had seen little change over the centuries.

Another country estate to be dramatically affected by the war was

Easton in Essex, the home of Daisy, Countess of Warwick. Daisy Warwick was also entertaining over the Bank Holiday weekend; Monday 3 August was the day of Easton's annual flower show. Four large marquees filled with displays of flowers and outsize vegetables were erected in Easton Park together with steam roundabouts and side-shows. To one young visitor all appeared cheerful and picturesque:

> it was a warm and sunny day, the villagers were in their Sunday best, and the distinguished visitors down from London were seated under the trees or walking around in pairs, the ladies in great 'picture' hats carrying parasols, the gentlemen in white, with panama hats, carrying elegant walking sticks.[2]

But some of the distinguished visitors were uneasy: George Bernard Shaw, staying at Easton Glebe, the home of H. G. Wells; R. D. Blumenfeld, editor of the *Daily Express* and a resident of Little Easton, and Taffy Gwynne, editor of the *Morning Post*. Their conversation was so disturbing that half-way through the festivities Daisy Warwick retired to the tranquillity of Easton Lodge. 'Less than four hundred miles away', as H. G. Wells later recalled, 'from a front that reached from Nancy to Liège, more than a million and a quarter of grey-clad men . . . were pouring westward to take Paris . . . to invade England.'[3]

In the small, half-timbered Sussex village of Fletching, Robert Saunders, the village headmaster, observed physical preparations for war, not just rumours: 'the reservists are being called up, all the railways are guarded, wire entanglements, trench guns etc. have been hurriedly put round Portsmouth, and even our post office has had orders to keep open night and day'.[4] Saunders was to be lucky in the war: three of his sons served in the armed forces for the duration but none was killed or seriously wounded.

Closer to the English Channel, Virginia Woolf found the village of Asheham practically under martial law: 'there were soldiers marching up and down the line, & men digging trenches, and it was said that Asheham barn was to be used as a hospital. All the people expected an invasion.'[5] In Devon, a young trainee architect, Frank Cook, was taking an evening walk on the deserted sands of Goodrington

Beach when he noticed the lighthouse on Berry Head had changed its signal.

The regular army, an expeditionary force of six infantry divisions and a cavalry division, began to mobilize on the afternoon of Tuesday 4 August. The Grand Fleet had been carrying out manoeuvres in the English Channel at the end of July and on Winston Churchill's orders was dispatched to battle stations in the North Sea. A correspondent for *Country Life*, ostensibly reporting on the Bank Holiday cricket at Canterbury, could not help but notice the battleships gliding past the Kent coastline, only a few miles from the cricket field: 'there exists a solemn and supreme feeling that cricket and everything must yield to the one thought, that England's hour of trial has indeed come'. Rudyard Kipling also watched the passing of the fleet. He was on holiday with his family, staying at Kessingland Grange, a lonely house perched·high on the edge of the Norfolk coast, lent to him by Rider Haggard: they sat in the garden looking out to sea with 'all the drama of the skirts of war laid out before us'.[6]

For most of the population, it was the calling up of reservists and members of the territorial army rather than the mobilisation of the regular army and navy which brought home the reality of war. There was no conscription until January 1916. The declaration of war coincided with the time of year many territorial soldiers were attending annual summer training camps. Robert Saunders' son Wally was studying to be a school teacher but the Bank Holiday found him at camp: instead of being sent home he was immediately mobilised and joined the 10th Middlesex Regiment. Another resident of Fletching (his father ran the village paint and paper-hanging shop), William Muddle, was called up and appeared in the village on 7 August to collect his uniform. 'He visited the Griffin and departed on a bike in a very excited state proclaiming loudly "well if he got killed he didn't care a damn".'

Charles Adeane of Babraham Hall, just outside Cambridge, was Chairman of the Territorial Association for Cambridgeshire and the Isle of Ely as well as being the owner of a large estate. He had known of the imminence of war several days before the declaration through a house guest, Lord Henry Bentinck, MP for Nottingham and brother of the Bloomsbury hostess Lady Ottoline Morrell. On Monday 3 August

Bentinck sent him a wire from London 'to say that there was little hope of peace'[7] and the next day Adeane organised the formation of an Emergency Committee to mobilise the Cambridgeshire Territorials. The battalion had only just returned from training in Ashridge Park so mobilisation was immediate.

At the same time a temporary telephone was installed at Babraham Hall, and paid for by the War Office. Throughout the war Adeane combined his responsibilities as a landowner and agriculturalist. He was Commandant of the Cambridgeshire Volunteer Regiment, in 1916 he was made Lord Lieutenant of the county and in 1917 he became President of the Royal Agricultural Society of England. It was fortunate for the future of Babraham that his only son Robert was a mere nine years old in 1914.

War had coincided with one of the busiest times of the farming year and in some areas there were not enough people to bring in the harvest. The dramatic impact of Kitchener's pointing finger and the words 'Your Country needs YOU', which first appeared on hoardings on 7 August, was primarily responsible: three quarters of a million Britons volunteered during August and September.

The two artists John and Paul Nash found themselves helping farmers in Buckinghamshire: 'novel amusement for me and great fun – Jack and I have worked hard – tossing sheaves onto a cart and pitching 'em off in the yard to make a rick'.[8] In Gloucestershire the writers Edward Thomas and Robert Frost also found themselves working on the land. Thomas was spending August with his family in lodgings on the farm of Mr Chandler, a veteran soldier with 21 years of service. Although Chandler was 44 years old, he was summoned to Hereford and had to leave his farm in literary hands. In Wiltshire, Devizes Urban District Council offered to lend the hard-pressed farmers horses and men in their employ at cost price. And in Northumberland miners came above ground to gather in the harvest. Coal was no longer being exported to Germany so alternative employment was welcome and some miners even took the opportunity to be retrained in agriculture at Armstrong College.

Not all countrymen rushed to volunteer. In September *Country Life* published a defensive explanation of the 'apparent apathy of the rural population to the call to arms', an apathy which the popular press had been quick to notice. 'In the first place, it was highly important that the harvest should be garnered; and, in the second place, news filters into the rural mind very slowly.' Though patriotism might be 'the marrow of the average countryman's bones' it appeared there were some English villages from which no one had enlisted. In an attempt to chivvy slow-witted Hodge into khaki, the writer of the article, J. L. Green, had organised a 'little army of recruiters' to spread 'a knowledge of German perfidy, German aggression and German malice' through the countryside. Green claimed to have got 10,000 villagers into Kitchener's new army in the first two weeks of his campaign.

In Somerset, a young member of the landed gentry was discovering this rural apathy for himself. Edward Horner, only surviving son of Sir John Horner and the heir to the estate of Mells, near Frome, nearly 7,000 acres of dairy pastures and woodland, displayed all the reckless bravery and chivalry associated with his class.

When war was declared he held a subaltern's commission in the North Somerset Yeomanry. He mobilised immediately and took his troop to Ashford Forest, near Winchester, for training. But 'the life is ghastly . . . No training only odd jobs and standing about amongst half dressed farmers who've refused to go abroad and only want to get back to their farms.' Frustrated by the reluctance of the Somerset farmers to leave their native land, Horner enlisted the help of his mother, Frances: 'getting out's the point beside which nothing else matters'.[9] Lady Horner pulled strings and through the help of the family friend Lord Haldane, who approached Kitchener, Horner was transferred to the Royal Horse Guards. He again appealed to his mother and finally obtained a commission in the 15th Hussars.

Edward Horner was a member of the 'corrupt coterie', a select and privileged group of young people which included the three daughters of the Duchess of Rutland, Marjorie, Violet and Diana Manners; Julian Grenfell, composer of the famous war poem 'Into Battle'; and Raymond Asquith, eldest son of the Prime Minster and Edward's brother-in-law. Mary Wemyss's eldest son Ego Charteris, married to Violet Manners, was also a member, together with his youngest brother Yvo and sister Cynthia, married to H. H. Asquith's second son, Herbert.

Between them, the young men owned or were heirs to large chunks of their country. They were representatives of a class which still held enormous social and political power and wealth. Some of the young men were already in the armed forces; the rest volunteered. Duff Cooper was the last to join up because his work at the Foreign Office was of national importance, a fact which probably saved his life as the majority of the men in the group were killed, including Raymond Asquith, Ego and Yvo Charteris, Julian and Billy Grenfell, Charles Lister, Percy Wyndham, Edward Tennant, Patrick Shaw Stewart and Edward Horner.

Ego Charteris, Lord Elcho, was heir to Lord Wemyss's five-thousand-acre estate in Gloucestershire and another 55,000 acres of Scotland, three substantial mansions and six castles. He was pursuing a legal career when war was declared but was immediately called up. He was already attached to his local Gloucestershire Yeomanry. On Sunday 9 August, Mary Wemyss went to Gloucester cathedral to watch the soldiers at church parade. 'Very moving', she wrote in her diary. She had heard the day before from her lifelong confidant Arthur Balfour, the former Prime Minister, that the Expeditionary Force had started for France. As she watched the 'quiet earnest faces' of her son and his troop praying in the ancient cathedral, 'it sank into my heart for the first time that they were going to fight'.

Unlike the farmers of the North Somerset Yeomanry, those in Gloucestershire, according to Mary Wemyss, 'left their corn standing and, inspired by disinterested zeal and unselfish devotion had answered the call of their country'. Hugo Wemyss gave a rousing speech in the tithe barn to rally recruits from his estate but the following day he backed up his rhetoric by threatening to dismiss 'all servants outside & in' if they did not enlist. Those who did enlist would have their places kept open for them and be paid half wages while 'away with the colours'. Mary managed to persuade her husband to withdraw the threat of dismissal. 'Those who give their lives should have the grace and glamour of doing so freely and not be driven like sheep to the slaughter.' She made her own recruiting speech, managing to find an excuse for Hugo's belligerence:

he gave notice of dismissal, not out of any wish to threaten or coerce but in order to make it easy for you to do what he thought it your duty to do – in order to make everyone realize and understand the extreme gravity and importance of the situation in which we now are placed.

Her tactic worked. By the end of August, a dozen able-bodied men, the first contingent of volunteers, left the haven of the Stanway estate. They marched away past the crossroads where, seven years later, a war memorial bearing a magnificent sculpture of St George slaying the dragon would be erected to the memory of those who never returned.

Hugo Wemyss was not alone in threatening his employees, it was common among the middle-aged landowners. Both the Earl of Lonsdale and Lord Rothschild threatened single men working on their estates in the Lake District and Hertfordshire with notice if they did not enlist. In contrast Walter Long, MP and Wiltshire landowner, relied exclusively on his powers of persuasion.

Better far to die shouldering your rifle in any fight for the liberties and rights of your country than live at home in ease, a craven at heart, knowing full well that the rest of your life would be spent in the miserable reflection that your country lost her position amongst the nations of the world because her young men preferred to live at home in a temporary ease … Here in this village and in other villages where I have influence I mean to have a great placard headed the roll of honour. On that will be inscribed the names of any man who joins the Colours; a copy of it will be sent to every house or cottage in which he has dwelt, and where his family are, and a permanent copy will be given to his family to keep as a lasting record of the fact that he did his duty.[10]

Charles Adeane went out recruiting with the mayor of Cambridge, who reminded his audience of their fighting ancestors. 'In the time of Cromwell the Ironsides came from Cambridgeshire and Huntingdonshire, and some of the finest soldiers the world had known had come from the Fenlands.' In the Civil War, however, some Englishmen had fought against, rather than for, their king.

Joseph Herbert Tritton of Lyons Hall, Great Leighs in Essex, gave his speech on 6 September in the lofty village barn. It was a day of intense heat, a deep blue sky, 'pastures and gardens burnt up by the long drought. Apples, pears and acorns falling prematurely.' Tritton tried to bring the war to the doors of his labourers' cottages. 'Think of what it would mean if we were to have our country overrun as Belgium is, and the scenes of horror there, of daily occurrence here.'[11] Tritton was supported on the platform by three majors, two baronets, the son of an earl and the vicar of Great Leighs, but his audience were unimpressed, irritated by the news that he had been putting pressure on his footmen at Lyons Hall to enlist. Nevertheless, within a couple days of Tritton's speech one of the strongest farm-hands volunteered from the village and others followed.

The Prime Minister was so impressed by the individual efforts of men of power and influence such as Lonsdale and Rothschild, Long and Adeane, in the first weeks of the war, that he set up a Parliamentary Recruiting Committee in September. Celebrities were also involved. Rudyard Kipling gave speeches in the neighbourhood of his country house, Bateman's, in Sussex as well as travelling further afield. His explanation for the reluctance of some of the country people to offer themselves was that Kitchener's call wasn't sufficiently bloodthirsty. 'It's from the country side that you will get good recruits', he wrote to the editor of the *Daily Express*; 'They don't want dope and soothing syrup.'[12] Adeane would have agreed with Kipling. After attending a meeting late in August at Romsey Town he noted in his diary 'poor meeting. The people do not in the least realize the serious nature of the contest in which we are engaged.' However, a visit to Ely on 5 September was more successful. Adeane drove over to the cathedral city with all his family, picnicking on the way by an old windmill, and persuaded 26 men to volunteer.

Throughout the country, in every sort of home, families were coping with the departure of husbands, sons and brothers, servants and tenants. All the young men volunteered from the village of Babraham, and the Adeanes' butler demonstrated to his former employees 'how to form fours in Army boots on the best parquet flooring'. Robert Saunders' son Ron enlisted in the East Surrey Regiment early in September. Saunders wrote 'Ma . . . is very upset about his going. She doesn't understand what a sacrifice it is on his part & doesn't feel proud to have all her sons doing something for their country.' Frank Cook responded directly to the Kitchener poster and enlisted in the Royal Engineers. He was 20 years old. 'When I told my Mother that I was enlisting, all she said was "I knew you would" and turned her head away.'[13]

The government was unable to cope with the number of men enlisting. Camps were hurriedly erected throughout the countryside but they almost immediately became overcrowded. There was a particularly high density of soldiers in the south-east of England and by 7 September Saunders was writing to his son William, who had emigrated to Canada early in 1914:

> there are 5000 at Sittingbourne and a similar number at every place of importance in the country. [17 September] In this district 6000 troops passed Piltdown on Monday; 2000 artillery with 4000 horses are quartered at Maresfield Park . . . Lewes is full, troops quartered in every house. [11 October] at Shoreham 40,000 men, Seaford 15,000, Crowborough and Maresfield 10,000.

Equipment and clothing for the vast numbers simply did not exist. Saunders noticed the majority 'simply had the clothes they stood up in when they marched off and for weeks the authorities have not been able to supply them. At Lewes . . . the people collected clothes, shirts, vests, pants, socks, etc. so as to enable the men to change.' In Suffolk there were complaints that the Foreign Service Battalion were housed in pigsties outside Bury St Edmunds and when Charles Adeane went to investigate he indeed found the men living under squalid conditions in 'filthy farm buildings'.

Salisbury Plain was inundated with troops. Large parts of it have remained closed to the civilian public almost ever since, with barracks, tin huts and tank tracks permanent features of the ancient downs. But in the first weeks of the First World War only tents were pitched on the springy turf. The weather was balmy and for Herbert Asquith, the Prime Minister's son, training at the Public Schools' Camp, romance was in the air:

the scene that I remember best was a march over the rolling slopes and ridges of the Wiltshire downs in the dusk of a moonless night when that long singing column of youth moved, rank on rank, passing over the hill like a company of shadows; as they marched at ease, their lighted cigarettes looked like a train of fire-flies moving through the darkness, and so, singing and smoking, but scarcely visible themselves, they crossed the upland turf beneath rollers of midnight cloud and the sparse, glittering lights of the September stars.[14]

With the approach of winter, huts were erected to replace the tents. The boyhood thrills of camping out in the open air shared by a generation brought up on Jefferies' *Bevis* and Ballantyne's *Coral Island* gave way to grumbles about the draughtiness of the hastily erected huts.

Guy Charteris, Mary Wemyss's second eldest son, was in Pembroke Docks with the Shropshire Light Infantry in December. The bad weather was making the progress of the men's huts uncomfortably slow. Guy commented 'the conditions under which the workmen labour are as bad as those under which the troops exist'.[15] Newspapers reported strikes by carpenters throughout the country and the efforts of trade unions to negotiate overtime for their members.

Such large numbers of men, horses and equipment reduced lush countryside to barren, muddy tracks and parade grounds. Their route marches, thousands at a time, through small towns and villages, could be equally disruptive. Robert Saunders' classes at Fletching village school were constantly interrupted by the passing of regiments of infantry and cavalry, Red Cross vans, ammunition wagons and guns. Not only the children rushed into the playground to wave. 'Teacher Kath generally manages to be in the playground when the RFA [Royal Field Artillery] go by on their horses and it seems to be the usual thing now as they reach the playground coming down from Piltdown for every man to "eyes left" to see if Teacher is looking.'

The peaceful country town of St Albans was typical in the transformation it underwent. Before 4 August 'on Wednesday morning sheep and cattle and pigs are driven in to the market place, and with them come the ruddy, sturdy Hertfordshire farmers, hard men to buy and sell with, yet hearty and jovial, exchanging plenty of chaff and witticism as they haggle over the prices for steer and hogs'. But with the declaration everything changed. Khaki became the dominant colour. The golf course was taken over by squads of men at drill and the first hole was surrounded by baggage waggons. The soldiers apparently benefited from the country air. A company of territorials from the East End of London were changed from 'pallid skinned, dull eyed' men to tanned, fit, erect soldiers 'all having that air of rude health which comes from constant work and exercise in the open air, accompanied by good and sustaining food'.[16] The country life was preparing men fit to die.

Not all recruits were as fortunate as the East Enders at St Albans. Disease and accidents became real hazards as the camps grew larger. One poor soldier at camp in Crowborough, Sussex, was destined never to leave England. He was crushed to death under the wheel of an ammunition wagon. There must have been other such accidents. Siegfried Sassoon sustained a broken arm while acting as ground scout during training in Kent. As he was jumping a fence a strand of wire tripped up his horse. It was an ironic fact of the war that the loss of farm labourers and the decrease in hunting encouraged farmers to increase the use of barbed wire around their fields. *Country Life* was particularly worried about the risk to officers returning home on leave and keen to join the surviving hunts. Just as the officers were the first to leave the trenches, the first to encounter the barbed wire stretched across no-man's-land, they also tended to be the first to jump fences on the hunting field.

> How many of them in writing from the front, have referred to the sport they love, and expressed the wish that they may find it going strong when they return . . . Let everyone, therefore, do what he can now . . . to keep their home at least as they left it, and leave barbed wire for its fit use – to protect war trenches and trip up enemies, not friends, nor the gallant lads who are fighting and dying for our homes and country, the home of the finest sport on earth.

The army camps and billets established over the countryside varied enormously in quality. Edward Horner decided not to take any chances and took his sister's horses, a man servant and personal cook with him. His attempt to maintain the semblance of a gentleman's life style was short-lived, however, as Raymond Asquith explained to Diana Manners: 'Poor old Edward went off to the North Somersets last week with Cicely's two best hunters and a body-servant and Mrs B. . . . all these conveniences have now been confiscated for the use of the Regiment, and old E. sleeps on bare boards.'[17]

Officers commanding the troops stationed around Cambridge – 20,000 by 20 August – were more fortunate. The Adeanes frequently invited them to lunch at Babraham Hall and afterwards 'we all used to have tea at a long table under the copper beech, and discuss the advance of the Germans into France'. However, Fraulein Baumann, the Adeanes' Bavarian governess, had to eat her meal upstairs and out of sight.

For some recruits there were surprising opportunities to pursue pre-war interests. Typical among the officer class were the brothers Geoffrey and Arthur Dent. Geoffrey found himself in Ireland, his needs catered for by two servants and with ample opportunity to hunt and shoot. 'There are simply millions of plover, golden plover and curlew on the Curragh, whose blood I thirst for', he wrote home in September. Later, from the trenches of the western front, he wrote 'had lots of good shoots. It is great fun seeing the Huns go down when you shoot at them.' Arthur spent the first months of the war shooting pheasants in Suffolk with the Essex Yeomanry.[18]

Walter Spradbery, artist and designer of London Transport posters, enlisted in September, joining the 3rd East Anglian Field Ambulance. Towards the end of the year he was billeted in the granary and stables of Burghley House, near Stamford, one of the country seats of the Cecils. He found the house 'most paintable from several aspects, full of quaint corners and handsome courts'. The marches through the countryside took him to villages and churches he could capture on his sketch pad. The Exeter Arms in Stamford proved 'a delightful little inn with beams across the Bar Room ceiling, and where we enjoyed home made butter, and the best of substancial [sic] English fare. The host was called Aldwinkle . . . His little daughter Fanny rode to hounds every week.'[19] Spradbery's experiences of 'Merry Old England' were exhibited at an art exhibition set up at the next billet in Peterborough.

Burghley House was one of many country houses, large and small, with out-buildings, parks and farmland which the owners made available to the army. Later in the war tanks rumbled through the grounds of Hatfield House, another of the Cecils' palaces. Daisy Warwick invited the Essex Territorials to train in Easton Park, though she was put out by their indifference to her carefully laid footpaths. Captain Gordon Bartlett exchanged the peaceful confines of his father's vicarage at Great Crosby, near Liverpool, for the unpredictable wild deer of Knole Park in Kent. 'We drill there & daily expect to be rushed at by some wild stag, they roar like a lot of young lions all day & night. The trees too are glorious.'[20] The deer of Duncombe Park in Yorkshire also played their part in training soldiers. The Earl of Feversham raised a battalion of farmers' sons and labourers from the north of England and made them practise advances against his herd. The deer counter-attacked and totally routed the yeomen.

Near Grantham, Lord Brownlow lent the park of Belton House for the training of some 15–20,000 men. The sandy bunkers of his golf course provided practice cover; the shallow River Witham, snaking through the park, offered 'bathing parade'; local tradesmen made a nice profit selling newspapers at the camp gates. By the following autumn, however, an officer in the 3rd Gloucesters found conditions were not so pleasant at Belton: 'Administrative chaos and confusion reigned. In addition, the site of the camp, normally parkland, became a quagmire of mud through inclement weather and the continuous traffic of army vehicles.'[21] Still, a quagmire of mud would provide a more accurate taste of trench life than keeping one's head down in a sandy golf bunker.

While thousands of volunteers were being trained in different parts of the country to go to the defence of Belgium and France, hundreds of Belgian refugees were arriving in England, bringing with them tales of the real horrors of war. Refugees began to arrive only days after war was declared. A War Refugees Committee was set up on 24 August: the Hon. Mrs Alfred Lyttelton, Viscount Gladstone and Lady Lugard were on the committee and Lord Hugh Cecil was chairman. On 9 September the Local Government Board took over control: 2,500 reception committees were established and by the end of the year some 100,000 refugees had been accommodated. They were scattered all over the country, wherever suitable homes could be found, and brought to the remotest parts of the countryside tales of the German advance and the loss of family and friends. The grim business of shot, shell, and bayonet at the front was brought into British homes with horrifying clarity.

It was to be a characteristic of the First World War that landed society, the 'upper ten thousand', took the lead not only in going 'over the top' first, but also in organising relief for refugees, offering their homes as hospitals and convalescent homes (after all they owned the biggest houses), training as nurses, setting up work parties in villages and towns to provide extra clothing for soldiers at the front and occupation for wives left behind.

Daisy Warwick, once a favourite of King Edward VII, found a new role organising the distribution of 30 Belgian refugees from the tithe barn of Easton Lodge. H. G. Wells described the eagerness with which the better-off families in the neighbourhood offered to help. 'There was something like competition among the would-be hosts; everybody was glad of the chance of "doing something" and anxious to show these Belgians what England thought of their plucky little country.'[22]

Punch revelled in the problems encountered between well-meaning British hosts trying to speak French with rural accents and their bemused Flemish-speaking visitors. A Scottish village devoted itself to the conversion of its Belgians to a taste for oatmeal but so far they 'have only employed it for baiting a bird-trap . . . we feel that their exile will not have been entirely wasted if they have learned to appreciate the purpose fulfilled by porridge in the Divine Order of things.' Weather was another problem, particularly in Scotland. 'They are puzzled, and after sixty-five consecutive hours of rain they wonder wistfully if it is always like this. We simply dare not tell them the truth.'

The feminist novelist Mary Cholmondeley took five Belgian soldiers into her country house after they had been discharged from hospital. 'After two days, Polydore courteously inquired how much longer they would have to drink our terrible English medicine with their breakfasts. This was the strong tea we had given them. Coffee was substituted for it, and smiles wreathed every face.'[23] In Great Leighs, Essex, a well-educated hostess was able to offer her refugees fluent French and

German. Unfortunately they spoke neither English, French nor German, only Flemish.

Mary Wemyss had to wait until Christmas for her Belgian family. Mr and Mrs Beyart, their two daughters and Mrs Beyart's mother were given rooms over the stable block of Stanway House. The coachman James Prew and his wife already occupied the flat but were moved back to their old cottage, not without some grumbling: 'they are not overpleased with "them Belgians"'. And Mrs Fletcher, the caretaker of Stanway House, refused to do extra work looking after the family so a local girl called Minnie Stratford was hired 'who undertook to work 3hrs a day for Belgians for about 5/2 a week – I should give it her in a present to avoid insurance'. The complications only added to the fun: doing up the flat was like arranging a dolls' house. 'Pamela [Mary Wemyss's niece and Charles Adeane's daughter] & I spent till 12 furnishing up the Belgians flat – the rooms look so wonderfully nice, no rubbish in the salon – nice cupboard nice writing table flowers – books & toys for children.'

Further west, Edward Horner's village of Mells in Somerset received its Belgian family. The Horners owned most of the village and offered Poyntz House to the Van de Werves, husband, wife and five children. (The former occupant of Poyntz House, the curate for Mells and Vobster had left in October for India with the 4th Somerset Territorials.) Food and coal were supplied by the better-off villagers: one of the Van de Werve daughters offered to help at Branch Farm. After the war Frances Horner recalled how fortunate Mells was with the 'charming' Antwerp bankers who stayed for two years:

> Looking back, I often think how uncomfortable they must have been, as the house they lived in was primitive in its equipment, but what they liked was having it to themselves; not being anyone's guests – and they nobly repaid the village hospitality in after years by contributing generously to its various charities.

The 'primitive' conditions involved no indoor sanitation. To the horror of the village the Van de Werves were spotted on at least one occasion emptying their chamber pots from the attic windows. When they returned to Belgium after the war, Pansy Helps, the daughter of the

Mells doctor, was invited to stay. In their family's several chateaux she discovered the grand style of living which the war had interrupted.

The nearest village to Mells is Kilmersdon. Lord Hylton, lord of the manor of Kilmersdon, provided a house rent-free for the refugees who became his responsibility. Longleat is only a few miles away from both Kilmersdon and Mells. There, Lord Bath made a farmhouse on his estate available to a family of Belgians. His head forester supervised the planting of the garden; his daughters, the Ladies Kathleen and Emma Thynne, arranged the furniture, no doubt in accordance with their own good taste.

While the titled ladies and gentlemen on the War Refugees Committee appealed for homes for Belgians, the Duke of Sutherland launched his appeal for country houses suitable for wounded soldiers, either as hospitals or convalescent homes. The response was overwhelming. He was offered 250 country houses almost immediately though in the end the government found few to be suitable.

Rauceby Hall in Leicestershire became a convalescent home for English and Belgian soldiers. Its position in prime hunting country offered familiar sport for the English officers although the Belgians must have been a little bemused. 'When the Belvoir Hounds met there was an assembly of wounded soldiers of both nations to look on . . . The pack, now running blood, stretched out across the Park to the Hall, where, at the very feet of the soldiers the hounds caught the fox.[24]

At Cheveney in Kent, Colonel Borton and his wife established a small convalescent home which remained open throughout the war. The first inmates, four wounded Belgian soldiers, were installed by 24 October. Gatcombe House on the Isle of Wight, the home of sir Charles Seely, was taken over as a Red Cross hospital. Sir Charles's son Jack Seely had resigned as Secretary of State for War just before the declaration and was on active service.

Wrest Park in Bedfordshire, the family home of Lord Lucas, was adapted for use as a hospital. Lord Lucas's sister Nan Herbert was in charge. The family friend, J. M. Barrie, gave generous cheques and frequently visited 'West in Beds', finding some consolation after the death of his adopted son George Llewelyn Davies by talking to the patients recovering in the statue-filled early eighteenth-century park.

Chapelwood Manor in Sussex, Lord and Lady Brassey's home, became a convalescent home. Siegfried Sassoon would spend a month there in 1917 among 'woods and sloping meadows and hedges in their young green, and growing wheat, with clumps of daffodils in the field beyond the gardens'.[25]

The Astors offered Cliveden, their Buckinghamshire mansion, for use as a hospital in October 1914, but the government considered it ill-designed for conversion. In November, however, the Canadian Red Cross decided to adapt the covered tennis court and opened it as the Duchess of Connaught's Canadian Red Cross Hospital on 20 February 1915. Meanwhile Cliveden was used as a convalescent home and the medical staff lived in Taplow Lodge.

Not every landed gentleman rushed to invite wounded soldiers into his home. Hugo Wemyss was horrified at the idea when his wife suggested as much only five days after war began. He spent the war years threatening to shut up Stanway House in order to economise. Mary Wemyss had to content herself helping at the local hospital in Winchcombe and entertaining the wounded to lunch, tea and entertainments in the tithe barn.

According to *Country Life* the landed gentry could help the wounded in other ways. Apparently game meat was particularly suitable for invalids. 'By the time the shooting season opens in October there will probably be far more invalids who are able to take advantage of the plentifulness of game.' So all sporting gentlemen too aged or decrepit to be useful on the battlefield were encouraged to carry on with the annual slaughter of pheasant and grouse in order to vary the diet of soldiers in hospital.

All classes of country men and women and children became enthusiastically involved in one or other sort of war-work: knitting and sewing garments for soldiers; helping with the harvest; guarding railway lines and reservoirs; attending Red Cross classes. Throughout the country, at least in the opening months of the war, people were brought together in a spirit of camaraderie, of community effort, of doing one's bit however insignificant. The feverish activity which overcame the nation was almost of carnival proportions. When Robert Saunders visited his daughter in London in September he found buildings decked with flags, appeals to enlist plastered on every available wall, photographs of the war displayed in shop windows, special constables bustling about showing off their newly acquired badges and khaki everywhere.

Newspapers and magazines made increasingly ridiculous suggestions as to how the population could help win the war. *Country Life* was under the impression that most boys owned ponies and suggested they should be used for dispatch-riding: 'a keen boy on a pony is really as useful as a man'. And could the government make use of the superior hearing of birds to warn of the approach of Zeppelins? There was abundant material for *Punch* to satirise. All the women on the Isle of Wight were busy making soldiers' pyjamas. 'One of the marks of patriotism amongst our ladies is the possession of a pair of pyjama legs. No picnic party is complete without them. When the men light their cigarettes the women bring out their pyjamas and add stitch upon stitch.' The sons of the Reverend Cushat, vicar of a village in the Midlands, were engaged in making saddle-pads for horses at the front. 'They try each pad out on our old Dobbin,' wrote Mrs Cushat to her friend Mrs Robinson, 'and are wild for him to go on service at once; but James has just decided that a Vicar's pony's place is in the last line of the Reserves.'

The Horner family were in residence at the Manor House, Mells, in August and Lady Horner immediately set up a work party for the women of the village. 'It seemed as if our obvious job was to help and organise there. I had a big Work Party for the village, and we started making shirts and socks, and sharing all the news.' Villagers anxious for the safety of husbands and sons serving abroad could rely on Frances Horner passing on information about the progress of the war gleaned from her friends, Asquith, Balfour and Haldane. 'We used to sit in the Loggia and sew, and I read aloud . . . I think the fact of working for their men, and hearing all the latest news I could get for them, was a great comfort to them all.' The men in the trenches received weekly parcels of food and comforts.

In Kilmersdon a Rifle Association was formed late in August. Lord Hylton was the president and offered to provide the rifle range for practising on as well as the rifles; members of the Association had to find their ammunition. The enthusiasm of the sharp-shooters was so great that the footpath leading to the designated field was reduced to a quagmire. A special meeting of the parish council met to discuss how the approach to the range could be maintained in a fit state. Lady Hylton gave the Asssociation one of their rifles. In late November she was selling cuttings of plants to help provide comforts for the 1st Somerset Light Infantry; by 1916 she was organising a local fund for buying Christmas puddings which the *Daily Telegraph* was sending out to the troops.

Ettie Grenfell, Lady Desborough, was another famous hostess of Frances Horner's and Mary Wemyss's generation. They were all three members of the 'Souls', a privileged and exclusive coterie of aristocrats who flourished around the turn of the century, and pursued more intellectual and artistic pleasures than the Prince of Wales's hunting, racing and gambling set. Ettie Grenfell set up her own work party at Taplow Court in Buckinghamshire and by 11 December 1914, 955 garments had been sent to hospitals and soldiers abroad.

As soon as the Kiplings returned to Bateman's from their interrupted holiday in Norfolk, sewing and knitting began in earnest. When Kipling's daughter Elsie slipped away for a holiday in Scotland she was pursued by her father's orders, to be fulfilled on her return:

> there is worrk, Madam – shirts and socks, Madam – to be undertaken. The fame of your socks has spread. Mummy's order for nine pairs (with shirts) has brought her a fresh order from the same troops – a modest man who says he is rather thin and five foot ten and 22 inches from elbow to wrist, or else it's shoulders.[26]

Colonel Henry Wemyss Feilden, a neighbour of Kipling's in Sussex, received a more bizarre request for help from the novelist, on the strength of taking part in a polar expedition as a naturalist forty years before.

> Dear Colonel Sahib,
> A demand comes to me to say whether sphagnum moss, of the sort that is being used for wound-dressings, grows in this country. Allah (and you) know that my botanical knowledge is nought, so I write you as the Ocean of Learning. If sphagnum don't associate with Sussex,

is there any other moss which baked and sterilised would make an efficient dressing?

The Red C. are collecting moss and a woman (once a nervous invalid) of my aquaintance is now jumping about bogs to collect it.

Please send me an authoritative line that will tell her whether she can hope to go moss-gathering in the county.[27]

Not far from Bateman's, in the village of Fletching, Robert Saunders' wife Elsie was panicking over the thirty knitted belts she had undertaken to make for the army. In the village school Saunders organised a penny collection to buy tobacco for old boys at the front. With the approach of Christmas, presents for the soldiers became the priority.

This week [4 December] we sent 3/- to the weekly Despatch Fund and they send for every 1/6 a Christmas box to any soldier you mention if you give the full particulars, a Briar pipe, a pouch, 2oz. tobacco, a packet cigarettes, a packet of matches. So we are hoping 2 of our boys, Bert Light, 2nd Coldstreams and Wm. Mitchell, 9th Lancers, will have something for Christmas from their old school.

Christmas presents were sent to France from every part of the country. Charles Adeane's wife Madeline, sister of Mary Wemyss, was President of the Ladies' Recruiting Committee for Cambridgeshire. Her committee organised the despatch of a gift to every soldier from the county, a total of 8,000.

In Blewbury, Buckinghamshire, another husband and wife were devoting their efforts to war-work. Kenneth Grahame, author of *The Wind in the Willows*, was living in virtual retirement beside the river he had immortalised. His wife Elspeth busied herself 'making crutches & splints, leg & back rests for base & ship hospitals – in the shed generally used for repairing agricultural equipment'. Kenneth joined the village's volunteer defence corps and spent every evening drilling with fellow veterans 'in a beautiful great framed thatched barn . . . The rats run in & out of the thatch along the rafters, and the barn cat, who ought to be attending to them, sits on wheatsacks and reviews us with great delight.'[28]

The women of Great Leighs in Essex knitted mufflers and mittens for the men in the regiment, the Coldstream Guards, in which the son of the lord of the manor was serving. Captain Tritton had written to his mother describing the intense cold in the trenches at night: she informed the vicar, the Reverend Andrew Clark. 'Poor things, I am afraid they can get very little sleep as the shells are constantly breaking round them at night.' In Mells, Pansy Helps was one of the village children knitting mittens for the troops. Hers were for the village postman and at the end of the war he brought them back to Mells.

While most people were confident the war would be over by Christmas, for some the realities of war were becoming all too clear. Mary Wemyss, riding through the Gloucestershire countryside in late August with her youngest son Yvo, found 'the country was magically beautiful silent waving corn & inviting distances, the wold had a strange unreal look . . . a *mystical* garb.' A few weeks later, her nephew Percy Wyndham, the only child of George Wyndham, the brother she had idolised, was dead. Percy (the family called him Perf) had gone to France with the Coldstream Guards immediately after the declaration. He was killed at Soissons, during the Battle of the Aisne, on 14 September. Perf's father had combined a political career with a taste for literature and became Chief Secretary for Ireland under Balfour. He succeeded to the family property of Clouds in Wiltshire in 1911 but died suddenly two years later. Perf was the owner of Clouds for only a year. Madeline Wyndham, the surviving grandmother, was left alone in Clouds. She had barely recovered from the premature death of George and was now 'quite crushed by the cruel war & all its horrors – & all the heart of her is broken by Percy's death – the end of her life is robbed of all sweetness & rest.'[29]

Perf was not the first of the upper ten thousand to be killed in the first few weeks, nor even the first of the 'corrupt coterie' to die. John Manners, the eldest son of Lord and Lady Manners of Avon Tyrrel, Hampshire, was killed on 2 September in the retreat from Mons. 'I find it terribly easy to be soppy about John', Raymond Asquith wrote to Diana Manners (John's cousin). 'You see he whipped the Greeks into a top hat at their own game – beauty, temperance, vigour and reserve – and all their tags . . . fit him like a glove.'[30] By the end of the year

Charles Adeane was pleading for landowners and their heirs serving in the forces to be exempt from death duties.

A man of the stamp we have described is usually intensely patriotic, but if he is patriotic the chances are that he is also tied to his estate by bonds that are not merely material. He looks upon it as a trust to be handed down by him as he had received it from his ancestors, and if he were hesitating as to whether it was or was not his duty to go to the front, he could be justified in taking into account the chance of the estate being mutilated and perhaps disposed of altogether should his life be lost. On the other hand, if the state acted more fairly by making such property immune from Death Duties, the fact would enable the owner to face the risks of war with a serene mind.

Of the peers and their sons who served in the war under the age of fifty, almost one in five was killed.

There were heavy casualties among the common soldiers too. In October alone there were 30,000 casualties and the standard required for entry to the army was lowered from 5 feet 8 inches to 5 feet 3 inches. Charles Adeane's daughter Helena recalled seeing 'the brave legless, armless heroes who found their way into the convalescent homes, hopping about in blue with bright yellow crutches, always smiling and joking about getting "A Blighty"'. Mary Wemyss helped to organise a memorial service in Stanway parish church for James Townsend, the first casualty among the 'men of Stanway' who had marched away on 31 August. Afterwards 'I gave the poor parents & the little brothers & sisters coffee & beef'.

Some of the first letters home from the front must have appalled the waiting families, particularly before censorship was imposed. The *Somerset Standard* published an account sent home by a Lance-Corporal in the 2nd Wiltshire Regiment.

I got wounded yesterday in a big battle. I had a shot go through my knee & another in my back . . . It is awful out here, & I shan't be sorry to be back & get all right again ... [The Germans] came in thousands & we were knocking them down like sheep.

[42]

Some country people had to rely on better-educated neighbours to read letters for them. *Country Life* published a fictional account of how a village responded to the news that 'our Ted's' name was in the newspaper. Unable to read, his family and friends assume he is dead until Sergeant Wills arrives with the correct version, 'mentioned in despatches for conspicuous gallantry'.

On 17 December death was brought into all English homes with the news of the shelling by German cruisers of the Hartlepools, Whitby and Scarborough the day before: 137 innocent men, women and children were killed, 592 were injured. Zeppelin raids did not begin until 24 December when a bomb was dropped on Dover but towns and villages were already preparing for the worst. In Mells 'the village was all darkened for fear of Zeppelins; even the Church wasn't allowed a hint of light to penetrate its stained glass windows'.

The sudden rise in food prices affected everybody. Only four days after the declaration Elsie Saunders was complaining: 'Beef is 11d. upwards, bacon 1/4 to 1/6, sugar just double'.[31] Daisy Warwick tried to alleviate hardship among her labourers in Essex by ordering the gamekeepers to thin her deer herd and offer the meat at 6d. a lb. Unfortunately the conservative countrymen refused to eat venison.

The requisitioning of horses, however, was particularly awkward for people living in the countryside, and most of all for farmers trying to gather in the harvest. While Elsie Saunders was grumbling about food prices, Mr Fenner of Church Farm, Fletching, 'was awfully cut up . . . as they [the army] came round and commandeered his black horse Kitty . . . They have been round taking everybody's horses that were suitable and at Uckfield they took the horses out of carriages and carts.' Exactly that happened in Paignton, Devon. 'Squire Churchward, who drove into Paignton regularly from the nearby village of Stoke Gabriel, had his beautiful carriage horses commandeered for the army when his coachman pulled up in front of Lloyd's Bank.'[32]

Siegfried Sassoon sold his favourite horse Cockbird to the army for £50 and another two horses for £40 each. Harkaway was too old and the 'plump mowing-machine pony' was rejected. Lord Ribblesdale, another keen huntsman, refused to allow his hunters to be sent to the front and had them all shot. His sentiments coincided with a journalist for *Country Life* reporting on the dozens of horses he watched being requisitioned in a hunting county, 'packed into the waiting trains and despatched to the scene of action . . . How many will ever hear again the sound of the horn.'

Threats of invasion and spy scares abounded in the early months of the war, sometimes adding to the excitement, the sense of emergency, but occasionally resulting in suffering and personal tragedy.

Captain Bartlett described the thrills he experienced while stationed at Whitstable in November:

> We had an exciting time on Tuesday . . . an orderly rode up with an urgent despatch from the General, be ready to man your trenches at a moment's notice, they feared that part of the fleet off Lowestoft would make a raid round here, all troops at Canterbury were hurried to the coast to make hasty trenches, I had to cart up alone, two waggons full of tools for our battalion. I had to take them three miles, fully armed and hand them over a very risky job, as plenty of spies might have been in ambush, waiting for us, they couldn't spare me a guard. Naturally we got no sleep that night.[33]

Two members of the civil guard had a far from pleasant experience when out patrolling a railway line near Frome in Somerset late in August. They came across the body of one of their comrades, lying beside the line, killed by a blow to the head administered by the open door of a passing train.

The *Daily Mail* carried on a personal vendetta against Germans unfortunate enough to be living in England at the time of the declaration. The leader on 16 October was uncompromising:

> The German spy network is so wide, so extraordinarily efficient, so immensely dangerous that it cannot be too severely repressed . . . Life and death are the stakes for which the nation is playing against the most determined, merciless and unscrupulous of assailants. The presence in our midst of 40,000 Germans and Austrians . . . must be a source of constant anxiety to the public.[34]

Popular fiction such as John Buchan's *The Thirty-Nine Steps*, published in 1915, which has Scottish glens bristling with German spies, reinforced the fear.

The result could be farcical. The inhabitants of one country village were firmly convinced that no one must eat blackberries that autumn believing the Germans had poisoned them. The local vet thought he had caught a spy in the Hare and Hounds Hotel, Shepton Mallet. The 'spy' turned out to be an inebriated officer in the 14th Company London Regiment Scottish Rifles, but before the police could arrive to give him protection his tyres were slashed. He was later charged with being drunk and disorderly.

The writers living under the Malvern Hills at the outbreak of war discovered that any unusual accent or unconventional behaviour could cause suspicion in the minds of their rural neighbours. Robert Frost was thought to be a spy because of his New Hampshire accent and stones were hurled at his cottage. Wilfrid Gibson's cottage came under suspicion after a Dutch poet came to stay 'whom the authorities took to be a German spy'. And after the arrival of Edward Thomas's party, which included a Russian boy from Bedales School, in the middle of the night 'all sorts of people joined in the hunt – the policeman, the retired clergyman, acting on the principle that "you never know what these naturalized Americans are"'.[35] It was ironic that writers so enamoured of the English countryside should be suspected of being spies and traitors by the rural people they honoured in their works and chose to live among. But even their late hours prompted the sending of anonymous letters.

A similar victim of rural xenophobia was the painter William Rothenstein in another part of Gloucestershire. He bought the decaying farmhouse of Far Oakridge together with 55 acres in 1912, choosing to leave London for the delights of the English countryside. With the outbreak of war the nearby towns of Stroud and Cirencester were filled with 'Officers in khaki ... examining horses, buying provender, recruiting men'. Rothenstein's parents were German born and he still had a foreign accent (he refused to change his name to Rutherston in 1916 along with his two brothers). When he was seen drawing a railway tunnel neighbours decided he must be a spy: 'rumours began to reach us – our house dominated the valley: we had laid down concrete floors, to be used for gun emplacements'.[36] It was only when Rothenstein's landlord, Lord Beauchamp – one of the few members of Asquith's cabinet to threaten resignation at the declaration – intervened on the artist's behalf that the rumours died down.

By the Christmas of 1914 the war was not over: England had become an armed camp, her countryside devoted to the training of soldiers and the production of munitions. *Country Life* reported

> the mutter of rifle-shooting and the roar of heavy guns have become more familiar to the ear than the whistle of the steam plough and the din of the threshing-machine . . . Quiet, secluded lanes daily witness the march of infantry and are churned into mud by the heavy artillery.

Three of Robert Saunders' sons were absent for Christmas, all in the forces, and the family had to make do entertaining seven homesick sergeants from the Lancashire Yeomanry.

Christmas at Stanway involved the usual party for all the families employed on the estate. The children dressed up as crackers, the church was decorated with holly. However, this year the guests included Belgian refugees from the next village. And the congregation who filled the church to celebrate the birth of Christ returned on Boxing Day to attend the memorial service for James Townsend.

Charles Adeane wrote in his diary on the last day of 1914: 'Babraham. We are now at the end of the fifth month of this terrible war. Nobody can tell when it will end.' On 1 January 1915, Mary Wemyss wrote in her diary: 'Sad year finished. What is to follow?'

Writers and Artists
in the countryside

Do you remember the still summer evening
When, in the cosy cream-washed living-room
Of the Old Nailshop, we all talked and laughed –
Our neighbours from The Gallows, Catherine
And Lascelles Abercrombie; Rupert Brooke;
Elinor and Robert Frost, living a while
At Little Iddens, who'd brought over with them
Helen and Edward Thomas?
. . . .

              'Twas in July
Of nineteen-fourteen that we sat and talked;
Then August brought the war, and scattered us.

     Wilfrid Gibson, 'The Golden Room'

T HE country-loving poets who moved from cities to settle
beneath the Malvern Hills just before the war thought, for a
brief moment, they had discovered a rural paradise. Their
cottages were old, thatched, half-timbered. The Gallows was named
after Jock of Dymock, executed on the site for poaching the king's deer.
Catherine Abercrombie cooked in the garden on fine evenings:
'Lascelles, John Drinkwater and Wilfrid Gibson would sit around and
read their latest poems to each other as I lay on a stoop of hay and
listened and watched the stars wander through the elms.'[1] The Frosts,
Americans, appreciated Little Iddens, three hundred years old with

brick floors and exposed beams and 'on a lane where no automobiles come'.[2] Elinor Frost described the countryside around to a friend in America:

> The pastures here are so rich that they are just as green as the mowing and wheat fields, and they are separated by dark green hedges and bordered by huge elms. Great flocks of sheep and herds of cows are everywhere. From a hill about four miles away, one can see the Severn River winding along, and the mountains of Wales in the distance.[3]

In August 1914 Edward Thomas made a third visit to his friends. The weather was idyllic, the harvest good: 'All day the rooks in the wheat-fields were cawing a deep sweet caw, in alternating choirs or all together, almost like sheep bleating, contentedly, on until late evening. The sun shone, always warm.'[4] The children's writer Eleanor Farjeon joined the party for the second half of August, taking lodgings in the village of Ledington. Her landlady, Mrs Farmer, 'had stepped out of a chapter by George Eliot, her husband out of another by Thomas Hardy'. The Farmers invited all their literary visitors to supper', forgetting the war for the moment with liberal quantities of home-brewed cider. The poets got very drunk, to Eleanor's amusement.

> I saw Edward and Robert stagger to their feet, clutch each other, and go down; they rose again with great caution, clinging together. On the other side of the table Gibson and Abercrombie were behaving similarly. Two brace of poets staggered out into the moonlight and went hilariously homeward like two sets of Siamese Twins.[5]

The writers walked the fields together while their children played. None were well-off. Abercrombie earned just over £200 in 1913; Thomas about £250. This was considerably more than an agricultural labourer's wage – low agricultural wages were one reason for there being so many cottages available for the poets to rent – but not much of an income for a middle-class intellectual and his family. However, the country was cheaper than the city, rents were lower, vegetables could be home-grown, inspiration was free and everywhere.

All the writers were very much in the vanguard of the Edwardian 'back to the land' movement. They were propagandists for the country-side, rather like Wordsworth and Coleridge over a hundred years before. For the rich, the newly discovered attractions of country life and English landscape were celebrated through the country houses and gardens designed by Edwin Lutyens and Gertrude Jekyll. Reading material for country-house weekends might include *Country Life*, the favourite also of those unable to afford their own rural retreat, or Edward Marsh's popular anthology *Georgian Poetry* to which Gibson, Abercrombie, Drinkwater and Brooke were regular contributors. Edward Thomas's rural essays *Rose Acre Papers*, *The Heart of England*, *British Country Life*, and *The Icknield Way* belong to the halcyon years before the war.

The first major effect the declaration of war had on the creative arcadia under the Malvern Hills was financial. Almost overnight their sort of writing was rendered unfashionable, irrelevant. Harold Monro, owner of the Poetry Bookshop in Bloomsbury, wrote to Edward Marsh on 19 August: '"business" has absolutely stopped. From the day war was declared scarcely any one has entered the shop.'[6] Frost realized the change of literary mood 'ends for the time being the thought of publishing any more books'.[7] He was even more concerned for his English friends who 'have all been notified by the editors they live on that there will be no more space for special articles and reviews till the war is over'.[8] Gibson agreed: 'there's no reviewing to be done'.[9] He was particularly worried about Abercrombie, who had been informed by his mainstay, the *Manchester Guardian*, 'that they would have no more reviewing while the war was on'. Catherine was expecting their third child in October and urging Lascelles to go harvesting to make some money,' but he simply hasn't the strength for that kind of work'.[10] Abercrombie applied to the Royal Literary Fund for assistance in September. 'We have not hitherto consciously applied to ourselves the terms "distress" & "destitution", but as the war goes on I guess it will amount to all that with us, financially if not emotionally.'[11] Momentary relief came with a grant in October for £100.

W. H. Davies, the one-legged super tramp, stayed at the Old Nailshop shortly after war was declared. He and Gibson were not the best of friends, jealous of each other's poetic abilities. Poor Davies had to limp three miles across the countryside in the pouring rain beside Gibson to visit the Abercrombie at The Gallows. His income was always small, only £40 in 1911, but the war had a calamitous effect. 'I don't expect to have anything in the magazines,' he wrote to Marsh, 'with the exception of a war-poem accepted by the Westminster – until all the trouble's over.'[12] Fortunately for him, Marsh was a friend of the Prime Minister: Davies's Civil List Pension was increased from £50 to £100 in 1915. But Davies's experience of only being able to place war poems was becoming all too common. Edward Thomas summed up the prevailing literary fashion.

> The demand is for the crude, for what everybody is saying or thinking, or is ready to be saying or thinking . . . It is the hour of the writer who picks up popular views or phrases, or coins them, and has the power to turn them into downright stanzas . . . Most [poems] seem to me bombastic, hysterical, or senseless.[13]

A year later, in November 1915, he wrote to Frost, who had returned to America, 'it is a pity Rupert Brooke is the only poet killed. I mean a pity for us readers.'[14]

Anthologies of war verse, slim volumes by public school subalterns, were snapped up by the public. *The Egoist* published its own comment in December 1914: 'Song: In Wartime' by 'Herbert Blenheim'.

> At the sound of the drum,
> Out of their dens they come, they come,
> The little poets we hoped were dumb,
> The little poets we thought were dead,
> The poets who certainly haven't been read,
> Since heaven knows when, they come, they come,
> At the sound of the drum, of the drum, drum, drum.

Contributors to *Georgian Poetry* were not averse to writing their own bombast. This, by John Freeman, before he went to the front:

> Happy is England in the brave that die
> For wrongs not hers and ways so sternly hers;
> Happy in those that give, give, and endure

> The pain that never the new years may cure;
> Happy in all her dark woods, green fields, towns,
> Her hills and rivers and her chafing sea.[15]

And this, by Harold Monro, who served his country on the home front. Called 'Carrion', it is a crude variation on Brooke's dead soldier whose rich dust will make 'some corner of a foreign field' for ever England.

> You are fuel for a coming spring if they leave you here;
> The crop that will rise from your bones is healthy bread.

Brooke was the first of the Georgian brotherhood to enlist and the first to die. His death brought together the ideas of dying for the English countryside and writing poetry about it: country poetry was fashionable again. As well as making his fellow Georgians popular again, however, his death was of considerable financial benefit to several of his closest friends, who were still just managing to make ends meet in their country cottages. His five war sonnets first appeared in *New Numbers*, a quarterly magazine produced through the combined efforts of Gibson, Abercrombie, Drinkwater and Brooke. It was printed at the Crypt House Press in Gloucester and distributed from 'The Gallows' to some 200 subscribers. Catherine Abercrombie kept the accounts; the poets packed the parcels and licked the stamps.

'The Soldier' achieved national popularity after it was included in Dean Inge's Easter Sunday sermon in St Paul's Cathedral and re-printed in *The Times* the following day. Brooke was by then suffering from dysentery on his way to the Dardanelles: he died of blood poisoning on 23 April. Back numbers of *New Numbers* were immediately sold out and the second volume of *Georgian Poetry* which appeared in October 1915 and contained the sonnet was an instant success. It was even considered suitable reading for the troops. An order came through to the Poetry Bookshop from the War Library for copies to be sent, at trade price, to the front and hospitals.

Brooke also named three Georgians as his heirs: Gibson, Abercrombie and Walter de la Mare were to receive royalties from his poetry for the rest of their lives. 'If I can set them free, to any extent, to write the poetry and plays and books they want to, my death will bring more gain than loss.'[16] The first collected edition of his poetry was published in 1915 and in June the three beneficiaries each received £58. 19s. 9d. Three impressions of *1914 and other Poems* were sold within seven days of publication. The three continued to benefit. In June 1916 they each received £267. 2s. 6d. and by 1921 they were struggling to avoid tax demands of £450. Marsh, one of Brooke's closest friends, came to the Old Nailshop in July 1915 to write a memoir and this was included in a second collected edition published in 1918. By 1926 nearly 300,000 copies of Brooke's poems had been sold: his patriotic response to war and his picture of an English countryside in which time stopped at ten to three still strike a chord in the hearts of poetry readers. His vision of the England worth dying for restored the popularity of poetry about the countryside: the longer the war lasted the more necessary were images of pastoral tranquillity.

The three beneficiaries were of course fortunate to survive the war to receive their royalties. Ivor Gurney, commenting on their good fortune in 1917, summed up the irony of it all: 'They have had £2000 each! That's why Gibson has not died, and his family. Poetry pays – it took a War to make it; but still, there you are.'[17]

Walter de la Mare was too old to be called up – he was born in 1873 – although he did work overseas for the Red Cross. Abercrombie, aged 34, tried to find work at Vickers Maxim near Barrow in July 1915 but was rejected. He then tried to join an artillery regiment in November but was again rejected. But at the beginning of 1916 he was at work in Liverpool, 4th class inspector of shells. It was a long way from The Gallows but he made the best of it. 'The interest of my works depends on the shells I am doing. Small shells are frightfully monotonous, the big ones quite interesting.'[18] Another Georgian, Gordon Bottomley, trapped on the edge of the Lake District by chronic ill-health, was appalled by Abercrombie's fate, doomed to live 'in a dreary brick-boxed road among trams, and grim grimy buildings, and grimmer trees in black gardens; with an office in Liverpool at the other end of his diurnal routine. This is among the most monstrous evils that the Germans have done'.[19]

Abercrombie never returned to live in the Gallows. In 1919 he was given a lectureship in literature at Liverpool University. He not only lost physical contact with the rich pastures of Herefordshire and

Gloucestershire; he also lost his poetic muse. 'Ryton Firs' is one of the few poems he wrote after leaving; a dream of a lost paradise in which 'Malvern Hills were with me all the way, / Singing loveliest visible melodies / Blue as a south-sea bay'.

Before leaving for the north, the Abercrombies shared The Gallows for a few months over the winter of 1914–15 with the Frost family. They were all trying to save money. Catherine found Elinor Frost's American habits strange, 'she kept her precious metal coffee pot going all day on the stove, and imbibed more coffee in the day than I did in a month'.[20] Frost was deeply attached to the countryside around. He declared his 'springtime passion for the earth' in one poem, in another he depicts a cow drunk on the Herefordshire cider he also enjoyed: 'Her face is flecked with pomace and she drools / A cider syrup'. But his relations with the local country folk were far from perfect. His strange accent and 'poetic' comings and goings, 'going off quietly for a few days at a time, and just as suddenly and silently reappearing aroused in the minds of a few suspicion that he was an enemy agent.'[21] Frost commented to an American friend, 'as writers we are a little mysterious to the peasant kind'.

Abercrombie and Gibson were allowed to walk over farms and woodland belonging to the local landowner Lord Beauchamp, but when Frost took off across the fields he came up against a bullying gamekeeper. Edward Thomas was with him and witnessed the gamekeeper, shot-gun in his arms, threatening Frost. The American's democratic principles were outraged. Gibson was regarded as gentry but 'me he called a "damned cottager"'.[22] Frost in turn threatened to beat up the gamekeeper and was then almost arrested by the local constable. A few days later he received a note of apology from Lord Beauchamp (the same Lord Beauchamp who came to the defence of William Rothenstein). The gamekeeper had been reprimanded by Beauchamp who apparently told him that 'if he wanted so much to fight he had better enlist'.[23]

Frost returned to America in February 1915. One of the last visitors to The Gallows was Ivor Gurney, who cycled over from Gloucester in April 1916, home on leave from the front. Only Catherine and the three children were there. Gurney was enchanted: 'all set in blue of the sky, green of the fields and leaves, and that red, that red of the soil'.[24]

But thereafter The Gallows slowly decayed. The elm trees around the cottage, also around the Old Nailshop, were uprooted in a violent storm only days after Gurney's visit: Gibson thought it symbolical. Now there is nothing left.

Gibson, the third of Brooke's beneficiaries, put off doing anything about the war until November 1915. He was called to Gloucester for inspection but rejected with bad eyesight. The following year he was operated on for appendicitis, his wife Geraldine had a baby daughter and in October he managed a reading-tour of America. This time Marsh had used his influence to keep Gibson out of the army, again for poor eyesight. He was less fortunate in 1917: by the end of the year he had said farewell (he would never return) to the Old Nailshop and was in the Army Service Corps as a clerk. He called it 'Hell' but loading manure was a far remove from the hell of the front-line trenches. Still he was unable to write any poetry. 'I grow duller and number & stupider every day . . . my nerves are all to bits.'[25]

However, before Gibson left the Old Nailshop he was able to write a series of 'war' poems almost as if on behalf of the countrymen who had been his neighbours, the 'Dymock boys, those simple, quiet, unlettered lads in Flanders mud'.[26] One hundred men left the village of Dymock to fight: thirty were killed and many more injured.

> Broken, bewildered by the long retreat
> Across the stifling leagues of southern plain,
> Across the scorching leagues of trampled grain,
> Half-stunned, half-blinded, by the trudge of feet
> And dusty smother of the August heat,
> He dreamt of flowers in an English lane,
> Of hedgerow flowers glistening after rain –
> All-heal and willow-herb and meadow-sweet.

Gibson's imaginative leap into the trenches compares favourably with many of the poems along similar lines being written by actual soldier-poets; for example 'Autumn in England' by Sergeant Colin Mitchell:

> Autumn in England! God! How my heart cries
> Aloud for thee, beloved pearl-gowned bride,

With tresses russet-hued and soft grey eyes
Which sometimes weep and sometimes try to hide
Sweet sadness in a smile of transient bliss,
Painting the West with blushing memories
Of Summer's hot and over-ardent kiss
Betokening farewell.[27]

The dead of Dymock included the village schoolmaster and one of the postmen who had stamped the parcels containing copies of *New Numbers*. The Mayo family and the Hardman family each lost three sons; the Hills family, in Dymock records for over five hundred years, also lost three sons. They were all of yeoman stock, and 'left the district but rarely to obtain wife or farm . . . having little or no desire to leave their heritage and the land they loved.'[28] Gibson was able to imagine their concerns in time of war.

I wonder if the old cow died or not?
Gey bad she was the night I left, and sick.

. . . .

And all I think of as I face the foe
And take my lucky chance of being shot
Is this – that, if I'm hit, I'll never know
'Till Domesday if the old cow died or not.[29]

John Drinkwater did not benefit directly from Brooke's death, but he had a comfortable war. He discovered his heart was weak in July 1915: 'Bed for a week, then rest for another month'.[30] His heart condition kept him out of the war for the duration – in 1917 a congested lung added to his physical disabilities – but he managed to continue as actor-manger of the Birmingham Repertory Theatre. When he wasn't working he stayed in a cottage in Gloucestershire at Far Oakridge, on the farm of his friend William Rothenstein.

Though Drinkwater did not fight for his country, he expressed his patriotic sentiments in his poetry to show he would, if he could, have defended his part of the English countryside from the German threat.

> I love my land. No heart can know
> The patriot's mystery, until
> It aches as mine for woods ablow
> In Gloucestershire with daffodil,
> Or Bicester brakes that violets fill.[31]

After the war he wrote a book all about patriotism in literature.

Life in his Cotswold cottage was, for Drinkwater, far from the momentous events proceedings overseas. The harvest appeared to be unchanged, the valleys 'happy with many a yeoman melodist', his own surroundings paradise itself.

> My garden is alight
> With currants red and white,
> And my blue curtains peep
> On starry courses deep,
> While down her silver tides
> The moon on Cotswold rides.[32]

Drinkwater's poetry may seem very bad today. But at the time it was well received: Drinkwater was a very popular writer. He provided what the public wanted: dreamy, escapist verse describing an unchanging and peaceful rural arcadia. Many of the Georgian poets followed his example, finally succumbing, according to Robert Graves, to a surfeit of nightingales.

Edward Thomas's poetry presents a rather different picture of the countryside at war. In 'As the Team's Head-Brass' poet and plough-man exchange words as the plough moves relentlessly up and down the field.

> . . . 'Have many gone
> From here?' 'Yes.' 'Many lost?' 'Yes, a good few,
> Only two teams work on the farm this year.
> One of my mates is dead. The second day
> In France they killed him. It was back in March,
> The very night of the blizzard, too. Now if
> He had stayed here we should have moved the tree.'

'A Wish'. Auto-lithograph by George Clausen. One of a group of four posters, published by the Underground Railways of London, Christmas 1916, and sent to British troops overseas, to 'waken thoughts of pleasant homely things'.

The Old Nailshop, near Ledbury, on the border of Herefordshire and Gloucestershire. The home of the poet Wilfrid Gibson at the outbreak of war and the meeting place for Georgian writers including Rupert Brooke, Edward Thomas, W.H. Davies and Robert Frost.

Little Iddens, near Ledbury. The cottage, 'on a lane where no automobiles come', rented by the American poet Robert Frost at the outbreak of war.

Weirleigh, near Paddock Wood, in the Weald of Kent. The family home of Siegfried Sassoon.

'Going Home. Anticipations of
Christmas leave by "A Subaltern,
R.F.A."'.

More sketches from the
subaltern, R.F.A. The subaltern
had been badly wounded and had
one of his legs amputated. But
'his splendidly buoyant nature
rises above even this misfortune.
. . . Like the great majority of
those who have suffered for their
country, he evidently is prepared
not only to take his misfortune
philosophically, but even to
discover a certain humour in it.'

Members of the Artists Rifles,
'cleaning rifles . . . somewhere in
the country to the east of
London'. Edward Thomas joined
the Artists Rifles on 14 July 1915.

The courtyard of Stanway House Gloucestershire, about 1900. Stanway House was built by the Tracy family in the 16th and 17th centuries. It passed, by marriage, to the Earls of Wemyss (the Charteris family), at the beginning of the 19th century. Hugo Lord Elcho, to become the 11th Earl in 1914, is *not* on horseback.

Stanway House, about 1904: the Charteris family, friends and staff. Hugo Lord Elcho wears the cloth cap; his daughter Cynthia (to marry Beb Asquith) is on his right. Mary Lady Elcho holds Bibs, her youngest child, on her lap; her children Mary and Ego are at her feet; her son Guy is seated holding a cigar; Yvo is seated in a wicker chair, wearing a lace collar and whistling. The family coachman James Prew stands at the back wearing a top hat.

Amisfield. The third country house (the second was Gosford) owned by the Earls of Wemyss. Designed by Isaac Ware, demolished by the 11th Earl of Wemyss in 1923.

Mells Manor House, Somerset, 1917. The Elizabethan manor house of the Horner family. Edward Horner would relax in the loggia in the balmy summers before the war. Frances Horner established the village work party in the loggia in 1914, reading news from the front as the Mells women sewed shirts for their soldiers.

Sir John Horner.

Frances Horner.

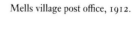

Mells village post office, 1912.

Mells village post office, 1915, immediately after fire almost destroyed the property.

Mells Park House, Mells, Somerset. The 18th century house of the Horner family, destroyed by fire in October 1917; 'an empty blackened shell with fallen keystones and inside piles of debris—like pictures of the Cloth Hall at Ypres' (France Horner).

We thank our friends in MELLS, VOBSTER and the neighbourhood for the help given by them on the night of Thursday October 11th during the fire at MELLS PARK. Had it not been for the courage and endurance of the many workers present neither pictures books, china nor furniture, could have been saved. This letter is an attempt to express our gratitude for the great efforts made on our behalf.

FRANCES HORNER,

JOHN FRANCIS
FORTESCUE HORNER.

The open letter sent by Sir John and Frances Horner to every family who helped save the contents of Park House.

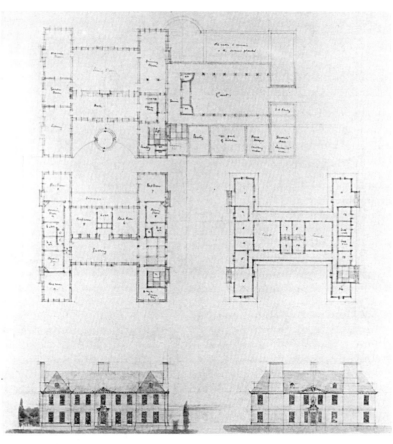

Preliminary designs by Sir Edwin Lutyens of Mells Park House for the
Rt Hon Reginald McKenna, 1925.

The newly completed Park House.

Descriptions of the landscape and country life are loaded with foreboding; imagery is inevitably ominous.

> And now again,
> In the harvest rain,
> The Blenheim oranges
> Fall grubby from the trees.[33]

> The cherry trees bend over and are shedding,
> On the old road where all that passed are dead,
> Their petals, strewing the grass as for a wedding
> This early May morn when there is none to wed.[34]

Thomas first considered his role in the war when walking over the fields of Herefordshire and Gloucestershire with Robert Frost and Eleanor Farjeon in August 1914: 'Something had to be done'. He was then 35 years old, with a wife and three children to support and he was offered the option of emigrating to America to live close to the Frosts. Instead he enlisted in the Artists' Rifles in July 1915. Unlike his fellow Georgians, Abercrombie, Gibson, Monro, he was not content just to play his part in the war effort on the home front: his intention was to go to the front: 'I want to see what it is like out there'.[35] At the same time as Thomas was choosing between enlisting and emigrating, he was also going through an astonishing metamorphosis as a writer. The impact of the war and the contact with Robert Frost turned Thomas from a hack-writer of country books into one of England's finest poets. Frost received batches of poems once he returned to America and he wrote to Abercrombie in September 1915: 'the war . . . has made some sort of new man and a poet'[36] out of Thomas.

During 1915 Thomas was commissioned to compile an anthology of poetry and prose to be called *This England*: the theme which linked the extracts was to be love of country. He preferred 'indirect praise' to 'professed patriotic writing', the latter usually being bad, and chose writers such as Hardy, Cobbett, Chaucer and Shakespeare. He also included two of his earliest poems, 'The Manor Farm' and 'Haymaking'. In both poems he emphasizes the indestructible features of country life.

> . . . a season of bliss unchangeable
> Awakened from farm and church where it had lain
> Safe under tile and thatch for ages since
> This England, Old already, was called Merry.
> The men leaned on their rakes, about to begin,
> But still. And all were silent. All was old,
> This morning time, with a great age untold,
> Older than Clare and Cobbett, Morland and Crome.[37]

Gibson and Abercrombie had found themselves unable to write but Thomas found the war 'has given me time to please myself with some unprofitable writing',[38] i.e. poetry. He was not starved of countryside for inspiration. The Artists' Rifles trained in Essex and in the autumn of 1915 *Country Life* visited their sylvan headquarters.

> . . . nowhere can there be a lovelier or more engaging spot. For some little way from the nearest station the road toils steadily up hill, with woodland on either side – twisted and fantastic oaks and thorns and birches and beeches, with a glimpse of bracken, and every here and there a green glade that goes tapering away into the distance of the forest. Locksley might have wound his bugle here, and the jolly clerk of Copmanhurst have brought down a fat buck by moonlight.[39]

In such a greenwood a country-loving English poet was being trained to fight for the land he loved. But for Thomas this wasn't so strange a concept. In his poem 'Lob' he describes the sort of country-man with whom he identified: 'as English as this gate, these flowers, this mire', with a face 'by life and weather cut / And coloured'. Lob is known by as many names as his kind have given to the flowers of the countryside. Throughout the centuries he has offered his life in defence of his land.

> The man you saw, – Lob-lie-by-the-fire, Jack Cade,
> Jack Smith, Jack Moon, poor Jack of every trade,
> Young Jack, or old Jack, or Jack What-d'ye-call,
> Jack-in-the-hedge, or Robin-run-by-the-wall,
> Robin Hood, Ragged Robin, Lazy Bob,

One of the Lords of No Man's Land, good Lob –
Although he was seen dying at Waterloo,
Hastings, Agincourt, and Sedgemoor, too –
Lives yet. He never will admit he is dead.

Though Thomas was killed at the Battle of Arras he achieved a lasting reputation as an artist through the poetry the war gave him the opportunity to write. The countryside that he wrote about in his poetry was more important to him than his own life: defending it was the finest gesture he felt he could have made.

Some of the Georgian writers were reluctant to rush off to fight for their country but none were pacifists. They were all unquestioning in their patriotism and in their support of the war effort. As they left their rural paradises for service abroad or in factories and munitions works on the home front, another group of artists and writers – Bloomsbury – were moving in the opposite direction. Vanessa and Clive Bell, Duncan Grant, David Garnett and other members of the group were leaving their London studios, houses and flats to settle in the English countryside, some reluctantly to work on the land as labourers rather than compromise their pacifist beliefs. Indeed, to join Bloomsbury during the war it seems the writer or artist was obliged to embrace the pacifist cause.

The principal and most exotic rural retreat of Bloomsbury was established before conscription was enforced. In May 1915 Ottoline and Philip Morrell moved from Bedford Square to their new permanent home at Garsington, a Cotswold manor house in Oxfordshire surrounded by two hundred acres of gardens and farmland. From the first days of the war, 44 Bedford Square had been a centre of pacifist activity. Morrell, Liberal MP for Burnley, ruined his parliamentary career by speaking out against the war on 4 August 1914. Bertrand Russell, one of their most frequent visitors, was deprived of his lectureship at Cambridge and was imprisoned in the last months of the war. He and many others opposed to the war flocked to Garsington: Lytton Strachey, Mark Gertler, Dora Carrington, Clive Bell, Katherine Mansfield and John Middleton Murry, D. H. Lawrence and Frieda, Aldous Huxley. In the idyllic pastoral surroundings of the Oxfordshire countryside they could air their political views and indulge in complicated sexual manoeuvres while Europe disintegrated into a bloodbath.

The Morrells held their first house-warming party in June 1915. Ottoline had painted the oak panelling of the drawing-rooms Venetian red and sea-green and arranged her collection of Samarkand rugs, silk hangings and lacquered screens around the house. Paintings by Mark Gertler, Augustus John, Duncan Grant, Henry Lamb and Charles Conder hung on the walls; classical statues lined the perimeter of the largest pond in the garden. Peacocks and guests strutted about the grounds; Ottoline's pugs yapped; Bertrand Russell helped to paint ceiling beams in the red drawing-room; the Lawrences had a fearful row and threw objects around their bedroom.

Later Lawrence wrote to his hostess in praise of the 'wonderful lawn, under the ilex trees, with the old house and its exquisite old front – it is *so* remote, so perfectly a small world to itself'.[40] But Lytton Strachey, visiting in July, commented 'the house is a regular galantry-show . . . very remarkable, very impressive, patched, gilded and preposterous'.[41] While Ottoline entertained, far away in the Dardanelles two of her brothers were fighting with the British forces.

Vanessa Bell created the other Bloomsbury retreat, in each of the three homes she established in the countryside during the war. The first was at West Wittering in Sussex, where Vanessa, Duncan Grant and David Garnett set up their *ménage à trois*. While Vanessa and Duncan painted and made designs for the Omega Workshop, David ('Bunny') modelled for them and pursued his own botanical studies (he was working under an eminent zoologist at Imperial College).

In June Bunny went to France with the Quaker War Victims' Relief Fund. He helped to build frame-houses in some of the devastated villages, including Sommeilles where 'up the main street there was one little house standing between the rows of burnt-out walls which stretched up to the top of the hill'. Letters from Vanessa described sailing excursions off the Sussex coast with Duncan, Clive and Roger Fry and a visit to Ottoline at Garsington. She wrote 'in spite of war and conscription and all horrors and disappointments . . . I have been extraordinarily selfishly happy lately . . . it has been hot and sunny and I sit out or in and paint.'[43]

Bunny returned to England in January 1916, the month Asquith's first Conscription Bill was passed, making military service compulsory for unmarried men. He immediately began to look, with Duncan, for somewhere congenial to work on the land so that their case for exemption might appear stronger when they made their inevitable appearance before a tribunal. Miss Florence Ewebank, an aunt of Duncan's, had recently died and they were able to take over her property, Wissett Lodge, in Suffolk, together with six acres. The early Victorian house had small, very dark rooms and was 'smothered with rambler roses and climbing plants'. Bunny read Florence Ewebank's journal, her household and cookery recipes, and felt her charm and spirit filling the house. He and Duncan set to work in the orchard pruning the apple trees and curing the blackcurrant bushes of 'big bud'. 'I was young and strong and this was my first falling in love with working on the land. I made plans, scoured the countryside for bees, went to market-day auctions at Halesworth and bought chickens, ducklings, and goslings.'[44]

Vanessa meanwhile filled the house with the atmosphere of Bloomsbury and Omega, painting the walls with brilliant lime-blue distemper and dyeing the chair covers with coloured inks. She wrote to Clive:

It is amazingly remote from the war and all the horrors, though Bunny saw a Zeppelin on Friday night and heard some explosions ... We hear rumours that one came down in the mouth of the Thames, but we get no papers – is it true? How absurd it seems that people shouldn't be allowed to live this kind of life in peace. One could be perfectly happy like this I believe. Only the time goes too fast.[45]

Other accounts of English life at this time, in town and country, give the impression that the whole nation was geared to the war effort, collecting and making clothes for refugees and soldiers, growing more food, learning first aid, joining the home guard if not the army itself, preparing for invasion. These artists needed to cut themselves off from the war, to bury themselves in their overgrown Suffolk garden. It was the privilege of genius, or so it must have seemed to Vanessa, who confessed to her sister Virginia Woolf, 'I see more and more that we are completely isolated from our kind'.[46]

Lytton Strachey visited Wissett: 'Everything and everybody seems to be more or less overgrown with vegetation, thistles four feet high fill the flower garden, Duncan is covered with Virginia (or should it be Vanessa?) creeper, and [Harry] Norton and I go about pulling up the weeds and peeping under the foliage'.[47] Leonard and Virginia stayed. Virginia was amazed by her sister's 'contented state of mind' and was inspired to write *Night and Day* in which the heroine Katherine Hilbery is based on Vanessa. Ottoline's visit was less successful.

> The weather was wet. The low-ceilinged little rooms would scarcely contain our magnificent visitor . . . I remember the feeling of relief when Monday morning came and Cutts drove his dogcart up to the door. Ottoline . . . suddenly appeared in a dress which she had not worn before during her visit. It might have been designed by Bakst for a Russian ballet on a Circassian folktale theme. Russian boots of red morocco were revealed under a full, light-blue silk tunic, over which she wore a white kaftan with embroidered cartridge pouches on the chest, on which fell the ropes of Portland pearls. On her head was a tall Astrakhan fez . . . off they drove looking exactly like the advertisement for a circus.

The increasing hostility of the locals was hardly surprising. They would come to the farm on Sundays – their day off work – to watch the artists trying to grow things. When Duncan and Bunny suspected their White Leghorn chickens were being stolen by their neighbours they painted their tails blue, which only made the locals more outraged. It seemed the Londoners were making a mockery of poultry-farming. When Duncan and Bunny appeared before the Blything Tribunal in May it was obvious that the Suffolk farmers on the jury suspected the young men had moved to Suffolk just to avoid call-up. Their appeal for exemption was rejected.

Later in the month the Appeal Tribunal at Ipswich granted Duncan and Bunny exemption from combative service but they had to show they were engaged in work of 'national importance' to avoid uncongenial labour. They could no longer be self-employed but had to become 'real' agricultural labourers working on a 'real' farm.

Virginia Woolf had written to Vanessa in May describing

Charleston, a farmhouse near her own Sussex country house: 'under the Downs. It has a charming garden, with a pond, & fruit trees, & vegetables, all now rather wild, but you could make it lovely'.[49] Vanessa decided to take it, finding work for her two young men on the nearby New House Farm. She moved in to Charleston in October 1915 together with Duncan and Bunny, her two children and three servants. The latter made it a lot easier to cope with the absence of piped water and electricity. Again Vanessa set about creating an arcadia in the midst of a world at war. The eighteenth-century farmhouse she found 'most lovely, very solid and simple, with flat walls in that lovely mixture of brick and flint that they use about here and perfectly flat windows in the walls and wonderfully tiled roofs. The pond is most beautiful.'[50] Bunny declared it 'the centre of slow-moving farm life'. And Virginia wrote 'Nessa seems to have slipped civilisation off her back, and splashes about entirely nude, without shame, and enormous spirit'.[51]

Duncan and Bunny might not be fighting, but working for Mr Hecks they certainly learnt the less-romantic side of rural life. They were paid 12s. 6d. per week with 5d. an hour for overtime and worked a 7½ hour day, half a day on Saturdays. It was hard work, pulling up turnips in the depths of winter, hoeing a ten-acre bean field in the spring, threshing, dung carting. The winter of 1917–18 was particularly harsh. Duncan lost weight alarmingly and suffered a severe attack of rheumatism so that he was eventually exempted from labouring in the afternoons. There was increasing personal tension between the three: Duncan was in love with Bunny, Bunny with Vanessa, Vanessa with Duncan. Bunny also found himself becoming increasingly depressed and angry about the war:

> hatred of the frenzied nationalism which had led the rulers of Europe to sacrifice the lives and happiness of millions for phantoms of Honour and Power . . . The knowledge that the majority of my countrymen would have thought I was a tick, if they had ever learned of my existence was not particularly consoling.[52]

Vanessa might have 'slipped civilisation off her back' but if she listened carefully she could hear the guns being fired on the battlefields of France. And her children suffered the abuse of their country neighbours. Quentin, then seven years old, remembers:

I knew we were wrong 'uns. We were really rotters. There was everybody else going off and getting killed in France, but we didn't. We weren't on good terms with local children because we were known as conschies and occasionally a brick would be thrown in one's direction.[53]

The war caused some privations: rationing affected the whole nation and at Charleston Vanessa kept chickens and rabbits and ducks; Bunny kept bees. But Bloomsbury friends would always arrive with chocolates, dates, cakes, copies of the *Tatler* and the *Burlington Magazine*, Clive with wine and cigars.

At least the work on the land was hard enough. Not so at Garsington. Philip Morrell had managed the farm at Garsington since taking over the estate and he was able to offer work to a number of conscientious objectors, putting them up in cottages close to the manor house. He made Garsington virtually self-sufficient in food during the war but this was not due to the efforts of his pacifist labourers, rather to the work of the regular stalwarts from the countryside around, those who were not fighting for their country of course. The harvest of 1915 was brought in with the help of Bertrand Russell and Charles Gore, the Anglican Bishop of Oxford, a combination which provided the locals with great amusement. One old lady warned the bishop of the wicked company he was keeping in the fields. Gerald Shove, a Cambridge economist, and his wife Fredegond were among Morrell's pacifist labourers, so was Clive Bell whose fiery pamphlet 'Peace at Once' had caused his father to temporarily cut off his allowance. Clive was apparently very popular in the hay and harvest fields with the local female workforce.

According to Ottoline, Gerald Shove was the laziest of the pacifists. An ardent socialist, he tried to organise a trade union but the Oxfordshire labourers were unenthusiastic. He was put in charge of the hens but egg production dropped. So:

he reeled off the contents of an advertisement for a famous egg-production nostrum which he had somewhere come across, and told Philip that he could not expect fowls to lay without it. Greatly impressed by this expert knowledge, Philip ordered half a ton of it – but no more eggs were brought in after its arrival than before.[54]

Finally, at the end of 1917, one memoir describes Shove storming into the manor house shouting 'down with capitalist exploits',[55] then decamping in a taxi along with several of the Garsington hens. The remaining fowls were found to be languishing in filthy roosts surrounded by rotten eggs.

The Woolfs visited Garsington in November 1917. Leonard was not a conscientious objector but had been rejected by the forces on health grounds. His description reveals the fictional quality of the set-up; unbelievable at the best of time, but during a world war quite incredible.

> The house, Philip and Ottoline, the kaleidoscope of their friends and guests formed a framed picture of a society and life unlike any which I have ever met anywhere else in the real world; but in the world of fiction I recognised its counterpart, for the people in Crochet Castle, Headlong Hall, Nightmare Abbey, and Gryll Grange would have felt quite at home and have fitted in beautifully at Garsington Manor . . . Ottoline was herself not unlike one of her own peacocks, drifting about the house and terraces in strange brightly-coloured shawls and other floating garments, her unskilfully dyed red hair, her head tilted to the sky at the same angle as the birds' and her odd nasal voice and neighing laugh always seeming as if they might at any moment rise with one of those shattering calls of the peacock . . . she was, like the motley crowd which sat round her breakfast table or drifted about her garden, a fantastic hotchpotch.[56]

No wonder D. H. Lawrence eventually rejected its seductive powers calling to him to 'lapse back into its peaceful beauty of bygone things'.[57] 'One's soul rebels', he declared, and withdrew to the rigours of the Cornish landscape. 'I like Cornwall: it is a bare, forgotten county that doesn't belong to England: Celtic, pre-Christian. There are very rough winds and very fine black rocks and very white bursting seas.'[58] Lawrence was not a conscientious objector, but he was bitterly opposed to the war. He called it a 'dreadful, colossal idiocy', 'creeping hell', 'a mass of destruction and disintegration'. He thought the sort of English life represented by Garsington would be destroyed by it: 'the great past, crumbling down, breaking down'.[59] And he included a cruel portrait of

Ottoline, as Hermione Roddice, and her country house life in *Women in Love*: lush, protective, artistic and ultimately sterile.

Lady Chatterley's Lover (1928) completed Lawrence's vision of the extinction of 'feudal' England. Wragby estate is inherited by Clifford Chatterley who is left mentally and physically crippled by the war, trapped in his wheelchair, unable to produce an heir. The war had itself hastened the end of the traditional life of the English country gentry: or so it seemed.

Lawrence had found no rural arcadia in which to develop his vision of England. Unlike the Bloomsbury pacifists he was without financial or political protection: his stay in Cornwall turned into a living hell. He was physically unfit for military service but his presence in Cornwall attracted unfavourable comment and suspicion, particularly after the publicity attached to the seizure and burning of copies of *The Rainbow*. His wife was a German; they were heard singing lieder at their piano; the locals suspected they were provisioning German submarine crews along the coast; policemen spied on them, following them on country walks, searching their cottage. In October 1917 Lawrence and Frieda went to dinner with the composer Cecil Gray who was staying near by at Bosigran Castle. Policemen burst in on the party, accusing the artists of signalling to German submarines – the wind had disturbed the curtains. Gray was fined but Lawrence, on 12 October, was ordered to leave Cornwall within three days, to avoid living in any prohibited area, and to report to the police whenever he moved. The couple left Cornwall on 15 October.

Cecil Gray described the Cornish people as being capable of 'the purest form of disinterested, impersonal malevolence that I have ever encountered'.[60] Their venom was directed at Lawrence throughout 1916 and 1917. His sojourn in rural England was very different from the experience of lesser Bloomsbury artists, Duncan Grant, Mark Gertler, Clive Bell. Wyndham Lewis, artist and soldier, summed up their war:

> all doing work of National importance down in some downy English county, under the wings of powerful pacifist friends; pruning trees, planting gooseberry bushes and hay making, doubtless in large sunbonnets.[61]

The quality of most of the work produced by the Bloomsbury writers and artists and the Georgians is similar in its range and achievements. There is little to choose between the art criticism of Clive Bell and the literary criticism of Lascelles Abercrombie: neither has made a lasting impact on twentieth-century culture. On the other hand the essays of Lytton Strachey and the poetry and short stories of Walter de la Mare are examples of fine writing from each clique, appealing to a small discerning readership.

During the First World War, however, the Georgians were in the cultural mainstream. Their poetry was sent out to the trenches and published in magazines and newspapers; they supported the war effort and those who were fit enough fought for their country. Their love of the English countryside inspired their writing and their patriotism. Ironically, most were forced to leave their country homes to take part in some sort of war work: many never returned to the rural life. Several members of Bloomsbury, however, discovered the attractions of country life for the first time during the war as they left their urban homes for pacifist retreats in the countryside.

Siegfried Sassoon, foxhunter, cricketer, hero of no-man's-land and Georgian poet, would seem to be an unlikely guest to encounter at a Garsington country weekend during the war. He had enlisted even before England declared war on Germany, professing his willingness to die for his part of the English countryside. Nevertheless Garsington did become a war-time retreat for the veteran of the Battle of the Somme.

Sassoon thought he was rather an odd guest, to begin with, and took his fox terrier Topper to steady his nerves. The dog at least

> showed no awareness of incurring any extra strain on his sensibilities while staying with the Duke of Portland's half-sister and being patted on the head by extreme pacifists who had 'accepted war work' on Mr Morrell's farm, and who came in of an evening to puff churchwarden pipes by the fire and talk cleverly in cultured and earnest tones about significant form in the Arts and the misdeeds of the Militarists.[62]

It was under the influence of the Garsington pacifists, Bertrand Russell in particular, and through his increasing awareness of the difference between life in the English countryside and life in the trenches zigzagging across France and Belgium, that Sassoon worked out his personal statement against the war.

Sassoon first heard from Ottoline Morrell in January 1916. She wrote enthusing about a poem of his published in *The Times*.

> I had received the letter when we were starting on a three days' march from rest billets up to the Somme trenches, and Lady Ottoline's large sheet of beautiful hand-made notepaper had seemed then something from another world.[63]

In August Sassoon was invalided home from the Somme. While convalescing in hospital in Oxford he was taken by his literary friend Robbie Ross to spend an afternoon at Garsington. He was overcome by the contrast between the utter tranquillity of the pastoral scene, 'as we halted under the ilex to admire the charming view' and the landscape in which he had been fighting for his life only a month before, where the few surviving trees 'harboured German snipers'.[64]

Garsington, apart from its pacifist residents, was part of the England he had joined up to defend in August 1914: the traditional rural England of manor house, parish church and tithe barn; thatch and half-timbering; harvest festival and Boxing Day meet. In 1916, before the Battle of the Somme, he was reading *Tess of the D'Urbervilles*. It reinforced his vision of the England he was fighting for. 'I had slipped a book into my haversack and it was a comfort to be carrying it, for Thomas Hardy's England was between its covers.' As well as visiting Garsington in August, Sassoon also went out to the Cotswold village of Burford to visit his uncle Hamo Thornycroft. Hamo had been a friend of Hardy for over thirty years; Sassoon and he talked to a Burford saddler who might have stepped out of a Hardy novel.

> Burford itself was like a welcome home from the war as I came to it through the ripened harvest landscape, and crossed the stone bridge over the little Windrush at the lower end of the steep street of grey houses. It was the first time I had fully realized what it meant to be

well away from the war, and its serenity seemed well worth preserving by such obscure personal efforts as one had managed to make [Sassoon had just been awarded the Military Cross].[65]

Hamo was sunburnt from his war-work, helping with the harvesting, 'proud of having already earned twenty-five shillings by piling corn-stooks on the local uplands'.[66] It didn't seem to matter that his efforts were amateurish and some of his stooks were already collapsing.

Sassoon found the whole day 'tranquillising', 'ideally pleasant', the afternoon suffused with 'dozy sunshine'. Only on his way home did the soldier-poet wonder how his uncle could manage to make the war seem so different from what it really was: 'there were vague stirrings of perplexity in my mind'.[67] After all, while Hamo was bringing in the harvest on the rolling Cotswold uplands, Sassoon's friends were fighting and possibly dying on the disturbingly similar rolling uplands of the Somme.

Confusion and perplexity pursued Sassoon to Weirleigh where his mother was still grieving over the loss of her younger son at Gallipoli the year before. One old man worked in the garden; all the horses had been taken by the army except for the old mowing-machine pony; the stables were neglected: 'a tin of Harvey's Hoof Ointment had obviously been there since 1914'.[68] Hunting was still being carried on although few turned up to chase the fox. Sassoon was able to enjoy a final day out with the hounds after being passed fit to return to his regiment.

Staring at the dim brown landscape I decided that the War was worth while if it was being carried on to safeguard this sort of thing. Was it? I wondered; and if a doubt arose it was dismissed before it had been formulated.[69]

In May 1917, after another spell at the front, Sassoon was again invalided home, this time convalescing at Chapelwood Manor, the Sussex home of Lord and Lady Brassey. Chapelwood was a relatively new country house, designed to fit into the landscape, with grey timbers, many gables, dark yew-hedges and formal gardens. Sassoon found himself cocooned in a pastoral arcadia, in a countryside being

used to nurse himself and a handful of brother-officers back to health
and to the trenches.

> I am a country wanderer once more – climbing gates and staring
> through tangled hedges at the mossy boughs of apple-trees laden
> with blossom, while the sun comes out after a passing shower ...
> And the sunsets are yellow and serene – never dyed with crimson or
> hung with banners of war.[70]

The very tranquillity of the Sussex countryside, the landscape Sassoon
had enlisted to defend, was making him brood continually on the fate of
his friends in France. On 15 June he wrote his statement against the
war in his diary; on 6 July he sent it to his commanding officer; on 30
July his statement was read out in Parliament and on 31 July published
in *The Times*.

The Garsington pacifists were delighted. Bertrand Russell had
helped to shape the statement, fuelling Sassoon with intellectual
arguments to bolster his emotional outburst against the war. Only the
intervention of Robert Graves saved Sassoon from court martial and
imprisonment: instead Sassoon was dispatched to Craiglockhart War
Hospital outside Edinburgh for shell-shocked officers. In 1918
Sassoon returned to the trenches.

While he was waiting at Weirleigh for news of his approaching court
martial – before the intervention of Graves – Sassoon was surrounded
by evidence of the durability of life in the countryside, the irrelevance of
war. His attention focused on the village church whose presence
seemed to offer a different, long-term view of life from his own.

> Butley church, with its big-buttressed square tower, was protectively
> permanent. One could visualize it there for the last 599 years,
> measuring out the unambitious local chronology with its bells, while
> English history unrolled itself along the horizon with coronations
> and rebellions and stubbornly disputed charters and covenants.[71]

The massive, all-embracing architecture of the church seemed to
suggest that even the horrors of a modern war, today's emergencies
would be absorbed, harmoniously, into 'the simple annals of this quiet

corner of Kent'.[72] The Roll of Honour inside the church and the village war memorial, both erected after the war, would suggest as much, carrying names to be found scattered on gravestones throughout the cemetery on the hillside beside the church.

Sassoon himself tried to return to the pre-war golden age which he created in his *Memoirs of a Foxhunting Man*; a golden age which, through his work, became the universally accepted vision of life before the war for a generation of disillusioned survivors. He settled in an old grey stone house in the Wiltshire countryside, hunting, playing cricket, writing poetry. But he seemed to 'walk in a dream through a dream world'. A few years before his death he was visited by Anthony Powell, who found him 'looking like a ghost haunting the fields of Passchendaele or Bapaume . . . For Captain Sassoon, though no longer himself involved in it, the first war was still in progress.'[73]

The ordinary soldier, however, who survived the war, looked upon Sassoon and his kind less kindly. As Frank Cook wrote: 'Sassoon made himself a nuisance to the Army when he was sent home, he did his bit but no more than thousands of others who did not rhyme about it.'[74]

Rudyard Kipling was already a Grand Old Man of Letters at the declaration of war. His only son John was killed fighting in France in October 1915. Kipling had to restrict his war-time activities to assisting the propaganda-machine of the allies; making speeches, writing, visiting troops in England and overseas – above all hating the enemy. His anti-Germanism verged on racist obsession: this, for example, from the *Daily Express*, May 1916:

One thing we must get into our thick heads is that wherever the German man or woman gets a suitable culture to thrive in he or she means death and loss to civilised people, precisely as germs of any disease . . . The German is typhoid or plague – Pestio Teutonicus if you like.[75]

When the *Daily Telegraph* published the Lansdowne Letter in 1917 Kipling's anti-Semitism was roused: the proprietor of the paper was after all a Jew; all peace plans were mad.

Unsurprisingly the story which Kipling wrote in 1915 to portray village life and village attitudes during the war is brutal in its hatred of Germans. The heroine, Mary Postgate, is the paid companion to an old woman whose nephew Wyn she falls in love with. Wyn is killed training for the Flying Corps and Mary has to burn his toys and sports equipment in the garden. She walks to the village to buy petrol for the fire as a stray bomb falls from the sky, killing a little girl. Mary returns home, to find the German airman lying in her laurel bushes, dying in great agony. Ignoring his cries, she sets fire to Wyn's relics. As the flames rise up, the German gives his death rattle. Mary goes indoors to enjoy a nice hot bath.

This sort of hatred – though we are meant to feel compassion for the lonely, frustrated companion – is what Lawrence encountered in Cornwall. It fuelled suspicions against William Rothenstein and Robert Frost. Kipling had it in abundance, especially after the death of his son. He wrote to Stanley Baldwin in July 1916 from his Sussex home, 'It's a curious thing that most of the Huns in our neighbourhood live on ridges facing the sea'.[76] In September 1918, on holiday in Cornwall, he again wrote to Baldwin describing the stoning by locals of some Germans living in a cottage. As far as he was concerned it was a jolly good idea to kill the Huns and their bitches. It would seem Lawrence and Frieda got off lightly.

The loss of his son was no doubt largely responsible for Kipling's violent anti-German attitude although 'Mary Postgate' was written several months before John's death. But Kipling's personal grief could produce the tenderness of the poem 'My Boy Jack', in which the poet speaks for every grieving parent.

> 'Have you news of my boy Jack?'
>   Not this tide.
> 'When d'you think that he'll come back?'
>   Not with this wind blowing, and this tide.

Kipling had seen something of the realities of war before his son. He was invited to visit the French Armies in the field in August 1915, just as his son's regiment, the 2nd Irish Guards, were put under orders for France. Wherever he went in France, Kipling came across young soldiers, English and French, who had been brought up on his books,

Stalky, the *Jungle Books*, *Barrack Room Ballads*. He wrote home from a villa in Jonchery:

> The General said to me, with a wave of the hand:- '*All* these men know your books'. I smiled politely. He turned on the nearest group and asked 'em! '*Yes*, oh yes,' said they, 'specially the Jungle Books!' He took me elsewhere and the sentries with their rifles told me the same thing. Weird Noncoms in dug-outs echoed it till I nearly thought it was a put up job of the General. But 'twasn't. 'Twas true. (The fuss about this tour is there's too much dam R.K. in it. I have to lead all the processions).[77]

Kipling was the poet laureate of the war. Poems such as 'If' had become part of the nation's consciousness. Woodrow Wilson confessed that 'If' had been an inspiration to him and wrote to Kipling for his autograph. Kipling was hardly flattered. He thought Wilson's policy of neutrality despicable: not at all in the spirit of 'If'.

Kipling's tour of the French armies provided him with plenty of useful advice to pass on to his son: 'I found boric acid in my socks a great comfort';[78] 'Don't forget the beauty of rabbit netting overhead against hand-grenades'.[79] When John was reported missing, Carrie Kipling continued to hope her son would be discovered alive and a prisoner: Kipling did not share her optimism. 'I've seen what shells can do, and I don't.'[80]

Kipling, Carrie and their daughter Elsie spent much of the war on their Sussex estate. Kipling had become a Sussex landowner in 1902 when he bought Bateman's, an Elizabethan manor house in the Burwash valley. 'It is a good and peaceable place standing in terraced lawns nigh to a walled garden of old red brick, and two fat-headed oast-houses with redbrick stomachs, and an aged silver-grey dovecot on top.'[81]

To begin with he owned only 25 acres of land but by 1925 he had increased the estate to over 300 acres. It was mostly worked by Carrie and a farm manager. At the beginning of the war the Kiplings were advised by their Sussex neighbour Colonel Feilden to buy some sheep. Kipling took the advice and bought forty, although he confessed 'I don't hanker after eternal mutton'.[82] He also bought some Guernsey cows to supply Bateman's with milk and butter. Dorothy Ponton, ex-governess to the Kipling children, described the activities on the thriving estate.

A Sussex herd of red Shorthorns roamed the pastures and were fattened for market, and two handsome dray horses worked on the farm to supplement the use of the mechanical appliances for farming. A poultry farm was run, and I was much impressed by the fact that the farm accounts revealed that geese cost next to nothing to feed, and sold at high price at Michaelmas. The orchards, too, provided good crops, and the piggeries yielded very profitable litters.[83]

It was all very different from the inefficient haphazard farming methods of Bloomsbury. The visitors to Bateman's during the war were also rather different from the guests of the Morrells and Vanessa Bell. A captain and five lieutenants were billeted at Bateman's in February 1915. They could enjoy the country fare and offer their avid host first-hand information about the war.

They turned up yesterday evening about 6.30 (having ordered dinner for that hour). They were preceded by a young transport officer (Preeston was his name) who rather reminded us of you [the Kipling's son John]. Also three or four soldier servants carried their kit to Bateman's – and you can imagine the joy of the maids . . . We gave them a decent dinner – tomato soup: fish: mutton: mince pies and cheese straws and unlimited ginger beer and cigarettes. They, naturally, talked shop *all* the time . . . Some of their tales would have made you faint.[84]

More soldiers stayed in 1916. They found themselves helping to scythe the grass, to cut hedges and cut the lawns with the hand-mower, or feeding the geese. MacIntosh was an 'immoral gander'; Bowser, one of his wives, took bread out of the hand and made 'snuffling noises like an affectionate puppy'. Kipling appreciated assistance around his estate but revelled in the stories he was offered in exchange for his hospitality.

We've just had a man down here fresh from the Jutland action – a destroyer commander. He was very well satisfied with what had been dealt out to the Hun and had a gay time *between* a couple of Dachshund cruisers at 200 yrd both of whom tried to ram him![85]

In June 1917 Kipling was approached to write a history of his son's regiment, the Irish Guards. John's young brother-officers became regular visitors to Bateman's, continuing to call after the war. One of the farmhouses on the estate was restored for the use of convalescent officers and their families. In September 1917 Kipling was again approached to write something for the war effort: inscriptions for the war graves which would eventually cover hundreds of acres of the war-torn fields of France and Belgium. Sir Fabian Ware came down to Bateman's to invite Kipling to become one of the Imperial War Graves Commissioners. He remained a member of the commission for the rest of his life. He proposed the inscription 'Their name liveth for evermore' at one of the earliest meetings of the commission, to be used on the Stone of Sacrifice in each cemetery; also every other inscription and form of words used by the commission. Kipling was also one of the originators of the plan to bury an Unknown Soldier in Westminster Abbey.

Much of this literary effort, to the memory of not just his dead son but all the men who died for their country, was made at Bateman's deep in the Sussex Weald. Kipling had fallen in love with this particular landscape long before he came to own his country estate. It gave him strength to cope with his personal grief and to represent, through his writing, the grief of the whole nation.

> Take of English earth as much
> As either hand may rightly clutch,
> In the taking of it breathe
> Prayer for all who lie beneath.
> Not the great nor well-bespoke,
> But the mere uncounted folk
> Of whose life and death is none
> Report or lamentation.
>   Lay that earth upon thy heart,
>   And thy sickness shall depart!

In the Manor House

Beyond the thunder of the guns,
  Beyond the flaming line,
Far from this sky of echoing bronze,
  The English valleys shine,
The gardens moated in the wolds
  By wind and water kissed,
And dainty girls, that England folds
  In sunshine and in mist.

Herbert Asquith, 'The Western Line. Flanders 1915'

WHEN Mary Countess of Wemyss wrote in her diary on New Year's Day 1915, 'Sad year finished. What is to follow?'[1] she could not have imagined how much she would have to suffer as a consequence of war. Two of her three sons would be killed, also three nephews, and there were many more deaths among her immediate family and friends. In this, she suffered about as much as other aristocratic mothers; the heaviest losses were borne by the class which went 'over the top' first. But there were also losses in the villages of Stanway, Didbrook and Stanton in the Cotswolds, and in Aberlady in East Lothian: family and friends, tenants and servants would be listed together on the village war memorials.

When peace was finally restored, Mary recalled the legend of the curse hanging over the Wemysses' ancestors, the Tracys, who first acquired the Cotswold estate of Stanway from Tewkesbury Abbey in the sixteenth century. 'I think they may have earned a double portion, not only for acquiring Stanway [from the church], but also for the heinous crime of William de Traci, one of the four Norman knights who murdered Thomas à Becket.' The curse also applied to her own family, the Wyndhams, and to her close friends the Horners, both of whom acquired their estates in Wiltshire and Somerset from the church at the dissolution of the monasteries:

> Wyndham, Horner, Popham and Thynne,
> When the abbots went out, they came in.

Her nephew Percy Wyndham, known to his family as Perf, was owner of Clouds for barely a year before dying in the Battle of the Aisne in September 1914. Edward Horner, the only surviving son and heir to Mells, was killed in November 1917. Her own son Ego, heir to Stanway and Gosford, died in April 1916.

The Wemysses and the Horners, linked by ties of friendship and marriage and owning sizeable chunks of the countryside, responded to the war with the same unquestioning patriotism. While their sons were leading their men 'into battle', Mary Wemyss and Frances Horner were devoting themselves to war work in their villages and in London. When their sons were killed, it was supposed they had died for Stanway and for Mells. At Ego's memorial service held in the small parish church at Stanway, the vicar recalled 'how absolutely he identified himself with all Stanway interests . . . he knew, and he loved to hear, the many things that make the details of the home-life of those on this estate.' Ego's wife Letty, hearing of Yvo's death, wrote to Mary: 'I thought of his love for you and all his family and of Stanway and the birds, and I felt that he must have almost *enjoyed* fighting for his "loves", and that he knew it *was* worth dying for'.

During the war country houses like Stanway and Mells were regarded as havens of stability and tranquillity, not only by those who lived in and fought for them but also in literary and artistic responses. In the two or three decades just before the war there had been a revival in all things rural: literary panegyrics of life in the countryside; the resurrection of dying village crafts; the preservation of footpaths and hedgerows; the establishment of the National Trust. Visitors to

Stanway were entertained with Morris dancers and trips to the Arts and Crafts Guild in nearby Chipping Campden; Mary Wemyss subscribed to *New Numbers*, the quarterly magazine of the Georgian poets living under the Malvern Hills at the outbreak of war.

The revival was largely a response to negative feelings about modern, industrial life: the factories and monotonous housing estates creeping across England's green fields were perceived as a threat to rather than as a part of civilisation. With the outbreak of war, the countryside became even more precious: manor houses, medieval churches, tithe barns and humble thatched cottages were all living symbols of an aspect of English life which must never be destroyed.

Describing Stanway's atmosphere of 'gentleness and peace' Mary echoed the words of Rupert Brooke, whom she had known before the war, in his evocation of the England he was prepared to die for: 'gentleness / In hearts at peace, under an English heaven'. The poet in her own family, Herbert Asquith (married to her eldest daughter, Cynthia), found Stanway and the Cotswolds to be a source of spiritual and physical strength and an inspiration to his muse. In November 1915 he came to Stanway to recover his health and sanity after a spell in the French trenches and spent six months cocooned within its 'ever-changing calm'.

Both Stanway and Mells are rich in history and legend. Dating back to before the English Civil War, they had survived political and social upheavals to emerge in the twentieth century as a vital part of Britain's heritage. Since its founding every issue of *Country Life* had featured a particular country house and during the war both houses were focused on: Stanway in 1916, the year its heir was killed; Mells in 1917, just eleven days after Edward Horner's death. St Clair Baddeley found a 'free yet firm and inseparable relationship'[2] between the manor house at Stanway, the parish church, tithe barn and Cotswold stone cottages. Mells has the same intimate plan: the tower of the medieval church, 'a symbol of strength and calm',[3] casts its shadow over manor house, cottages and gravestones. They are seen as relics of 'Merrie England'.

The architectural unity of the villages of Stanway and Mells, the closeness and interdependence of manor house, church and cottages, were reflected in the united responses of all the inhabitants of the villages to the war. The manor house and church were the centres of organisation in the war effort but every level of the rural hierarchy became involved, from landless labourer and servant to tenant farmer, village school-teacher, vicar and landlord: growing more food, making shirts and blankets, knitting socks, nursing, taking in refugees, entertaining wounded soldiers, mourning their lost families and friends.

The way of life and the attitudes of the Wemysses and the Horners during the war epitomised the special relationship which existed between the gentry and their estates: a relationship based on service, self-sacrifice and patriotism.

Hugo and Mary had only just become Earl and Countess of Wemyss when war was declared. The tenth Earl, Francis Charteris, died on 30 June 1914. He would have been 96 years old on 4 August. For years he had predicted war with Germany. He was convinced the Germans would make their first landing at Aberlady, on the east coast of Scotland, and turn his Scottish mansion Gosford into barracks. (Instead, his other Scottish mansion, Amisfield, was to become a billet for British soldiers.)

Stanway House and estate had been given to Hugo by his father. The couple married in 1883 and Stanway remained their principal home even after they became Earl and Countess. In 1886 the tenth Earl also gave Hugo a house in London, 62 Cadogan Square, and at his death, Hugo inherited Gosford and Amisfield, together with 55,000 acres of land in Scotland, another London house (23 St James's Place) and half a dozen ruined castles.

Although the land brought in a rental income of around £55,000 a year the Wemysses were not fabulously wealthy by the standards of their class. The 1894 Budget was the first to impose death duties on agricultural property (the tenth Earl called the budget 'burglarious . . . it would pauperize the rich')[4] and the rate was increased in 1909. Also in 1909 provision was made by the Liberal government for a valuation of all land in the United Kingdom for the imposition of an Undeveloped Land Duty, heralding the sale of large chunks of the countryside by many worried landowners even before their sons died in the war.

Hugo had to pay £28,000 in death duties for eight years, starting in 1915. However, his Scottish factor George Connor glumly informed him that he was £23,000 short of the required amount if both Gosford and Stanway were to be kept open and the regular allowances paid to various members of the family (Hugo received £2,000 and Mary, for running all their households, paying school fees and university expenses, travel expenses and servants' wages, £5,400). The tenth Earl had left unsettled personal estate of nearly £100,000 but out of this many bequests had to be paid, including £10,000 to Ego, £1000 to George Connor and dozens of smaller amounts to his servants. The Wemysses were not only responsible for the upkeep of their estate and for paying the wages of their servants; they were also patrons of Stanway parish church and Stanway and Aberlady village schools. In addition, major repairs and extension work had just been undertaken at Stanway House and completed in the summer of 1914. The guests who had assembled at Stanway for August Bank Holiday in 1914 were meant to be celebrating the reopening of the house. And like all owners of agricultural land at this time, the Wemysses were victims of inflation: incomes from land were not keeping pace with the cost of maintaining an aristocratic way of life. In 1873 the rents from the Stanway estate had been £6,900: in 1909 the rents had fallen 48% to £3,652; an annual profit of several thousand pounds had turned into a loss of almost one thousand pounds.

Financial worries were to be a constant source of friction between Hugo and Mary throughout the war years. Hugo would accuse his wife of being unreasonable when she pleaded for Stanway to be kept open as the family home or tried to stop him selling off land and family heirlooms. Mary commented in her diary 'how much easier to fight Germans or Turks than to manage every day life – one is "at the front" nearly all the time'. She had reason to worry as Hugo's past financial record was hardly reassuring. His alarming tendency to gamble with stocks and shares had reached a climax in 1899 when he lost a staggering £80,000 on the Johannesburg Stock Exchange.

But Mary was herself something of a liability. She was a notorious collector of problems – her immediate plan to turn Stanway into a hospital when war was declared was typical – and she filled her country home with a variety of refugees. When a decrepit horse was delivered to Stanway in 1916 even she realised she was going too far:

a gaunt hairy humerous swelled legged weak hocked cab horse
arrived . . . I'd love to keep her but what will Hugo say if I become a
hospital for dogs & horses old men Belgians & invalids & grand
children, instead of having a small efficient establishment run on
business lines!

In 1915 Hugo was still paying off his speculating debts. The sale of
the tenth Earl's London home in July realised £10,000 which Hugo
immediately planned to invest. Mary objected, no doubt remembering
past 'investments', and suggested, to Hugo's intense irritation, that he
should pay off some of his debts, thus saving interest payments of £600
a year. Later in the year Hugo was badgering his eldest son Ego, serving
in Egypt with the Gloucestershire Yeomanry, to give his permission for
some of the Wemysses' art collection to be sold. Ego agreed but was
perhaps a little waspish in his reply:

I am sorry I have not answered your letter sooner but I have been very
hard worked for the first time in my life in a responsible position, and
found it very difficult to switch the mind off horses, picketing-pegs,
head-ropes, cardigan jackets, Balaclava helmets, razors, hair-
combs, toothbrushes, etc. on to landed Estates.

The contents of Stanway had been left in the tenth Earl's will to be held
by the trustees (A. J. Balfour, Alfred Lyttelton and George Connor)
'upon trust as heirlooms for the life rent use of those who succeeded to
the title',[5] which was bad luck for Hugo.

Many owners of country houses were 'saved', temporarily, by the
war. Houses and parks they could no longer afford to run themselves
were graciously offered to the nation as hospitals, convalescent homes,
training grounds and barracks, or were simply rented out to wealthy
Londoners fleeing German Zeppelins.

The Lothians and Border Horse were the first regiment to rent
Amisfield from the Wemysses in 1914; the Argyll and Sutherland
Highlanders moved in the following year. Occupancy by the army was
not without risks and when the Wemysses found a Highland major
using the drawing-room for his bedroom they quickly removed the fine
art and better pieces of furniture, including a pair of priceless Chinese

Chippendale day-beds. A less valuable 'Chinese bed', now at Gosford, bears the marks left by the soldiers striking their matches on its end-posts.

The Horners were considerably poorer than the Wemysses and their 6,700 acres in Somerset brought in rents of just over £10,000 a year. Sir John also received a stipend of £1,200 a year as a Commissioner of Woods and Forests. The Horners owned two large houses in the same village. A wealthy eighteenth-century ancestor had built himself a brand-new mansion, Mells Park, outside the village, at the same time demolishing half the Elizabethan manor house. When Frances Graham married John Horner in 1883 the agricultural depression had taken its toll:

> all the cottagers on the property . . . just lived on us. Their rents were a shilling or eighteenpence a week . . . as the cottages were very old there were constant repairs to be done; and none of the farms were in good order. Beef was given away at Christmas at a cost of nearly a hundred pounds. We had to roof the Park House, and lay on water. It was one long struggle against debt, which mounted slowly up.

As a result the Horners moved back into the old manor house in 1900 and let Mells Park together with the shooting. Their tenant was Gilbert Thompson Bates, second son of Sir Edward Bates, a wealthy Liverpool shipowner. Bates took his role as temporary owner of a large country house and estate seriously. In December 1914, just after hearing his son had been wounded at Ypres, he still led the annual hare-coursing meeting on the Mells Park estate. Unfortunately the ground was too wet so the hares did not 'sit tight', which was 'all against the dogs'.[6]

In September 1914, when a Mrs Agnes Cookson wrote to enquire whether the manor house itself was to let, the Horners moved up to their London house for six months. Mrs Cookson wrote 'so many people are letting one of their houses, if they have two, this winter'. The Horners had three and let two of them. There was some quibbling about the price – Sir John wanted 200 guineas – but it was finally settled at six guineas a week for twenty-two weeks, and a further nine guineas a week for two more weeks. Sir John's agent explained Mrs Cookson's responsibilities to her:

> the tenant to pay the gardeners' wage there are 2 men & a boy & to have the produce of the garden – I may say that the head gardener has charge of the electric lighting – Sir John would like to leave his head housemaid in the house, he paying her wages & the tenant her keep.

The following autumn Sir John was able to install central heating in the manor house, no doubt thanks to the additional income from rent.

Renting out property was not without its hazards, however. Mrs Cookson entered into the life of the village with enthusiasm, helping with children's tea parties and annual prize-givings, alongside members of the Horner family and the Belgian refugees. But in March 1915, while the Cooksons were still occupying the manor house, a fire broke out in the chimney of the library. The Frome Fire Brigade arrived just in time else 'there might have been a serious conflagration and a valuable staircase was endangered'.[7]

Yvo Charteris, Mary Wemyss's youngest son, was still at Eton when war was declared. In December he was given a place at Balliol College, Oxford, but by February 1915 he had enlisted and received a commission in the King's Royal Rifle Corps. 'These last few months here [at Eton] have been dead and listless. This place seems to me terribly irrelevant.' Meanwhile his mother, as if foreseeing the future, had ordered the gardener at Stanway to plant an avenue of trees, *Pyrus malus floribundus sanguineus*, leading from the house to the tithe barn. 'I call it the bl . . dy row', she wrote, 'because it is planted in war time and is so rosy red.'

In March Yvo was confirmed in Winchcombe parish church, a few miles from Stanway, by the white-haired Bishop of Gloucester. Yvo had specifically asked to be confirmed as close to his home as possible. The Bishop appealed to the young soldiers among the candidates to 'fight for God by fighting for your country'. To his mother, Yvo was already the perfect chivalrous knight: 'Yvo's fair face and slender figure, kneeling, khaki-clad, made a never-to-be-forgotten picture of consecrated youth'. A friend of Yvo's with whom he played war games recalled Yvo himself imagining he was a knight of romance: 'he loved to picture himself taking part in the old French wars ... the days of knighthood and chivalry when lance met lance and sword met sword, and he would have gone with joyful heart and merry jest.' When he left for France in September he took with him his initialled copy of *The Happy Warrior*, 'Daily Thoughts for all who are serving their country', compiled by the Hon. Mrs Gell and with a foreword by the late Field-Marshal Earl Roberts.

On 27 March a telegram arrived at Stanway House for Mary. It was from her brother Guy Wyndham: his eldest son George had been killed in France. Though Mary's background and upbringing had instilled the traditional beliefs in sacrifice for country, public duty above personal emotion, her response to the loss of her nephew was real and painful. 'I woke up often during the night & hoped & wished Guy's telegram was not true, but a nightmare, to fade with dawn – but I know it's true.'

She then had to watch Ego's midnight departure on 8 April, together with her youngest daughters and Ego's wife. When she had heard Ego was to be sent to Egypt she wrote to him, 'I've been trying hard to make myself behave like a mother in the days of the old crusades'. The scene as she depicted it was invested with mythological proportions, the countryside becoming a backdrop to Arthurian legend:

At first the men were singing, or crooning a wild rather lovely murmuring song which mingled with the tramping of the horses and the clinking of their bits ... What music there was in the jingle of the harness, what romance in the clank of accoutrements and the thud of the horses' feet. The beauty of the stern pale faces of the men, full of quiet resolve or grim determination caused feelings far too deep for words or tears.

When Ego came by there was a slight pause for a last farewell, and looking splendid, he rode away into the darkness.

Last of all came the creaking transports, and then silence; the place was utterly deserted. The gallant, glittering Gloucesters passed out of our sight and we went sadly home to bed.

Mary was doing pretty well at being the mother of a crusader. She would have known the chances of Ego being killed were extremely high but she uses the language of romance, heroism and legend as a way of controlling and coping with her fears.

She never saw Ego again. The Gloucestershire Yeomanry rode in triumph through their home villages in the Cotswolds, cheered on by family and friends. They embarked at Avonmouth, bound for Egypt and the Dardanelles.

On 7 May, 1915, Mary and her sisters attended a dedication service at their parents' home of Clouds in Wiltshire. Unlike Stanway and Mells, Clouds was a new country house, designed by Philip Webb in the 1880s for Percy and Madeline Wyndham. It was meant to look as if it was part of the countryside, built of the local materials, with rambling servants' quarters; a suitable seat for a liberal landed gentleman keen on hunting, concerned for the welfare of his tenants and an active member of the Society for the Preservation of Ancient Buildings. Percy Wyndham had died in 1911 and his son George inherited the estate.

George Wyndham, 'the handsomest man in England', had been tipped to become Prime Minister at the beginning of his political career. He had wealth; good looks; considerable abilities as a writer and a soldier; wit; a fine intellect. However, the pressures of public duty proved too much for him and he died in 1913 aged only 49. Just before his death he had built a chapel at Clouds for his wife Sibell Grosvenor and erected a cross in the nearby cemetery of East Knoyle to mark his father's grave.

On the day the *Lusitania* was torpedoed, members of the Wyndham family remembered their dead as the Bishop of Salisbury dedicated chapel and cross. For Mary 'it was a beautiful day, & there was a lovely mass of bluebells on the hillside where the oaks had been felled'. But on the wall of green sandstone (the same stone used to build Clouds) which George had erected round the family plot at East Knoyle were four inscriptions, 'my father, George, his son Perf, & Guy's son George Heremon, all within the space of four years'.

Almost immediately the Wyndham family received the news of the lucky escape of Guy's younger son Richard, to whom Perf had left Clouds. He wrote to his grandmother Madeline from Rawal Pindi Hospital in Boulogne:

I was just having my after-lunch Benson and Hedges cigarette, when they attacked again. This time it was more serious . . . I had just got up to the top [of the dam] when I was hit . . . Luckily my scalp proved too hard a nut to crack, so the bullet only cut the scalp and knocked me out. My asphyxiating gas-pad and my hat also protected me, for the bullet came through both.

Richard survived the trenches of France to take up his inheritance, but as well as Clouds he inherited considerable death duties. A special Death Duties (Killed in War) Act had been passed in 1914, reducing and postponing duties on estates which passed to wives or lineal descendants. However, Richard was Perf's first cousin. Charles Adeane of Babraham (Mary's brother-in-law and Richard's uncle by marriage) writing in *The Field* in 1915 used the example of Clouds to plead for exemption from death duties for anyone killed in the service of their country:

> . . . a well-known estate in the South of England, long enjoyed by a public-spirited country gentleman who died only three or four years ago. It passed to his son, one of the most brilliant and best-loved Cabinet Ministers of his day. He in turn died suddenly a year before the war, and was succeeded by his son, a gallant young soldier who has since been killed in France, leaving only a collateral to bear the unreduced charges on an estate already crippled.[8]

Richard Wyndham was still lucky to be alive, estate duties not withstanding. But as the news of his escape reached his family in 1915, they heard, at the same time, that Edward Horner was in a convent hospital at Bailleul, so seriously wounded that his parents and sister had been given permission to visit him. For weeks he was gravely ill – he had been shot in the stomach and lost a kidney – but finally he returned to spend midsummer at Mells.

Even greater anxiety was experienced by Lord and Lady Desborough, friends of the Wemysses and the Horners. Their eldest son Julian Grenfell was wounded in the head on 13 May and spent thirteen days in a Boulogne hospital lingering between life and death, his mother at his bedside, before dying on 26 May. Ettie Desborough was another mother of heroes: she covered his grave, high on a hill on the edge of Boulogne, with oak leaves and wild flowers. Mary Wemyss visited her at Taplow, her country house in Buckinghamshire, early in June. She found Ettie 'quite wonder – calm. Unemotional & upheld by a sense of Julian's continual presence & love – she deserves the wonderful reward of courage & faith – I feel I could never be like that – I hope the power will not fail.'

Worse was to come. On 30 July the second Desborough son, Billy, was killed on the western front. His body was never found. Mary's daughter Cynthia had known Julian and Billy since childhood. She wondered how their parents could face 'such utter desolation, such extinction of joy, glamour and hope. I remember them so well as little curly-headed boys in white the first time they came to Stanway.'[9]

Against this background of increasing anxiety and loss, Yvo was preparing to leave for France. He had transferred from the King's Royal Rifles Corps to the Grenadiers in June with the help of his uncle Jack Tennant, Under-Secretary for War. On 11 September the 1st Battalion left for France, Mary waving farewell to her son, 'his young fair face & beautiful figure elastic tread broad shoulders slender waist & quite serene'.

Yvo left behind at Gosford a family far from serene. When Hugo was not wrangling about money with Mary, he was arguing with his mistress, Lady Angela Forbes. Beb Asquith was home on leave from the front but tetchy and irritable; grieving for the dead and wounded. On 13 September Frances Horner arrived with Edward, still convalescent, to stay for a few days. Edward was a keen sportsman so was taken out shooting by Hugo. Unfortunately Edward managed to pink a keeper in the ear at the same time as killing a few birds.

Yvo survived just a month in France. His letters gave some idea of the macabre conditions he found around the trenches near Loos.

We have got a delightful sight in our graveyard here, from one of the graves the tombstone has been laid open by a shell – the coffin-lid has been torn off showing the skeleton of a man – a toad is sitting on his chest and little brown mice are playing in his bones – R.I.P. says the tombstone.

[87]

The landscape was similar to coal-mining areas near Gosford, 'unspeakably desolate, not at all like "La Belle France", full of great slag-pits like pyramids and dirty little houses and muddy roads not unlike Port Seton or Portobello'. On 18 October Yvo's sister Cynthia ordered him an 'ear-shield' in Harrods but the day before Yvo had been killed by machine-gun fire, leading a party of bombers in a 'gallant and futile attempt' to capture a German trench.

The depleted, grieving family assembled at Stanway for the memorial service. Ego was in Egypt, his wife Letty and sister Mary in the Mediterranean on their way to join him (and Mary to marry a fellow-officer, Tom Strickland). Mary wrote to her mother from the ship, 'I saw a darling little grey wagtail on deck yesterday morning which reminded me so of Stanway and Yvo. He and I used to go down the Sling [stream] to look for the grey wagtail's nest.'

Every inch of the house reminded Cynthia of her brother, 'sometimes as a child, sometimes as a youth. Yet, in a way, the atmosphere is healing.' On Sunday 24 October the rain poured down. 'Stanway was weeping.'[10] The service was held at six o'clock. A bier stood in the chancel with a Union Jack spread over it and a laurel wreath leaning against it. Grace Wemyss, the second wife of the tenth Earl, wrote in her diary 'it was very simple and impressive & Mr Allen preached such a pathetic little sermon about him. He was the very incarnation of youth & strength and had grown into such a fine looking youth.'[11]

On the Thursday after Yvo's service, Mary Wemyss took out three soldiers, one without a leg, from Winchcombe Hospital, for a drive through the Cotswolds and tea. The next day she gave them tea again, this time at Stanway, and on Sunday Bibs put in a day's work at the hospital as a scullery maid. One way of coping with the loss of family and friends was to care for the living and at Winchcombe Hospital all the non-fighting members of the Wemyss family served on the 'home front'.

The VAD Hospital was first established in the infant school in Winchcombe, catering for 25 wounded soldiers. It opened in May 1915 and closed in November 1918. The commandant was Eliza Wedgwood, great-great-grand-daughter of the founder of the pottery firm, who lived in the neighbouring village of Stanton. Nicknamed the

'Queen of Stanton', she devoted her life to good works in and around her village, including the initiation of dental treatment for the children, and invariably enlisted the help of Stanway House. Mary and Cynthia helped with administration and nursing at the hospital as well as entertaining the soldiers; two of Mary's nieces, Pamela Adeane of Babraham and Richard Wyndham's sister Olivia also nursed; to her annoyance Bibs was considered too young to nurse, instead she leant a hand cleaning floors and peeling potatoes; Hugo lent his car.

Many accounts of the home front – memoirs, biographies, poems such as Siegfried Sassoon's 'Does It Matter' – give the impression that those left behind were unaware of the horrors of the trenches or, if aware, refused to face up to the plight of the ordinary soldier. A family such as the Wemysses not only suffered personal loss in the war, but also learnt of the agony, the fear and the bravery of the ordinary Tommies through their involvement with the hospital.

In November 1915 Cynthia dropped in on a concert in full swing in one of the wards and found it 'a most delightful and touching atmosphere: most of them had such gentle faces, one felt the horror of their returning to such Hell. They sat about in groups with arms entwined like affectionate monkeys.'[12] She found herself crying when they sang 'When the Boys come home'. On one occasion Mary talked to a soldier returned from the Dardanelles, 'a dear who had been buried up to his head for 48 hrs', and on another she welcomed to Stanway 'a poor man without toes . . . he had had an awful time in Gallipoli in blizzard & is all frost bitten & neurasthenia'. The hospital régime at Winchcombe was strict. The men were allowed no alcohol and were confined to the hospital grounds unless they had an escort, so outings with the Wemysses and Eliza Wedgwood were important in their regimented lives.

Clouds, the home of Mary's parents, was turned into a convalescent home for wounded soldiers in 1915. Madeline Wyndham occupied the suite of rooms off the main hall which had been her husband's; her son Guy and his wife Edwina helped to run the house until the war ended and their son Richard could take up his inheritance.

Letitia Fowler, granddaughter of Edwina by her first marriage, was only seven or eight years old when she stayed at Clouds and helped to steer the blinded soldiers around the gardens. 'Every nook and cranny in the house was stuffed with soldiers![13] Once or twice a week villagers from East Knoyle would come up to the big house to help roll bandages using a special machine clamped to a table in the kitchen. Olivia Wyndham worked with the wounded at Clouds as well as helping at the Winchcombe VAD hospital.

Christmas 1915 found the soldiers from Winchcombe involved in all sorts of entertainments at Stanway House, mixing with the family, their servants, tenants and village children. Mary sent them a present of a ping-pong table though she wondered whether there was room for it, 'but if they do operations and eat there there won't be much room for ping pong'.

It was the first Christmas without Yvo and the poignancy of the occasion was intensified by the presence of the convalescent soldiers and by Beb Asquith who had returned from the trenches, physically and mentally scarred. Madeline Adeane wrote to her sister from Babraham: 'it breaks my heart to think of your Stanway & Christmas time & your Beloved Baby Ivo gone out of your life . . . *lovely* Stanway all the more lovely in its *tragic loss*.'

Stanway House was full: Mary and Hugo; Grace, Dowager Countess of Wemyss; Hugo's brother Evan Charteris; Cynthia, Beb and their sons Michael and John; Bibs, Ego's sons David and Martin; the daughters of Lady Angela Forbes (who was off running buffets in Boulogne for British soldiers). On 20 December a party was held in the neighbouring village of Didbrook to celebrate the retirement of Mrs Alcock, village schoolmistress for thirty-five years. She was presented with a purse, Hugo gave a speech and Flavia Forbes recited. Then the local policeman, notorious for composing risqué songs, entertained the audience with his latest composition, suitably laced with nods and winks: 'The lads in their trenches / They think of their wenches,' and so forth.

Beb was in the throes of composition himself. His first collection of verse, *The Volunteer* (containing his tribute to Yvo, 'The Fallen Sub-altern'), had just been published and he had been asked by the family friend Philip Burne-Jones to write a poem called '1916' for the *Sunday Pictorial*. The fee was £50, only slightly less than an agricultural labourer's annual wage and, as Burne-Jones pointed out to Beb, ten times the amount Milton was paid for *Paradise Lost*. Cynthia, however, was worried her husband might find it difficult to write to order even though they were permanently hard-up: 'I don't know how to coax Pegasus back into his room and wonder what atmosphere is most conducive to Beb's muse.'[14]

While Beb struggled with his muse, Hugo was sampling contemporary fiction. Cynthia had lent him the latest work by her close friend D. H. Lawrence. *The Rainbow* produced many protestations of disgust from Hugo but he nevertheless offered Cynthia £5 for her copy, reckoning it might just be a good investment.

Hanging up the stockings on Christmas Eve was a melancholy ceremony, Cynthia struggling to be jolly for the sake of the children, Mary thinking of Yvo all the time, 'Ego thank God safe & well'. The local doctor dressed up as Father Christmas to entertain the patients and nurses at Winchcombe on Christmas Day. On Boxing Day Evan Charteris left for London. He had been suffering a guilty conscience ever since his maid had declared 'you're a man of pleasure and you drink champagne in wartime'.[15] He was a barrister at the Parliamentary Bar but he had now sent in his application for a commission in the artillery even though he was over 50.

On New Year's Day Mary wrote in her diary: 'I go into a year that Yvo didn't know from here – & every second I miss him'. She recalled attending midnight service at Stanton with him the previous New Year's Eve. This year she sat on the doorstep of Stanway House looking out at the black tower of the church outlined against the starry sky. At midnight the bells clashed out and one of her chows howled dismally.

But on New Year's Day Mary was up and about organising tea for nearly a hundred guests, doing her bit as the resilient lady of the manor. The children dressed up as Time, War and Peace. Young David Charteris, only three years old, represented the New Year – the year he would lose his father and become heir to Stanway and Gosford.

The German army launched their attack on the fortress of Verdun on 21 February 1916. While thousands of men were being killed in the struggle which only finally petered out in November, Britain and Europe were experiencing a particularly harsh winter and spring. Deep snow covered the Cotswolds for weeks and on 28 March a ferocious blizzard buried sheep and lambs, brought down trees and damaged sprouting crops. Describing the way the blizzard dealt with elm trees, *Country Life* might almost have been in the trenches:

> the roots came away leaving a crater in which you might conceal a horse and a load of hay. The top crashed to the ground . . . And now the wind, as if still further maddened by the victory, rushed at another elm in the middle of a grass field . . . and slew it, too, almost immediately.

The effects of the weather in Stanway were felt as far away as Romani in Egypt, where the Gloucestershire Yeomanry were stationed. Ego Charteris had to take the news to Bruce Dudfield, one of his men, that his father Benjamin had died in the storm. Dudfield had dropped dead of a heart attack after spending hours digging his sheep out of the snow. Bruce was given leave to return to Gloucestershire. He later wrote of Ego, 'I shall always feel I owe [him] my life, for without his kind interference I must have shared the fate of April 23rd'.[16]

Another fortunate victim of the bad weather was Mary Wemyss's second son, Guy. He had been sent out to the Somme at the beginning of the year but was invalided home in March with a third severe attack of rheumatic fever. He would miss the Battle of the Somme which began on 1 July.

War work carried on in Stanway, even in the worst weather. The ladies of the neighbouring villages collected wool and material from Mary, returning with finished stockings and shirts ready to be sent to soldiers at the front. Once the snow had gone, Stanway's gardener reluctantly set about planting lettuces and radishes instead of antirrhinums. The bad weather meant food prices had risen sharply – hay for the ponies £6 a ton – and the Wemysses were doing their best to cut costs. There was excitement on 8 April when the local hunt killed a fox on the tennis court: young David Charteris was blooded.

Easter 1916 fell on Sunday 23 April. On the 22 April cheques from Connor arrived for Cynthia, Bibs and Guy. Yvo's money had been divided among his surviving brothers and sisters, £97 each. Cynthia was deeply depressed. She had been walking through the estate grieving over her 'favourite childhood trees' blown down by the storm.

Then, during the night, Mary dreamt of Ego. She wrote in her diary the next day:

> the atmosphere of the room seemed to quiver with excitement – I felt the stress and strain and *saw*, as if thrown on a magic-lantern sheet, a mass of black smoke splashed with crimson flame . . . I saw Ego standing, straight and tall . . . Round his chest was wrapped a golden banner, its colour very beautiful, it swathed his body in spiral folds and seemed to protect him as he stood there with his face set and stern.

Even in her dreams Mary unconsciously called up motifs from Arthurian legend. The names of her sons – Ego, Guy, Yvo – belong to the pages of Malory, Walter Scott and Tennyson: the children of the Souls were seen off to war like knights of the Round Table, riding away (many were in cavalry regiments) to right the wrongs of the world.

Mary spent Sunday afternoon at Winchcombe Hospital – the apple trees in the little garden were in blossom – but all the time 'I felt as one in a dream . . . I believe that I knew, without actually realizing, that Ego was dead.'

The Wemysses had to wait until 1 July for confirmation that their eldest son and heir had died on 23 April at the Battle of Katia. For weeks conflicting reports reached them. First he was wounded, then in a hospital, then a prisoner. Visiting Gosford in June, Mary heard from the Red Cross in Damascus that Ego was definitely alive. She sat in Aberlady church, 'waves & wells of gratitude seem pouring out of me & over me . . . to think that he will possibly probably outlive the war & live for England – its wonderful'. Then the Red Cross confessed to a mistake and the doubts returned. 'One must have been *very rich* to be able to lose so much – two *such* sons.'

Mary and Bibs were staying at Clouds when the telegram arrived from Hugo on 1 July: '*Les officiers à Angora certifient que Lord Elcho fut tué à Katia*'.

> Ego & Yvo – Yvo & Ego, I feel as if I had *always* known they would go – I knew it when I looked at Egos face in Glos. Cathedral, after ch. parade his beautiful serious face with the lovely smile & the eyes where the spirit of truth did dwell.

Cynthia was in London with Hugo. 'Oh God – Oh God, my beautiful brother that I have loved so since I was a baby.' Together they went to Montagu Square and found Letty playing the piano to David and Martin.

> Papa went up – I waited downstairs. The music stopped and I heard a gay 'Hulloa', then silence. I rushed up and found Letty clinging to Papa. It's indescribable – it was just like somebody in a fearful, unimaginable, physical pain . . . The children were scared. 'What has happened to you, Mummie? What is the matter with you? Will you be better in the morning?'[17]

Ego's memorial service was held at Stanway on 16 July. *The Times* published a tribute to Ego on 7 July, reiterating the theme of sacrifice, of knightly heroism. 'None surely of those who have given their lives has more faithfully embodied the heroic spirit of the younger generation.' Down at Stanway Mary picked bay leaves and crimson roses for his wreath; Letty arranged his sword and spurs in the church. Centuries old ritual controlled and contained appalling grief.

To Cynthia her home seemed to belong to the dead. 'Its spirit seems broken – lush, heavy, almost black-green midsummer everywhere, and the cricket field a jungle.'[18] Ghosts inhabited the cricket field where Ego had played for the village, also the field where the Gloucestershire Yeomanry had trained before the war. 'The men had such shaggy steeds', Mary recalled, 'but they became the finest possible Brigade,' only to be wiped out at Katia. In the tithe barn the memories lingered of Letty, the young pretty wife of the heir to Stanway, handing out prizes won in the yeomanry sports and making a gracious speech.

Raymond Asquith was behind the lines on the Somme front when he heard of his friend's death. He wrote to Lady Diana Manners, Letty's sister:

> Ego is irreplaceable . . . A blind God butts about the world with a pair of delicately malignant antennae to detect whatever is fit to live and an iron hoof to stamp it into the dust when found. It seems amazing that the bony fingers of fate and spite should push into what seemed the safest field of all the War and nip the finest flower in it.[19]

He was right to regard Egypt as a relatively safe field; the Somme was not. The first of July, 1916, the day Ego's death was confirmed, was also the first day of the Battle of the Somme. On that day there were 50,000 British casualties; of those 20,000 dead.

Raymond was fortunate not to take part in the first push: he waited behind the lines, dreaming of 'woods and hay fields in England' and visualising his wife and children playing in the hollyhocks and dahlias in Mells' garden. But on 15 September Raymond was killed. And over the next few days the news came to the Wemysses that their nephew Bim Tennant, Lord Glenconner's eldest son and heir, had been killed; also Mark Tennant, brother-in-law of their son Guy.

Mary was staying up at Gosford. The Prime Minister wrote to her from Downing Street: 'There's [sic] has been a happy & glorious lot. The sadness is for us who remain, & for the world, which is being drained of all that was most bright & loveable – the promise of the future.' H. H. Asquith's daughter Violet Bonham-Carter also wrote to Mary: 'one must invest all one has got left in people of your David's age – they are our only future left'. Mary's sister Madeline Adeane spelled out the full list of their family's losses:

I can imagine beautiful Gosford as you say a dignified & huge white Tomb of Hope & Joy & those *Darling* children of *Beloved* Ego . . . just wonder at our *splendid* children with all they have to do & bear & see & hear & the sons – your two, George's one, Guy's & Pamela's [all five dead].

Mary wrote in her diary 'none will care to read this diary now'. She returned to Stanway in October and was in time to attend a memorial service at Didbrook for Alfred Alcock, the son of the retired school-mistress, killed fighting for his country. The Alcocks had chosen a hymn sung at Ego's service in the summer, 'Oh Love that wilt not let me go'.

Rationing did not begin to affect the population until relatively late in the war. Mary makes her first reference to food shortages in her diary in November 1916. She was travelling from Stanway to London and had a cup of tea on Oxford Station. She was amazed & distressed at the wastefulness of the English as a nation, 3 lumps of sugar had been shoved into the saucer & was rotting & wasted; the railway people might have read of the fuss in the papers about sugar.

To her delight official limits were imposed at the beginning of 1917. 'Thrilled at the meat sugar & bread limit in papers yest. Shall be very stiff & hope the servants will co-operate!' Unfortunately the servants were not as patriotic as their mistress. She had a trying interview with the kitchen maid, finally deciding on two meatless days a week, and then found Alfred, one of the servants, 'cutting off seven slices of bread for lunch'. Harry Last, the Stanway gamekeeper, found himself breeding chickens instead of pheasants. He had to arrange the chicken coops discreetly around the stone pyramid in the grounds to make sure they were not seen from the house.

At Clouds, a strict routine was initiated by the Wyndhams. Bertha, the housekeeper, formidable in her starched white cap, weighed out the butter in the still room once a week. It was delivered from the Home Farm. Each member of the family, the servants and the convalescent soldiers were given their correct allowance according to the government rules.

Of course the Wemysses and the Wyndhams suffered no real privations, indeed their diet was healthier for the restrictions. In January 1918 Mary found she had exceeded the flour ration so cut down on the bread sauce and reduced the scones to twice a week. Hugo got in some exercise digging a bed for the potatoes at Stanway and then, in April 1918, got in a row with his wife over the use of his butter ration. To his annoyance his uneaten London ration had been used for cooking down in Gloucestershire. These were minor inconveniences. At Mells, however, Frances Horner and the ladies of the village organised a soup kitchen for the poorer families. Hot meals were provided in a small building on the village green: after the war the building became the meeting place of the Mells Women's Institute.

In 1917 the Horners unexpectedly got back their spare country house. Gilbert Thompson Bates, the Liverpool shipowner who took a lease on Mells Park in 1907, died, suddenly, in March. His son had been killed in May 1915: now his widow decided not to remain. Gilbert Bates left a fortune of over half a million pounds and many of his possessions were sold in an auction in July.

Edward Horner, who had only just rejoined his regiment in France in the spring of 1917, was jubilant. 'I've always longed for the Park empty again and this seems an opportunity and with the hard court and all we shall surely enjoy Mells this autumn.' Edward was a keen sportsman and relished the idea of being able to shoot on the Park estate once more.

Edward was pulled up by his parents reminding him of their financial problems. Mells Park had been let out of necessity. He wrote to his mother on 2 July:

> I am wretched you are worried about finances again, and fear my reiteration 'don't let' must have sounded silly (to say the least of it). But, on looking back on it all, I do think the situation of lessor and lessee in country houses is almost intolerable if they meet at all and so would rather sell now or live on capital to recoup by selling some day than both let and live in Mells the next few years ... sell ... things or even bits of land to relieve pressure ... Anything is better than you and Daddy having to be uncomfortable now in order that I may be less so one day.

Edward had always been wildly impractical about money – one of his friends described him as 'so ancestral'. At school and university he had spent money recklessly, well beyond his and his parents' means. But he was correct in pointing out that the Horners had a lot they could sell apart from the spare mansion. Frances Horner's father William Graham had left her a considerable part of his collection of Early Renaissance and Pre-Raphaelite paintings.

The possibility did not arise, however. Almost as if Edward's letter were a premonition, the problem was solved. On 11 October Mells Park was destroyed by fire.

The family had just started entertaining in the house. Edward had leave in September and spent a few days shooting pheasants instead of Germans: 'a bad year for partridges, but *very* good for wild pheasants'. Duff Cooper joined in, one of the few remaining of the coterie set who had not yet been sent abroad. The Horners were anxious to improve the sport on the estate which they thought Gilbert Bates had allowed to suffer:

> . . . he would not try to *walk* after partridges *at all* but always tried to drive them. Even in a good year there are not enough partridges in this county to make 'driving' really satisfactory, and there are not enough turnip fields.

Back at the front Edward was sustained by memories of killing birds at home. France, by contrast, was 'very peaceful in our pretty farms'. On 28 September he wrote hoping his father was not tiring himself shooting too many partridges, 'always acceptable here – better sent half cooked'. Sir John was also organising the fishing of one of the lakes on the estate. On one day 4,000 fish were caught: 500 were immediately sent to Frome to a jumble sale; the rest were distributed throughout the village in two carts driven by Richard Hames, the head-keeper, and his daughters Violet and Ada.

Then came the news of the fire. At first Edward thought it was the old manor house. *The Times* confused the two, describing the fire as being in the old Elizabethan mansion at Mells Park. Edward wrote home:

> It is the crushing summit of our troubles. I don't feel as if anything could have happened that I minded more or that we shall any of us ever be able to bear seeing Mells again . . . Curiously, I used to think of two things as so impossible to bear if they happened that they surely wouldn't. One was Raymond's death, the other, this. It seems wrong to couple them, but, I somehow did.

The Times was still misinformed on 16 October. Their correspondent waxed lyrical over Parochia Mellis, 'the village of honey'.

> Mells in its winding, rocky valley, with its thatched cottages and roses, its true Somerset air of comfort and peace, is still beautiful, a place of honey. But the chief glory has gone. Worse things have happened and are happening in Belgium and in France. Yet one cannot but sigh for the loss of one more link with the past of England.

Like Edward Horner, the correspondent reveals as much feeling for a country house, a part of 'Old England', as for the men dying for their country overseas.

Edward was enormously relieved when a telegram from his parents explained Mells Park had been destroyed. 'I've not the same feeling about it as the other', he wrote, then got on to the subject of money. 'I assume it's well insured in which case we ought to have something to play with. I presume, in the circs, Daddy wouldn't be induced to rebuild.'

The fire had started late at night on 11 October. Frances Horner had gone up to London saying 'wish I could stay in dear old Mells where nothing ever happens'.[20] The doctor's young daughter Pansy noticed the ceiling of her nursery lit up by the red glow from the burning house. Mrs Sharman, wife of the postmaster, received the call to send for the fire brigade. It was a wild, blowing night and the fire brigades at Bath, Shepton Mallet and Radstock were unable to offer help. The Frome Fire Brigade tried to get some sort of haulage power – horse, steam or petrol – but all were refused or not available. They finally managed to obtain two government horses but these took hours to catch. The distance between Frome and Mells is only four miles but the fire engine arrived over three hours after the call for help was made. There were only three servants in Mells Park – one without a leg – and once the water in the house gave out, nothing could stop the flames spreading. The whole village tried to help, even colliers from the Mells coal mine, rescuing books, paintings and china. Sir John rushed to and fro outside the burning house shouting 'mind the paint, mind the paint,[21] as his family heirlooms were brought out on to the lawns. After it was all over, each family in the village received a commemorative poster from the Horners in gratitude for their assistance.

Frances described the scene to her daughter Cicely.

The house was *too* terrible – an empty blackened shell with fallen keystones and inside piles of debris – like pictures of the Cloth Hall at Ypres.

She could still joke about some of the paintings:

most of the Italian pictures saved – and all the worst family portraits of course: Granpapa and Grandmama Horner survived, smelling horribly – nothing will ever destroy them.

The house and its contents were insured for some £40,000 but the Horners did not rebuild. Edward was given special compassionate leave at the beginning of November and stayed at Mells for a few more days shooting. Back in France he was sent a letter from his mother written on 21 November, 'we loved your leave ... you were very beloved' and one from his father written on 22 November, speculating on the prospects of good sport at Christmas. Edward, however, was already dead. He had been killed on the 21st. Later Sir John was able to say of the burning of Mells Park: 'After all if it hadn't been for that we should never have had Edward with us for the last time, so perhaps it was almost worth losing the Park House.'

But with Edward 'perished the last hope of direct male succession in an ancient and honourable English house'.[22] The Horners' friends shared in their grief. Cynthia Asquith remembered her youth spent with Edward and Katharine, Raymond and Ego: 'all so interwoven. Soon there will be nobody left with whom one can even talk of the beloved figures of one's youth.'[23] F. E. Smith (Lord Birkenhead) wrote a tribute to Edward in *The Times*: 'to those who survive him his death seems to bring twilight into their world and to be the breaking of a last link with the happy past.'

On 8 August 1917 Mary Wemyss wrote to her cousin and ex-lover, Wilfrid Scawen Blunt. She apologised for not visiting him at his country house in Sussex that summer: her life was just too complicated. She was exhausted emotionally by the continuing news of deaths at the front and exhausted physically by war work in the village and at Winchcombe Hospital; Hugo had returned unexpectedly from visiting Angela Forbes at her soldiers' buffets in France; Cynthia's son John was causing the family anxiety, his remoteness and fits of temper early symptoms of mental illness; and Stanway had become refuge for another victim, Angela McInnes (later Angela Thirkell, the novelist), granddaughter of Edward Burne-Jones, who was fleeing from her drunken, violent husband.

When Mary finally managed to visit Blunt in the autumn, the escape from responsibilities was overwhelming.

I *loved* slipping back into the centuries leaving clattering & vulgar Vauxhall – & finding myself in the 16 or 17 century driving yr Arab geldings through Primordeal forest and visiting my Poet Patriarch . . . arab shek my cousin & my Friend.

Their brief love affair had taken place in the Egyptian Sahara over twenty years before and their daughter Mary was now married to Tom Strickland, one of Ego's officers, who had survived Katia but was immured in a Turkish prison. Ever since, Mary treasured memories of the desert, the bohemian life she had experienced, and would dream of returning there when her responsibilities became overwhelming. And now her eldest son was buried somewhere in the desert to the east of the Suez Canal.

Back at Stanway, she offered support and comfort to more casualties of the war. No sooner had her servant Alfred, 'a clean quick worker', gone off to the front than the news came that Mrs Thombs's boy had been killed. 'We all liked him so bright & nice looking – its Mrs Thombs youngest she lost her eldest 13 months ago.' 'Poor 1917 slunk away in silence shame & sorrow.'

On 13 February 1918 a woman from Cutsdean called at Stanway House. Her husband's brother had lost a leg fighting in Egypt and the family needed help getting him into a convalescent home. Also in February the Wemysses found a job for a shell-shocked sergeant as caretaker at Gosford House.

On 31 March the vicar of Stanway took seven services for the dead. Mary noted 'All today the fighting is fiercely continuing – the fate of the world is in the balance.' The last great push by the Germans was spilling out into Stanway. Winchcombe Hospital was filled with fresh wounded. Cynthia and Mary worked there regularly. On 9 May Cynthia spent her first night duty, worried by her sister Mary's gruesome 'stump talk': one of the patients, 'poor little Harris', had had more taken off his leg after the first amputation proved insufficient 'and he has nearly died of haemorrhage ever since'. 'Pray God I never have to see that naked stump.'[24]

Cynthia's first night was eventful. One soldier sleep-walked, believing he was still at the front, 'hurling missiles about in the delusion that they were bombs'. Her favourite patient was called Morris, 'who does beautiful elaborate embroidery with an admiring audience standing round'. She at last dressed Harris's stump, 'I won my spurs', but immediately received a telegram from Beb at the front, 'a small splinter in his arm'.[25] She found herself crying over the soldiers getting better only to return to their hell – once a month a captain inspected them, marking out the men fit for the trenches.

The soldiers at Winchcombe had some impact in the country community, showing the countryfolk what the war did to men, but also disturbing the passions of the local girls. A soldier called Overton was particularly mischievous, one afternoon falling through a skylight in the hospital, then nearly getting caught by the sister playing billiards after lights out. His biggest problem was how to deal with his two girl friends.

He had been carrying on with another 'young lady' in Winchcombe, and was embarrassed to know how to square her now his official one had arrived. I [Cynthia] afterwards heard that his second string saw him in the lane with his first string and cut up terribly rusty, poor thing. She went so far as to mutilate his photograph – sticking pins through his eyes.[26]

A nurse in the hospital was more fortunate in the relationship she struck up with one of the patients. She was herself a Belgian refugee and became engaged to a soldier from Australia.

Increasing numbers of women, many of them daughters of the landed gentry, were nursing in France. While Mary and Cynthia worked at Winchcombe, Mary's niece Pamela Adeane was in France. By the end of the war she would be mentioned twice in Haig's dispatches for her nursing services.

Katharine Asquith was also in France nursing. Her three children spent most of the time at Mells, looked after by Frances Horner and their nanny. But the letters which reached Katharine continued to record losses. The children were enjoying the hawthorn blossom in Mells Park when they met Richard Hames, Sir John's gamekeeper. Hames was in suspense over the whereabouts of his son Wyndham, later to be declared dead. He was also to lose a son-in-law in France. The return of the warmer weather brought poignant memories of past summers in Somerset to Frances Horner and she wrote to her daughter:

> I associate Edward so with summer – lying in the loggia rushing to the bathing sweating joyfully at tennis – & all that is left of our beloveds the vision of a grave in France . . . Oh darling how cruel it is to be at Mells without Edward or Raymond: I am glad you have children: if there were no children growing up it wd seem more unutterably useless still.

At Babraham, Pamela Adeane's home, weeds began to appear on the once-neat paths and in the flower beds. All the younger gardeners had joined up, leaving four old men to do the work of twelve. Even the odd-job boy, 'a little homeless waif called Crick' had enlisted. Pamela's youngest sister Helena remembered Crick going to the front, reported 'missing' and never heard of again. 'It seemed that he had come from nowhere, to enjoy alone, a short span upon the earth, before vanishing to some gaping grave, deep in the mud of Flanders.' For her, Crick was the unknown soldier.

At Stanway, the cricket field remained uncut. Dandelions flourished, 'silence reigned instead of shout and laughter'. The only cutting was of Lidcomb Wood – the wood to be sent to France – the last sacrifice made by the Wemysses for the war effort. Mary took a final look at the trees in July, 'looking too lovely . . . my heart is broken for Lidcomb . . . Lidcomb must go, as all good & beautiful things have gone.'

When Armistice finally came on 11 November 1918, the families shared relief but no great joy. Frances Horner felt a 'strange mixture, which was too poignant to be relief, and too thankful to be sad but it was hard for those who had gone through the anguish of War to face rejoicing without pain'. Charles Adeane found the change from war to peace an extraordinary experience. He walked out into the Cambridgeshire countryside and found himself instinctively looking for search lights, the moon is looked at with suspicion and then one remembers that the war is over and there will be no air raid. The telephone no longer rings at midnight to say that Zeppelins have crossed the coast.

Mary was staying at Gosford with her family. The house was semi-shrouded and most of the electric light supply cut off. Cynthia found it strange and creepy. She viewed the approach of the Armistice with anxiety, 'one will at last fully recognise that the dead are not only dead for the duration of the war'.[27] On the 11th of November Mary walked into the village of Aberlady and saw a few young children singing and waving flags. She wrote in her diary:

> This is the greatest Victory – it is also the *saddest* peace & except for a few Babies in their teens, *no one* can feel light of heart & to most of us, almost the hardest part is now beginning – we miss our shining victors in the hour of Victory – Everyone is War weary & the Peace with all its new problems will bring much confusion.[28]

Mary had lost two sons in the war. She had helped to nurse wounded soldiers; she had attended memorial services, visiting grieving friends and relatives, given support to bereaved tenants. And also, unlike many of her class, she was well read. She could not have been unaware of the bitter and satirical poetry of writers like Siegfried Sassoon. Despite all this, when she comes to write about her own loss in her personal diary, she still appears to maintain the persona of the crusader's mother, blithely unembittered by the reality of war.

In the Village

O N 18 September 1914 the *Somerset Standard* reported on the response of Somerset villages to the nation's call for volunteers. Mells, home of the Horner family, showed exemplary patriotism. Forty-six men from the village were already serving in the Navy, the Army, or Reserve Forces. The neighbouring town of Frome, on the other hand, was less impressed by the call to arms.

Being happily far removed from the seat of war, from the sound of guns and the clashing of arms, it is difficult for an inland town like Frome, which is not even in close touch with the serious business of training troops for the Front, to be deeply impressed with the overwhelming danger that threatens our beloved country. [20 November]

In May 1915 a reporter from *The Field*, too old himself for military service, went to Castle Combe, one of the prettiest of the Cotswold villages, to discover how its inhabitants were coping with the strains of war. He was dismayed to find the community carrying on as if nothing had happened. Able-bodied young men were delivering goods to the cottages as usual:

I saw a scene which would, in peace-time, have been idyllic. A stalwart young man of magnificent physique was lazily rolling a tennis lawn with a very light roller which the pretty girl by his side might easily have pushed with her little finger. The sight suggested to me the hymn, 'Peace, perfect Peace,' but I could have wished that it suggested Lovelace's line:

> I could not love thee, Dear, so much,
> Loved I not honour more.

Also in May 1915, Andrew Clark, vicar of Great Leighs in Essex, was reporting that thirty-six men had enlisted from his parish but that another thirty-six, all fit to fight, had not yet volunteered. Both Clark and Robert Saunders, headmaster of the village school at Fletching in Sussex, in common with many of the older generation, thought the sooner conscription was brought in the better. Saunders commented, in February 1916, 'that a Compulsion Bill was needed is now patent to everyone, the Papers are full of the applications for exemption that are coming before the Tribunals and the miserable excuses put forward make one's blood boil to think Englishmen are so degenerate.'

The situation had changed by the time *Punch* included a poem called 'Our Village' in a number for September 1918.

> Our baker's in the Flying Corps,
>   Our butcher's in the Buffs,
> Our one policeman cares no more
>   For running in the roughs,
> But carves a pathway to the stars
> As trooper in the Tenth Hussars.
> . . . .
>
> The postman, now in Egypt, wears
>   A medal on his coat,
> The Vet. is breeding Belgian hares,
>   The Vicar keeps a goat;
> The schoolma'am knits upon her stool;
> The village idiot gathers wool.

After four years of war, the sleepiest, remotest villages had become involved. Cottage windows all over Britain displayed cards, sometimes as many as six per household: 'NOT AT HOME A man from this house now serving in His Majesty's Forces'; 'FOR MERIT Serving his King and

Country'. The villagers who were left behind had become part of the home front.

Mells in Somerset, Fletching in Sussex and Great Leighs in Essex are three typical southern English villages. In all three it is possible to follow the gradual changes which the war brought to their traditional rural life: the effects of the pressure on farmers and local industries to produce more with a reduced workforce; the increasing involvement of the older men, the women and children in various sorts of war work, on the land and in home defence; the response to recruitment campaigns, to conscription and to the news of casualties; attending memorial services in the parish church to mourn the village dead.

Andrew Clark described his village during the war years as being 'singularly isolated', even though it is only thirty-seven miles by road from London. No resident travelled regularly to the capital, the village was some distance from any railway station, and the work was 'self-centred, on the farms, in the smithy, the wheelwrights and carpenters'. The population was 614 in 1914. J. Herbert Tritton of Lyons Hall was the squire and major landowner as well as a partner in Barclays Bank. His mansion formed a close unit with the church and the rectory. There were three public houses, two shops, a church school and a council school, a blacksmith's and an undertaker's, one policeman and the services of a visiting doctor. Clark had been the incumbent since 1894, his rectory a substantial and attractive Georgian country house.

Mells was larger than Great Leighs in 1914, with a population of 1,416. It is four miles to the west of Frome and used to have its own station two miles away. The fifteenth-century church tower dominates the village and is a landmark for miles; inside the church was decidedly chilly c.1914, so much so that a vestry meeting in April 1915 voted to install a more efficient heating system. The Horners had been lords of the manor for nearly four hundred years and played an active part in all aspects of village life. Farming was the chief occupation. There was also coal mining, a wheelwright's, a mill and a limestone quarry. The colliery was under intense pressure throughout the war to produce as much coal as possible. Nevertheless when many of the skilled miners enlisted in the armed forces, the directors responded to their patriotism by agreeing to pay their wives 3s. 6d. per week during their absence, plus the usual bag of coal. If the wives of reservists and widows whose sons were reservists lived in company houses they were to be exempt from paying rent.

Mells had its own doctor, blacksmith, bootmaker, baker, policeman, painter and decorator; also a village shop and a Post Office – with a red hawthorn tree blooming outside, one public house, a Public Elementary School taking over 200 boys and girls, and a community Reading Room over the doctor's stable, where whist and cribbage competitions continued throughout the war between teams from rival villages.

Fletching had a population of 1,116. Sheffield Park was the nearest railway station, two and a half miles away; Uckfield, four miles distant, the nearest country town. Two families owned most of the land in the parish: the Maryon-Wilsons of Searles and the Soameses of Sheffield Park (the last Earl of Sheffield had died in 1909). As in Great Leighs and Mells, agriculture was the principal occupation and the main crops grown were wheat, oats, barley, beans and hops. There were two public houses, two grocer's shops, three blacksmiths, two millers, a doctor, butcher and baker, a tailor, plumber and decorator, a shoemaker, dressmaker and carpenter. Robert Saunders' Public Elementary School could take over 200 pupils. His wife was the schoolmistress.

The villages were all virtually self-sufficient. There was little need and often little desire to visit the nearest town, let alone London or other parts of England. In Mells a carrier called Francis Lacey went every day to Frome to buy unusual items requested by the villagers. Every Monday he collected laundry from any cottage displaying a card with the letter L in its window; the laundry was returned on Friday.

The doctor, George Crawford Helps, held a surgery every morning including Sundays, in Bilbao House. In the afternoon he did his rounds of the area on a bicycle while his chauffeur, Mr Baber, tended to the doctor's vegetables. On other occasions, when the car was out of action (Baber was delighted when 'them plugs' played up), Trilby, the doctor's pony, was harnessed up. Dr Helps had a busy practice during the war, especially delivering the babies of wives of soldiers at regular intervals after home leave: 'That's what leaf does'. His chauffeur's two daughters helped to deliver the village mail; their brother fought and was killed in France.

The Horner family provided Mells with much of its entertainment. Famous politicians, artists and writers who stayed at the manor house could be seen in church on Sunday. Venetia Stanley, confidante of H. H. Asquith, spent part of her honeymoon in Mells in 1915 with Edwin Montagu. The Horners were themselves curiosities. Sir John's brother George, former vicar of Mells, was renowned for his smelly feet; his sister Muriel could be seen in church hunting through six layers of petticoats to find her collecting money.

The incumbent of Mells during the war was also involved in organising the cultural life of the village. The Reverend Edward Lear and his wife led a flourishing dramatic society. All members of the village took part in annual productions of the plays of Shakespeare. Three new street lamps were erected just before Christmas 1914, paid for out of the profits from the previous summer's production of *The Merry Wives of Windsor*.

Amateur theatricals were a feature of life in Fletching until the death of the last Lord Sheffield. Performances took place in Sheffield Park; also annual maypole competitions. The village flower show took place at Searles.

Most residents of Fletching had more than one job or role in the village. Mr Grover the butcher kept dairy cows and Lily Mainwood delivered their milk in a special bucket with a measure hanging inside. William John Stevenson who kept the Griffin Inn also ran the coal business and a horse wagonette in which he took passengers to and from the railway station for 7s. 6d. Joseph Weston, proprietor of the Rose and Crown, delivered bread. It was brought from Uckfield by horse and trap, left on a scrubbed white table in his public bar, then distributed in a small hand-cart. Joseph and Tom Bellingham grew hops on Parsonage Farm and kept a dairy herd; Mrs Joe Bellingham owned a sweet shop in the village.

Many of the countrymen who joined up voluntarily or who were conscripted into the armed services had never left their homes before and knew little of other parts of the country, let alone France, Belgium or Gallipoli. Their knowledge of the world was dramatically widened by the war; if they returned their own villages seemed different.

An article in *Country life* on village life in war-time suggested that the farm labourer's experience of life in the army gave him new ideas and ambitions; the education and the opportunities offered within the rural community appeared inadequate and restrictive by comparison. Two men who were invalided home to their village apparently even volunteered to go out again, saying: 'The squire's wife, she's just splendid to us – but it's too homely like with the old street ascending the hill, and the ol' mill sails going round and round.'

Andrew Clark, however, found the men from Great Leighs were not so keen to go out for a second time: 'they know what it means'.[1] And leaving Fletching had quite a different effect on one of the old boys from Robert Saunders' school. The boy's mother called on the headmaster to apologise for her son's not visiting him when home from the front 'where he had been two years before getting leave. He is in the 16th Lancers and she said she nearly cried to see the change in him, all the Boy being gone. He couldn't bear to come down through the street to see anyone & was very downhearted to go back.'[2]

Both Saunders and Clark tried to acquire as much information as possible about the war from those who left for the front. Saunders could rely on his three sons who were in the services to keep him informed, but he also wrote to his old boys 'so I get a good deal of information that doesn't appear in the papers'. Clark kept an extraordinary personal record of the war, a diary, letters and newspaper cuttings and circulars which finally amounted to ninety-two volumes, over three million words.

But for many left behind on the home front, the old and infirm, the women and children, it was virtually impossible to find out what momentous events were taking place on the other side of the English Channel once censorship was imposed: instead of being widened their knowledge of the world was narrowed and restricted. In the first few weeks of the war many local newspapers attempted to give full details of the progress of the war, as well as publishing interviews with soldiers home on leave and letters from the front: 'it is awful out here, and I shan't be sorry to get back'; 'sometimes the slaughter is terrific'. But censorship was imposed on the newspapers as well as on the soldiers' letters home. Instead of being packed with war news, many local newspapers shrank to less than their pre-war size, the *Somerset Standard* included. Interviews with survivors of the war became stereotyped, timid. Soldiers all seemed to be 'of a bright and fearless type'; a Dardanelles veteran 'except that he still limps on the left foot as the result of his wound . . . appears to be in the pink of condition'.[3]

A sense of the gulf which could develop between home and abroad can be recovered from the letters collected by three sisters living in Ashurst Wood, East Grinstead, not very far from Fletching. The Miss Lucases regularly sent out parcels to men who had enlisted from their village and carefully preserved the letters sent back to 'Bramblehurst'. Early in 1915 a grateful Captain Habgood was able to report that his Worcester Sauce had arrived at the front uninjured. In return he enclosed 'a piece of a German aeroplane which was brought down behind our trenches'. This was obviously received with enthusiasm by the Lucases because in October he sent another piece of aeroplane: 'I thought you might like it as the black piece is part of the Iron Cross which is painted on them'.[4]

The same month a rather less jovial letter arrived from Private Arthur Tomsett with the Mediterranean Expeditionary Force, 'thousands of miles from dear Ashurst Wood. I might mention that only three of the A. Wood boys are left, George Skinner, Arthur Lindfield & myself, the remainder either being wounded or sick.' Tomsett was himself wounded in September 1916 but he continued to write, next time from Minehead Red Cross Hospital, a Somerset beauty spot.

Private Charles Syms, serving with the 7th East Surrey Regiment, was lucky to survive the Somme. The 8th Battalion East Surreys had taken part in the attack on the German trenches at Contalmaison, led by Captain Nevill, kicking a football. The Miss Lucases might have read of their exploits in the *Daily Mail*.

> On through the hail of slaughter
> Where gallant comrades fall,
> Where blood is poured like water,
> They drive the trickling ball.
> The fear of death before them
> Is but an empty name;
> True to the land that bore them,
> The Surreys play the game!

Syms wrote to Bramblehurst in November 1916 not of his experiences in that dreadful battle, but full of congratulations on hearing of the success of the Ashurst Wood Bazaar and particularly the hard work put in by the Lucases on their stall. He concluded, however, 'I am glad you found the Somme film interesting, it is all very interesting in reality but so terrible to witness at the time.'[5] What more could he say that would be fit for village spinsters to hear?

For most on the home front, the facts of war arrived gradually, a stealthy invasion of ordinary life. There was no radio or television, newspapers and letters home from the front had been subject to censorship since the end of 1914. Knowledge of the war depended to some extent on geographical location. Those living in south-east England, for example, grasped something of the reality of war almost immediately because they could hear the ominous sound of guns being fired along the Western Front. Throughout the war Robert Saunders commented to his son in Canada on the persistent rumblings, 'like the thud of some giant propeller'; 'the continued pulsation, like the sound of a great propeller on a Mammoth steamer', which reverberated around Fletching. Walks through the Sussex countryside were ruined by the reminder of the war pulverising the countryside in France.

> The country round is really & truly a picture that gladdens the heart. The Cuckoos are in great force this year & for a wonder everybody agrees they never saw or heard so many.
> The great blot on everything is the Thud & Throb of the guns, night & day in France, & yesterday I could even hear them in-doors.

In June 1917 when high explosives were detonated under the Messines Ridge, Saunders were intensely relieved that his son Ron was in England. The mother of one of his old boys was not so fortunate: 'the sound of the guns all day when she was alone nearly drove her mad thinking of her boy out there'.

Air raids began in December 1914, bringing violence, destruction and death directly into the village, the town and the city. The counties of East Anglia, Kent and Sussex were particularly vulnerable. Great Leighs was close to two major centres of war industries: Braintree had

Lake & Elliot, Courtaulds and Crittalls; Chelmsford had Cromptons, Hoffmanns and the Marconi Works, all targets for German Zeppelins. But even in Knafferton, East Yorkshire, a village schoolteacher called Albert Copps was shaken out of his sleep by the noise of a Zeppelin dropping a bomb near Driffield Station.

In the summer of 1915 Albert Copps took his family south to Hertfordshire to help with the harvest on his parents' farm. But their pastoral holiday was rudely interrupted when bombs were dropped on the market town of Ware.

> While the evening prayers of the family were in progress I detected a familiar drone in the air. My wife had also heard and she pointed to the lighted lamp. In response I pressed the extinguisher for the windows were innocent of blinds. When my father had finished the prayer the family wanted to know if this was my idea of a joke, but I bade them listen, for the noise was growing and then they knew fear.[6]

Fascination seems to have been the most common response to Zeppelins, also the desire to collect souvenirs if an air ship was actually hit. The general opinion of the villagers of Great Leighs was that 'those Zeppelins don't know their business. Why don't they drop their bombs on Parliament – when the MPs are there? A lot of them could be spared.'[7]

A raid over Great Leighs on the night of 31 March 1916 brought Andrew Clark out of his bed and into the garden.

> It was a starlit night, slightly foggy. By this time the Zeppelin was roaring like a railway train somewhere near by, apparently just over the Rectory stables . . . I tried every way to locate it against the stars, but did not succeed. Then the noise began to be louder and louder as the machine began to move from over-the-stables way to over-the-stable-yard way. The movements were ridiculously, so far as could be judged from their sound, like those of a crow, flying over a pasture field.

The vicar's daughter called out that he must put out his cigarette as he was showing a light. Then the gate of the rectory clicked and Clark's neighbour Major William Brown arrived to join the watch. A little later the Zeppelin returned and they finally saw it, 'a long, black thing against the stars' hovering over the Stokeses' cottage. 'A window was heard to open in the Stockeses' cottage, and Miss Stokeses voice call out shrilly to her mother (who is rather deaf) – "I can hear the sound, but can't see anything." Little wonder, since the Zep. was then directly over the cottage.'

The Clark family, their servants and neighbours finally retired to bed in the early hours of the morning after more Zeppelins had passed over accompanied by sizzles and bangs. The damage had mostly been done in Braintree. The home of Clark's favourite stationer had been bombed and five people killed in Martin's Yard. Next day the town was packed with sightseers. 'All Braintree had gone to Sudbury (to see the damage there). All Essex had come to Braintree.'

There was a gruesome side to air raids: not just casualties on the ground but casualties among the crews. In September 1916 a Zeppelin was hit over Essex and fell burning into a field not far from Billericay. One of the soldiers sent to guard the wreckage arrived while it was still burning. 'What a sight it was! What a sight!'

> The worst bit was gathering up the crew. The ground was very soft where they fell and when we picked them up there were indentations in the soft soil of the shape of their bodies, arms, legs, everything – a mould of the bodies really. We carried them to the farmhouse. We picked up wicker chairs, loaves of German bread and bits of burnt silk and pieces of aluminium – all sorts of stuff. It kept us in beer for months! Everybody wanted souvenirs.[8]

The German crew were buried in the village churchyard. The officiating clergyman altered the words of the Burial Service from 'our brothers here departed' to 'these men here departed'. The crew ended up buried in the green fields of the English countryside, presumably 'some corner of a foreign field' forever Germany.

Zeppelins never got as far as Somerset, though Percy Long, the Mells painter and decorator, blackened out the church windows in anticipation. Nevertheless fear of air raids was intense and by the beginning of 1915 some country men and women were erecting their own air raid shelters. In one village near Frome the wife of a retired bank manager was killed while helping her neighbour to excavate the trench for his shelter. She was crushed to death when the woodwork for the shelter collapsed on top of her.

Many rural areas of Britain were affected by the construction of aerodromes, munitions factories and military camps: in the Home Counties, East Anglia, Wiltshire and Hampshire farmers lost valuable agricultural land, and country towns and villages had to cope with living in close proximity to thousands of soldiers in training, waiting to be sent overseas. Although this made the scale of military operations all too clear, it often caused more local tension and drama than awareness of what lay in wait for the young men across the Channel. It could even provide entertainment for rural backwaters: sometimes English villages appear to have become settings for farce.

Frome experienced the antics of the North Somerset Yeomanry in May 1915. A squadron was sent to defend the town against a mock attack by the rest of the regiment. Unfortunately the defending soldiers chose the wrong point at which to base their defence and the rest of the regiment simply marched straight into the town, 'in fact they may be said to have been in possession of the town before the defenders were aware of their presence'.[9] Not a shot was fired, even in pretence.

A temporary camp was established at Lyons Hall Park, Great Leighs, in May 1916, for the artillery section of the Lowland Brigade: 12 anti-aircraft guns, 600 men and their horses. The peace of the village was at an end. There was shouting and raucous singing from the camp and from individual groups of soldiers walking through the village on their way to and from one of the public houses. The opening hours of the pubs were reduced and military police were posted at the camp gates to keep the men in after 10 p.m. (10.30 on Saturdays) but many still managed to slip out.

On one occasion, an Inspecting Officer called unannounced at the camp. The colonel in charge had gone off to town on self-granted leave, so the Inspecting Officer, who was himself a general, put the officers left in camp through their paces. Their horsemanship was so execrable that he exploded with rage and foul language. Thomas Stoddart, land steward at Lyons Hall, happened to be present and confessed later he 'felt it wrong in him as a Churchwarden, to hear such language used in the parish'. He rapidly withdrew.

The Trittons, owner of the park, were invited to tea in the Mess Tent, only to witness the bad manners of the high-spirited young subalterns. Andrew Clark found the antics of the soldiers amusing but Mrs Tritton, who was deeply religious, was always trying to bring a little sobriety into their lives. She was unsuccessful in getting prayers to be said every night at the camp but she did erect a 'Quiet Tent' for private worship. She encouraged the men to sign the 'War Roll', a teetotallers' pledge. 'Just to oblige the lady', several signed, each adding the names of half a dozen of his comrades, 'just to see what would happen'. They were taken aback when Mrs Tritton invited all the soldiers whose names were on the list to tea in Lyons Hall. When the cunning men twice managed to invent excuses not to come to tea, Mrs Tritton forlornly expressed her disappointment to the vicar: 'on each occasion they have been unexpectedly called off on military duty and so unable to come.'

The lady of the manor was undeterred. She brought to the camp an American evangelist from the Coldstream Guards who had been a protégé of her dead son (killed with the Coldstreams in France in December 1914). According to her 'he thrilled the men: tears were running down their cheeks'. But the soldiers gave a different account. They agreed the American had an attractive voice but thought he was 'an evangelistic liar of exceptional daring and ingenuity'.

Robert Saunders' nearest camp was at Maresfield Park. It was not a typical English country estate. The absentee landlord was a German, Prince Munster. Once he had bred prize cattle in the park and questions were asked in the Commons in 1915 as to whether this valuable herd 'was being preserved intact for its enemy owner'. But Prince Munster's herd had gone long before the army arrived: four cows remained according to the Home Secretary and these were 'doing their utmost for the benefit of British subjects'.[10]

The army camp at Maresfield was much larger than at Lyons Hall with 10,000 soldiers installed by October 1914. Five miles of roads had to be constructed between the huts at the beginning of 1915. At one time Canadians filled the camp and Saunders worried that 'the sound of the "Nasal" will corrupt the pure throaty Sussex in time'. They grumbled endlessly about the 'rotten' English climate and drank too much. Their cavalry were ruining the countryside and added to the general sense of desolation which overcame Saunders in the autumn of 1916. The Battle of the Somme was still raging.

> The last time I walked round Daleham I couldn't help comparing it with those of former years. The sky was cloudy and made every thing look desolate and sombre, the trees were losing their leaves, the flowers were gone save a few thistles, ragwort, & groundsel. The only birds I saw were 3 goldfinches that suddenly flew up on the Common by the Star. The ground here which used to be covered with grass and furze, is now perfectly bare, being used as a practice ground for the cavalry at Maresfield Park.

Noises from the camp were worse than rumbles from France. 'Every day there is Bomb practice at the Camp & some of the Bombs make a big noise, then there is the rattle of Machine Guns, forcing you to remember we are at War & taking your attention from country sights and sounds.' As far as Saunders was concerned Sussex was no peaceful rural paradise. But his daughters and other local girls enjoyed the bustle. Every time a group of soldiers marched through Fletching, Saunders noticed how much interest was shown in the motto written on the front of his house. Then he realised his two youngest daughters were looking out of the window, engaging in nods and winks with the soldiers.

The entertainment provided by soldiers was a widespread feature of their presence in the countryside during the war. Many rural communities suffered from a lack of social activities. The Women's Institute was itself a product of the war, set up by and for the women who were left behind. Middle-class city workers might seek the peace and tranquillity of the village but villagers often found their life deadly boring. One of the reasons for the increasing depopulation of the countryside in the decades just before the war had been the rival attractions of city life, of music halls and football and cinema. Ironically the war itself offered several years of entertainment coming directly into the village.

In Lincolnshire, for example, in the first half of 1915, an imaginative colonel took soldiers of the 3rd East Anglian Field Ambulance on regular visits to the villages. First they would be treated to tea and cakes on the vicarage lawn. Then the musician in the regiment would give an organ recital in the church. This was followed by a demonstration of stretcher drill, squad drill and other games in front of the delighted villagers. The transport section would give exhibitions of riding and 'newcomers were put through their paces to amuse the crowd by falling off'. The village of Northborough got more than it bargained for, however. In the church crypt there was a great pile of bones and skulls but after the visit of the soldiers, 'it is said the pile was depleted by a bone or two'.[11]

Australian and Scottish soldiers were billeted on the country town of Romsey in Hampshire in May 1915. The inhabitants could choose between the bagpipes of the Scottish soldiers and the brass band of the Australians, both tried out in the market place, and bringing 'new life and stir' to the 'pretty, drowsy' town.[12]

The Army Service Corps provided a baffling sight with their haybalers as they travelled throughout the countryside harvesting fodder for the army horses. Pulling up in a Sussex village for dinner, one team was forced to leave a guard beside its haybaler. The guard then proceeded to tell the curious villagers outlandish stories about the machine. One group was told it was an anti-aircraft gun that had been used in London during the recent air raids; another was told it was part of a tank and the team were going over to France to take part in the fighting. The gullibility of the villagers would confirm *Punch*'s frequent picture of the countryside being inhabited by yokels with straw in their hair capable of believing any cock and bull story they were spun by sophisticated townies.

When John Buchan's novel *The Thirty-Nine Steps* was published in 1915 it was an instant success. The adventures of Richard Hannay, the perfect English gentleman and patriot, thrilled a nation at war. To the enthusiastic veterans who became special constables or joined the volunteer regiments, Hannay's stalking German spies through the Highlands of Scotland was of immediate relevance. Night after chilly night, men too old to fight guarded railway tunnels and bridges, telegraph posts and reservoirs, on the look-out for real-life spies and saboteurs.

Within a few days of the declaration of war special constables were being enrolled to assist the overworked police force. In the country town of Tewkesbury, Gloucestershire, John Moore's father, aged 50, 'put on a red armlet and drilled twice a week with a Boer War rifle, or guarded railway bridges against imaginary and ubiquitous "spies".'[13]

Twenty-two men from the Great Leighs district, including Andrew Clark, turned out for their first drill on 14 September. They arrived at the pre-selected field on Mr Brown's farm, only to find it had been heavily grazed and manured by a herd of cows. They then tried a field on Mr Stephen's farm:

> . . . the surface of the field was very uneven; there was blowing a gale and the drill-instructor's voice was mostly inaudible; the instructor is not a tall man and he stood beyond much taller men than himself so that his demonstrations ('You move this way', 'You wheel that way') were invisible to three-quarters of the company. The right-about movement produced time after time the most ludicrous clumps or dispersed confusions which produced shouts of mirth on the part of the company when they took breath to see the tangle they had got into.

In the early months of the war the special constables were intensely keen. They saw spies everywhere. An unfortunate Ordnance Survey reviser fell victim to the diligence of the Great Leighs special constables in October 1914. He was seen asking questions, making notes, lingering in the country lanes, until six special constables, one after another, arrested him in their respective districts. Finally he fled to one of the stately homes to seek the protection of its owner who was a Justice of the Peace.

Andrew Clark was dubious about the usefulness of the special constables. 'There is nothing in Great Leighs that it would benefit an enemy to destroy.' He was forced to give up drilling in May 1916 as he was too deaf to hear the commands. His fellow constables were denied the pleasure of shoving their vicar around the Essex countryside. The village blacksmith was also critical of the constables and openly facetious in the pub about their supposed bravery. In return tricks were played on him in the night. On one occasion a rope was tied to the handle of his front door, then taken around the house to the handle of the back door, with the result that he was unable to get out in the morning.

But the blacksmith's derision was not entirely misplaced. In October 1915 a group of extra-special constables was formed in Chelmsford to warn the inhabitants of the approach of Zeppelins. They were issued with long poles with pads on the end with which to reach up to tap on upper-storey windows. It was pointed out that this was quite daft because anyone woken up in such a way would light gas or a candle and open the window, thus illuminating entire streets. While the people of Chelmsford suffered taps on their windows, some of the villagers in Great Leighs lay in fear and trembling of the night patrols. 'They hear the sound of measured footsteps pacing along the road past their house, where no passer-by is expected, and they lie and tremble, questioning whether it is tramps or invaders.'

There was another side to these night patrols. Many of the constables enjoyed unexpected communion with their natural surroundings: watching by deserted railway tunnels could be rewarding for nature lovers and philosophers. Andrew Clark regretted he had forgotten his boy's knowledge of the stars, some nights the moonlight shone 'sweetly-bright' and he heard the 'sighing of the telegraph-wires in the soft breeze'. H. G. Wells, also living in the Essex countryside, imagined similar communings for the hero of his novel *Mr Britling Sees It Through*, special constable for the village of Matching's Easy.

As he prowled the countryside under the great hemisphere of Essex sky, or leant against fences or sat drowsily upon gates or sheltered from wind and rain under ricks or sheds, he had much time for meditation and his thoughts went down and down below his first surface impressions of the war ... he faced the deeper riddles of essential evil and of conceivable changes in the heart of man.[14]

The Volunteer Home Defence movement was well under way by the beginning of 1915. Thousands of men spent their weekends drilling, camping out under canvas or in barns, learning to dig trenches and

Clouds, Wiltshire, 1915. Designed by Philip Webb for Percy and Madeline Wyndham.

The west corner of the drawing room, Clouds, shortly before the war.

Clouds, 1910. The celebratory meet for the coming-of-age of Percy (Perf), only child of the Rt Hon George Wyndham.

(*Below left*) The Rt Hon George Wyndham and his son Perf outside the south-west door of Clouds, shortly before the war. George Wyndham had succeeded to Clouds in 1911.

(*Below*) Lieutenant Percy Wyndham. Perf succeeded to Clouds in 1913 but was killed at the Battle of Aisne in September 1914.

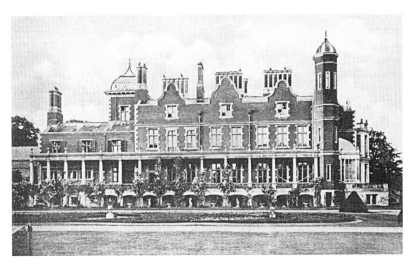

Babraham Hall, Cambridgeshire. The Jacobean style home of Charles and Madeline Adeane.

Charles Adeane C.B. During the war he was Lord Lieutenant of Cambridgeshire and Ely, President of the Royal Agricultural Society of England, Commandant of the Cambridgeshire Volunteer Regiment and Secretary of the Agricultural Relief of Allies Fund.

St Mary's, Fletching, Sussex. The home of Robert Saunders, headmaster of Fletching School. The motto on the front of the house reads 'Res non verba'.

'The Cottager's Roll of Honour' The cottage is in Eartham, nea Chichester.

'Woman-Power'. *Punch* 15 May 1918.
Ceres 'speed the plough'

'Deserving the Medaille Militaire'.
A French woman at work on the land.

ss Marjory Maxfield, Miss Hilda Hobson and Miss Phyllis Hobson with Dexter-Angus bulls at Sandringham.

Sketch by Ms C.M.M. Prunell, who worked on the land 1917–18. 'Punch rebellious, kicking . . . & in between sleeping, until I got a switch from the hedge-row. . . . An aeroplane came and stopped her engines to do spiral dives and twists & most marvellous evolutions in the air exactly over our field. Once she came whirr-whirring so near over the rake and so low that Punch snorted with fright & remained awake for the rest of the afternoon.'

Cecil Aldin, 'A Land Girl Ploughing'.

Randolph Schwabe, 'Hoeing'.

Randolph Schwabe, 'The Women's Land Army and German Prisoners'. 'What the blighters are doing is making a straw stack after the corn has been threshed' (Randolph Schwabe).

'Binks's Patent Futurist Scarecrow'. *Punch* 17 July 1918.

Frank Cook's paint box. 'Filthy and lousy as I was, I managed to keep my sketches intact with all my battle kit'. ($3\frac{1}{4} \times 1\frac{3}{4} \times 1\frac{3}{8}$ inches)

Neuf Moulin, near Abbeville. Sketch by Frank Cook, 29 September 1916.

Vauchelles, Somme. Sketch by Frank Cook, 16 July 1916. 'We rested here after the first Somme Battle. The Division was badly knocked about but after making up our strength we were soon back again.'

Zouave Wood, Ypres Salient. Sketch by Frank Cook, winter 1915. 'The duckboard track leading to Regent Street communication trench. We worked in this wood every night for three weeks in bitter weather.'

build bridges. *Country Life* made them sound like overgrown Boy Scouts, 'squads of more or less elderly gentlemen ... enjoying a surprising renewal of youth'. When the war ends 'they will remember the swing and lilt of the route march on a fine day, the jolliness of lunching out of doors, even perhaps the uneasy slumber in a hayloft'.

Robert Saunders discovered he was completely unfit when he had an attempt at drilling so he gracefully withdrew. He encountered his fitter neighbours on their first route march in the summer of 1915. His impression was rather different from *Country Life*'s.

> The Fletching V.T.C. indulged in extensive cursing on Bank Holiday when they had their first Route March. It was raining and they had to march from Searles through the village to Piltdown, on to Newick, out to Chorley, back to Sheffield Park, Sheffield Arms, round Bray's Lane (Witches) to Searles where refreshments were promised and turned out to be ginger ale and cake.

Not exactly the refreshments Sussex farmers of mature years were expecting after devoting their energies to King and Country. One Fletching man summed up his opinion of the Volunteers: 'If England has to fall back on they chaps, we be done'.

Punch delighted in poking fun at the Volunteers in a series of fictional pieces. A Major Chrustie of Tiffin Lodge organised his villagers into the Larkfield Dare-Devils. They were better equipped than the Volunteers from the neighbouring village of Sloshley, however: they had uniforms. Also 'we have been promoted to aim at the running perambulator drawn by a long rope'. Sloshley were still at the 'haystack stage'. Blanche, a silly female snob and a regular feature of *Punch*, reported on the volunteer movement in her Kentish rural retreat. Her elderly butler had joined up, but 'what with drilling and route-marching all day with the Village Veterans he's so tired by dinner-time that he regularly falls asleep as her serves the barley-water'. One evening he nods off during dinner, dreams he has captured a German spy and tries to strangle one of the guests. The Duchess of Clackmannan, a dear friend of Blanche's, forms her own Yeowomanry. They are the proud possessors of a machine gun and are 'hoping to make it go off soon'.

While *Punch* was publishing farce and *Country Life* was describing gallant attempts to carry on hunting and local newspapers reported on flower shows, raffles, bring-and-buys, those left behind in however sylvan surroundings could not shut out the facts of war for ever. As the years passed and the numbers of casualties increased, the mood of many on the home front became at best stoical, at worst embittered, cynical and angry. The imposition of rationing and the effects of food shortages only intensified the general misery and suffering. Nothing could compare with the bloodbath across the channel, but village life on the home front was grim enough.

Food rationing did not begin in earnest until 1917. However there had been shortages, rising prices and profiteering since the beginning of the war. Andrew Clark noted criticism of the government's economic policy as early as January 1916.

The village gossips are much exercised over the Government's exhortations to practise economy, addressed to a village like this where no-one has ever done anything else and where there is no increase of money received, since no-one has war-work, and appeals to invest money in the war-funds, where no-one has any reserve either to give or to invest. They have an instance in point, if extravagance is sinful (as the Government says) why did Mr Asquith not check it in the case of his daughter's marriage. If the national funds are in such need as the Government says, why doesn't Mr Asquith sacrifice a tenth of his large income, and other members of the Government likewise, to the national need?

Bread rationing hit the rural poor particularly hard. Many poorer families relied on bread, it was 'in a very realistic sense the staff of life in the cottage',[15] so the prospect of being allowed only a fixed weight of bread was alarming. A family of seven which normally consumed 32 one pound loaves per week was to be allowed only 28 one pound loaves. One village baker in East Anglia profited by charging different prices to particular customers. Those living within delivery range of the competing town bakers were offered their bread at a penny less per loaf than those customers living in remoter areas who could not reach the town.

As the train fares had increased by 50 per cent, the average farm labourer could not possibly afford to call on the town baker and was forced to pay the higher price for his bread.

Andrew Clark was irritated by the circulars he received from the Food Controller urging ministers of religion to encourage their parishioners to cut back on food consumption. A circular from the Ministry of Food arrived in June 1917 offering a purple ribbon to anyone who reduced their consumption of bread. 'Waste of paper; useless expenditure of clerks' time and of postmen's time as though everyone had not heard the whole story over and over again or had any trust in a government office.'

Robert Saunders was becoming more and more angry about the fixing of prices and profiteering going on in his part of Sussex. When he tried to buy tea in October 1917, an item with a maximum price fixed by the Food Controller, he found 'the shopkeeper tells you he has no controlled Tea . . . at 2/4 per lb. but has only been able to buy a small chest of China Tea at 4/- per lb. & as a great favour he will let his regular customers have 2 ounces.' In August 1918 Saunders managed to get some currants from his grocer, the first for over a year, 'so had some currant buns. The bread is still very far short of pre-war times & I don't eat more than an oz. a day as a rule, using porridge for breakfast & milk pudding for supper.'

Dr Helps in Mells was fortunate during the war because he was sometimes paid in kind by the farmers he ministered to, mostly with milk and eggs. Less welcome were the goats brought to the surgery by the gypsies who had a semi-permanent camp near the village (and who, according to villagers, were always giving birth). For poorer families in Mells, hot meals were provided in a small building on the village green (it became the Women's Institute after the war), organised by Frances Horner and other ladies of the neighbourhood.

Such assistance was necessary. A national survey undertaken for the Agricultural Wages Board in April and May 1918 revealed that many families were in need. On average, 'families were eating only about four-fifths of the meat they had consumed in 1912, less than half the cheese, and about three-quarters of the fats'.[16] A Suffolk wheelwright and blacksmith recollected with bitterness the unfairness of food distribution in his area.

I can remember being really hungry ... Rations! That was a joke. We never saw sugar at all. We used to have golden syrup in our tea and if we couldn't get that we had black treacle ... The farmers' houses were full of food, dairy butter, sweet cakes, meats – everything. They got it off the shop-keepers. They had some kind of mutual arrangement.[17]

Wounded soldiers were dispersed throughout the countryside, not only to the larger permanent hospitals but also to the many newly created Voluntary Aid Detachment hospitals, to enlarged cottage hospitals and converted country houses. The presence of the limbless, the burnt and the blinded brought the tragic aspects of war into every village.

The village of Fletching laid on entertainment for a group of war-wounded in August 1917.

Last Thursday a gentleman at Piltdown invited 'Arms & Legs' i.e. soldiers who had lost an arm or a leg to play a Cricket Match in the Recreation Ground against a local team. They came up from the Pavilion at Brighton in big Motor Charabancs & as the day was fine had a very enjoyable ride. There was a big crowd to see them & the school children at Lu's instigation all brought fruit, Plums, Apples, & Pears which they carried round & distributed ad. lib. I stood & watched for a time but it was too worrying to see a man on one leg trying to bat though Jim Faller our captain told the bowlers to bowl easy balls. Some of the women cried to see them but they were as cheerful as crickets & hopped on one leg from the Pavilion with their one leg & without crutches. You know how our ground is situated a lovely view of the Downs, Ladies in white, sitting round the Ground & the wounded who were not playing, scattered here & there receiving plenty of sympathy from all the girls. All the time the big guns were roaring in Flanders so we could hear the war & see the sad results of it.

Death was never far from the experience of Andrew Clark, right from the beginning of the war. He regularly gave memorial services for the young men from Great Leighs who died fighting for their homeland. On 10 January 1915 he gave a service for Captain Alan Tritton of the Coldstream Guards, son of the lord of the manor, who was shot by a sniper just after Christmas; also for Private Dick Fitch of the Essex Regiment who was killed in October 1914 and his brother Private Arthur Fitch of the Royal Marines Light Infantry, who went down with HMS *Formidable* on New Year's Day.

Clark was specially requested by the Tritton family to include the Fitchs in the service; Mrs Sophie Fitch was asked to choose a hymn. Her husband Walter (he lost two more sons in the war) was an agricultural labourer and they lived in a cottage near the Dog and Gun. Officers and privates, lords of the manor and labourers were brought together in similar memorial services throughout the war: death in war broke down the rural hierarchy for a few hours at least.

When the curate of Mells left his village in October 1914, bound for India with the 4th Somerset Territorials, his parishioners presented him with a pair of field glasses. The following month the village heard the news that Captain Bates, son of the tenant of Mells Park House, had been wounded. At the same time, a letter published in the *Somerset Standard* from a trooper in the North Somerset Yeomanry bluntly informed readers, 'It's not war but hell'. The year ended with the tragic death by drowning of a young man in the Mells coal mine, only a few days before he was to be married.

In April 1915 a young wife from the Frome area tried to kill herself by cutting her throat. She had been suffering from depression ever since her husband went away with the National Reserves. Then, in May, the news came to Mells that Edward Horner was seriously wounded; Captain Bates and Captain Long had been killed.

Arthur Long had served with the North Somerset Yeomanry in the Boer War and joined his old regiment in 1914. He was one of the most popular men in the parish and left a widow, daughter of the Horners' gamekeeper, and three young children. He and his brother were the village builders and decorators, but Arthur also played a prominent part in the Rev. and Mrs Lears' theatricals. He had starred in *The Merry Wives of Windsor* in the summer of 1914. The local paper recorded his and Captain Bates' memorial service:

the village of Mells, in its sylvan setting, never looked more beautiful and picturesque . . . The bell from the tower of St Andrew's Church tolled slowly and solemnly, and knots of people, all clad in the sombre garb of mourning, were wending their way to the ancient fane.[18]

Frances Horner sent a message to Arthur Long's widow, 'Dear Mrs Long, my heart is with you to-day'.[19] She was unable to attend the service because she was with her wounded son in France.

By July 1916 seventy-four Mells men were serving in the armed forces. The numbers of casualties were increasing too: the village memorial would record the total of twenty-one dead. But the curate returned, alive, in 1917, with the Military Cross, awarded for saving the life of a wounded soldier. He was given his own living not far away at Norton St Philips.

The pressure of conscription and then death came into Andrew Clark's home in 1916 when his groom-gardener, Charles Henry Ward, was called up. Ward joined the Royal Field Artillery, leaving the vicar to fend for himself, scything, carrying and sawing wood, burning rubbish and mending fences ('I am very pleased with my rough fencing'). Clark found the primitive water supply at the rectory particularly burdensome. A heavy wheel had to be turned two to three hundred times three times a day to draw water from the well up to a cistern in the roof. Impudent sparrows made fun of the portly vicar from their perch on the gutter.

By the summer of 1917 Charlie Ward's father, a labourer on one of the Great Leighs farms, was dying of a painful malignant internal growth. His mother was utterly dependent on her soldier-son so applied for a separation allowance with the support of the vicar: 'It is a most deserving, as well as a necessitous case.' Clark included Charlie's letters to him in his war-journal: this, for example, written on 3 November 1917, and 'very typical of a village lad's letter'.

Dear Sir
I now take the Pleasure in writing a few lines to you trusting you are getting on alright and keeping well . . . I am afraid you have been working very hard since I left . . . I expect you are having some cold

weather at home now it is very cold out here one or two mornings of
white Frost it is getting quite winter now it will be a blessing when we
can all get back for good the time soon flys past it cant last forever I
must now close as I cant find any more to say to night.
Yours obediantly
Charlie Ward

On 16 November Charlie was dead, killed in a train accident. His
funeral, at least, was fitting for a village lad. The whole population of
the village of Seurre where he had been billeted came to the funeral and
covered the coffin with flowers. Charlie's father survived until a few
weeks after the Armistice.

By the last year of the war Robert Saunders had had enough of the
incessant noise both from the military camps near Fletching and from
across the Channel. Almost every family he knew seemed to have
suffered a loss. 'Every day we hear casualties among people we know.'
He had accidentally witnessed the news of the death of the butcher's
youngest son being delivered by the postman in May 1917.

> On Wednesday morning while I was dressing I was looking out of the
> window as the Postman came along. I saw him give Grover the
> Butcher some letters and among them, an Official Envelope. This he
> put down thinking it was from the War Office about sheep & cattle as
> he had had several. They let it lie till dinner time then opened it &
> found it was a notice to say Harry, the youngest boy, was killed in
> France . . . Poor old Grover was so upset & can't seem to get over it,
> if any one tries to sympathize he stands & cries.

Saunders attended a particularly impressive memorial service in
Fletching parish church in July 1918. The church was packed, the
atmosphere 'full of feeling. There were special Hymns, Psalms,
Lessons, then Chopin's Funeral march, & the Last Post sounded by
Trumpeters from the camp, followed the reading of the names of those
who had fallen.' A poem in *Country Life* describing war-time in a Kent
village summed up the feeling of inadequacy of those left behind, the
emptiness of the streets, the special symbolic role of the church.

Up the one street the old folk slowly move
To find their peace, where prayer is made; the Church
Has aisles invisible, where village lads
Now by the Nile, or windy Trojan plain,
In God are very near.
Soon through the trees the crescent moon will gleam
Like burnished copper on the homeward road,
Where village girls walk back from Church alone.

In Great Leighs the war came to an end with a sad incident involving one of its families. Louis Percy Wright went out to France with the Essex Yeomanry early in the war. In May 1915 he was fortunate to survive a particularly bloody engagement – he had been sent back from the front line in charge of the colonel's horse. Wright continued to be lucky right up to the end of the war. Meanwhile his only son Louis Walter had taken up war-work at Lake & Elliot's in Braintree. In July 1918 his employers failed to get him exempt from military service and in October Louis Walter was at home on 'final leave'. He had already been in hospital with severe bronchitis and his mother couldn't 'think what good a lad with so weak a chest will be in France in the winter'.[20] Louis Walter never got to France. On 9 November he was dangerously ill with double-pneumonia. His mother and sister were themselves ill with influenza so unable to visit him in the Sheerness hospital where he died, on 11 November, the day the armistice was signed.

Young Louis Walter was given a military funeral, with six bearers, a firing party of fourteen, a bugler and sergeant in charge. He was buried in Great Leighs but without his father being present. Wright Senior didn't receive the telegram in time. He had been carrying a German bayonet around with him for several weeks, intending to bring it home as a souvenir for his son. But when he finally heard of Louis's death he threw the bayonet away: it was just as his regiment entered Brussels in triumph.

Sixty-seven men finally joined the armed services from Great Leighs. Nineteen of those died, their names and their sacrifice recorded on the war memorial. In Fletching the cross erected beside the church and opposite Saunders' home contains the names of thirty men who died. Most were former pupils of Saunders; all were from families he knew well. As Saunders led his schoolchildren to the church on Armistice Day 1918 and joined in the singing of the National Anthem, he found himself musing over the loss of so much youthful promise:

As I look back over the last 4½ years I can see so many tragedies in families I know well, & I can see so many of my old boys who are dead or wounded, or dying of consumption & recall them as boys at school where I used to urge on them the duty of patriotism, so that at present, it doesn't seem right that those who have escaped shall give themselves up to Joy days.

A strange ceremony took place at the same service. It is best described in Saunders' own words.

On the day War was declared the Gloves under the Armour [the Nevill Accoutrements of the Earls of Abergavenny] fell to the floor. Mr Hood made a lot of the coincidence imagining the spirit of the old Knight in the Gloves, and said he would restore the gloves to their place on the day the War ended, but as you know he died last year. The present Vicar, however, carried out his wishes, & carefully refixed the Gloves, while the children watched. Then we sang the National Anthem and the children formed a long procession & marched up & down the street singing till it was time to go home. After tea our Church Clock, which had been silent all through the War struck at 6 & has continued striking day & night . . . sounded like the voice of an old friend returning from the grave.

On the farm:
the fight for food

It is my sincere conviction that it may be on the
corn-fields and potato lands of Great Britain that
victory in the Great War may be lost or won.

Rowland Prothero, President of the Board of
Agriculture, Dec. 1916

Up and down the furrows went Harry, with his head
hung low, in his ears the mutter of the guns, so faint on
the windless April noon that he sometimes thought
they were just the sorrowful beating of his own heart –
up and down, scattering seed into the earth, leaving his
token of life in the fields he loved before he was himself
taken up and cast, vital and insignificant as a seed, into
the furrows of Aceldama or the Field of Blood.

Sheila Kaye-Smith, *Little England* (1918)[1]

O N 1 July 1916, the first day of the Battle of the Somme, Lord
Selborne, President of the Board of Agriculture, declared 'the
turnip is just as important as the shell and the Army'.[2] Not
everyone agreed. Throughout the war a mostly bloodless but often
bitter struggle took place on the pastures and cornfields of Britain
between farmers, labourers, the government and the military machine.
Farmers were asked to plough up their pasture land, to grow more
grain to compensate for the effects of the German submarine blockade.

[130]

But at the same time they were asked to supply men to fight – agricultural labourers and farmers' sons made excellent soldiers – and to supply land on which military camps, munitions factories and airfields were erected. In exchange they were offered temporarily guaranteed prices and a motley collection of unskilled labourers – women, prisoners of war, pacifists and schoolchildren.

At the outbreak of war Britain was not self-sufficient in food. In the previous forty years of more or less continual agricultural depression three million acres of arable land, mostly in the Midlands and western counties, had returned to pasture. The ridges and furrows of centuries of ploughing are still visible in many grassy fields. British farmers produced only a fifth of the wheat consumed by the nation in 1914: the rest was imported. Nearly half the supply of meat and over three-quarters of cheese were also imported. British farmers provided enough food for only 125 days of the years.

However, most farmers were by no means badly off in 1914. The agricultural depression had been at its worst at the turn of the century, but prices had begun to increase in 1906 and in 1908 the decline in the acreage under cereal crops was halted. John Moore described a typical Christmas Fair at Tewkesbury, Gloucestershire just before the war:

Here was the annual harvest of the great stock-fattening farms which lay in the rich valleys of the two rivers; here was a season's consummation, the happy outcome of the marriage between English weather and English soil, delivered by the skill and patience of men whose grandfathers had owned their farms before them.[3]

A. G. Street, in *Farmer's Glory*, recalled 'if one attended to one's business decently, one got along all right'. 'Granted, there were occasional instances of farmers going bankrupt, but these rare cases could always be traced definitely to drink, gambling, or some other vice or extravagance causing neglect of the farm by the master.'[4]

By contrast the life of the agricultural labourer was far from comfortable. Between 1900 and 1910 the cost of living rose by 10 per cent but average wages in England and Wales rose by only 3 per cent. Almost all agricultural labourers were below the poverty line in 1914;

their living conditions were often inadequate and their prospects negligible. Rural depopulation continued to empty the countryside of its traditional workforce: no one stayed who could possibly find employment elsewhere. Young men and women with energy and enterprise thankfully exchanged the life of the fields for the life of the town. Many who remained on the land joined the newly formed National Agricultural Labourers' and Rural Workers' Union: strike[5] action was a feature of farming life in the 'golden' era before the war.

While labourers were expressing their dissatisfaction with the conditions of working on the land, new suburbanites were singing the praises of rural life as they perceived it. The countryside was seen as a place of retreat and recreation. As the thwarted and embittered labourers thankfully moved out of their damp, insanitary cottages, their places were taken by readers of *Country Life* and *Georgian Poetry* who relished the exposed beams, smoking fire-places and ancient thatch. The inheritors of uneconomic chilly country mansions played hosts and hostesses to architects in search of something vernacular, designers seeking out vanishing rural crafts, composers eager to take down original folk songs before the gnarled and wizened singers dropped down dead from a hard life on the land. Country life was never more desired than at the moment when it appeared to be on the brink of extinction.

When war was declared many labourers found the army an acceptable alternative to rural life – they enlisted not so much to fight for their countryside as to escape the stultifying hierarchical system. A labourer from Ronald Blythe's 'Akenfield' was paid 11s. a week before the war. 'When the farmer stopped my pay because it was raining, and we couldn't thrash, I said to my seventeen-year-old mate, "Bugger him. We'll go off and join the army."' After four months' training in the army he realized 'for the first time in my life there had been no strenuous work'. Both he and his fellow labourers 'were all damned glad to have got off the farms'. The magazine *Punch* provided its version of why the labourer enlisted. A farmer says to his ploughman, 'What do you mean by knocking off work at this time of day?' The ploughman, who has just witnessed an aircraft bomb drop in the field where he was working, replies: 'I be goin' to 'list for a soldier. If I be goin' to be killed, danged if I'll be killed ploughin'.'

Their places were often taken by country-loving townies, eager to get back to the land at a time of national crisis. William Rothenstein, who had acquired his farm in Gloucestershire in 1912, put down his paint-brush when his labourers joined up and 'joined in weeding and hoeing, in haymaking, in picking up stones, in planting potatoes, and, later in the year, in binding and propping up sheaves to dry, in carting them to the rickyard, and in threshing operations'. He found the work 'exhilarating and satisfying'[7] and could not praise the skills of his labourers too highly. But they remained at the bottom of the wages' scale, owning neither home nor land.

The first month of the war coincided with the harvest. The weather was unusually fine, the harvest bountiful. Sir Thomas Middleton, later to master-mind the plough-up campaign, noted 'a percentage of our younger men had already gone, and in certain districts many of our horses had been requisitioned, but otherwise a casual visitor to our harvest fields would have detected nothing very different from usual'.[8] Home supplies of grain plus foreign supplies already stored in the country ensured there was sufficient for five months. This would be ample if, as many thought, the war was going to be over by Christmas.

Lord Selborne set up a consultative committee of experienced agriculturalists in the first week of the war. It was generally agreed that food should be grown which produced the greatest possible amount of calorific energy – wheat, oats, potatoes: the acreage of cereals should be increased wherever practicable. But the government decided it 'would not be justified in holding out a financial inducement to farmers to increase their acreage of cereals'.[9] Instead it appealed to the farmers' patriotism. One Leicestershire farmer was unimpressed: 'To my mind they consider farmers a lot of asses.'[10] But others, knowing prices would rise even without government intervention, did plant more so that the 1915 harvest of wheat was increased by 20 per cent. This was achieved in spite of, rather than with, the assistance of the government.

Since the declaration of war the military had been churning up farmland in central and southern England. Fences were torn down, gate posts knocked over, trenches dug across prime agricultural land, freshly sprouting crops flattened by horses and gun carriages. A farmer in East Sussex lost 100 acres of land around his house.

[133]

Roads had been driven all across the place, and the farmyard was like a rolling sea of mud. They had put up rifle ranges across the arable land and entrenched 30 acres at the south end of the farm. The whole place was turned upside down and torn to pieces in a way that was perfectly heartbreaking.[11]

Equally heartbreaking was seeing much loved farm horses being taken away by the army and exposed to the shell-fire on the western front. By June 1915 about 8 per cent of heavy horses used on the land had been taken, and a quarter of saddle horses. As Pamela Horn points out, 'each horse requisitioned meant the loss to its owner not only of power for harvesting, carting, and ploughing, but also the loss of a known and often well-loved character, skilled in carrying out the tasks required of it'.[12]

Compensation was eventually paid to farmers for their losses and damage caused. The experience of Albert Copps, the Yorkshire village schoolteacher who enlisted in 1915, when training in Wiltshire in May 1918, suggests that by the last year of the war some farmers even managed to benefit from the recklessness of the army.

I worked under Lt. Godfrey Tearle, the well-known actor, and Major Blackwell – a wild Irishman, who on one occasion took me, as his aide, in a cycle combination. Sighting his O.P. – a haystack in the middle of a field, he did not stop to open the dilapidated gate, but charged through it. 'What the—' I began, but he merely growled, 'There'll be a bill for the bl— thing, so we might as well have our fun.' He was referring to the practice of farmers, who found it profitable to have their old gates replaced by the government.[13]

The submarine blockade began in the spring of 1915: food shortages were a distinct possibility. But the recruiting campaign of the government, supported by many landowners, was stripping the land of skilled labourers. By the end of April, 40 per cent of the male population of military age in Dorset had joined up, 35.5 per cent in Westmorland, 34.6 per cent in Norfolk and 39.6 per cent in Flint, all predominantly rural counties (London, by way of comparison, had produced 36.3 per cent). The Tritton daughters of Lyons Hall, Great Leighs, were typical

[134]

of their class, pestering the labourers out in the fields, plastering the neighbourhood with recruiting posters. *Punch* made fun of such activities through its fictional character Blanche. She writes to her dear friend Daphne from Curfew Hall near Puddlebury Parva, where she has been out and about in the villages helping with recruiting.

'Now,' I said to the young natives standing about the village streets, 'you boys have got to leave your hedging or your digging or whatever it is you do, and offer yourselves to your country. I'm quite *quite* sure big, strong, brave fellows like you aren't going to stand by while other men do your fighting for you! So come along with me *at once* to the recruiting office!' And they shuffled about and gurgled in their throats and nudged each other and grinned – but they came along.

But the reality of such coercion could be serious. The foreman of Lyons Hall Farm despaired of the activities of the Tritton women. 'Enticing more men away from the land, when too many have gone already; if the government want more men let them take idlers, not workmen. Unless the war is over before August, and some of the men come back, there will not be enough men to get in the harvest.'[14] The posters around Great Leighs were all torn down.

The government responded to the crisis by setting up a committee under Lord Milner (to become Minister of War in Lloyd George's coalition government), to study the country's food production 'on the assumption that the war may be prolonged beyond the harvest of 1916'.[15] An interim report was made in July, which insisted the farmers had to be given financial inducements to plough up their grassland.

To obtain any substantial increase in the production of wheat, oats and potatoes ... it will be necessary for farmers to sacrifice the comparative certainty of their present profits, to change some of their methods, to alter their rotations, and to increase their area of arable cultivation in the face of a shortage of labour. In addition, they will have to run the risk, not only of uncertain seasons, but also of a fall in the price of wheat at the conclusion of the War ... in order to ensure a general movement in that direction we consider it essential to guarantee a minimum price for home-grown wheat for a period of several years.[16]

The Milner Committee was far-sighted. But the government responded only to the short-term: in the summer of 1915 the submarine threat abated so adequate supplies of grain were obtained from the United States and Argentina; also the harvest at home was very good. Lord Selborne made the usual ineffective appeal to the farmers' patriotism, 'you who live by the land to assist your King and Country by producing as much food as possible in the coming year'.[17] But nothing was done about guaranteeing prices. Not surprisingly farmers responded by inaction: they grew just what they had always grown; pastureland remained untouched by any ploughing-up campaign; the overall arable acreage actually dropped back below the pre-war average. With no guaranteed minimum prices and little confidence that more men would not be taken from the land farmers were in a difficult position.

The government did introduce a policy of 'starring' skilled workers in agriculture to ensure they would neither be accepted as volunteers nor even approached for recruitment. But one angry Kent farmer wrote to Lord Selborne in October 1915 that a recruiting officer had visited his farm and

persuaded against their will to join the Army, the second horseman, the thatcher and my first dryer under head hop-dryer, he also went to two lads at the plough and tried to persuade them, also my first waggoner. Three were married men. If we are to have our farms depleted of workmen, it will be impossible to carry on the work.[18]

The government did make extra labour available for helping with the harvest of 1915. Soldiers not actually being trained were granted special leave, or furlough, of up to a fortnight, helping with the harvest and autumn cultivation. The availability of the soldiers was extremely haphazard, however, and farmers were made to pay for the soldiers' transport from the nearest railway station to the farms.

Many women wanted to help on the land but the farmers were, as yet, unwilling to take them on: they wanted skilled labour. One brave farmer employed four women in 1915 but was left declaring he had had 'enough women to serve him a lifetime'. The girl who professed to be able to plough 'insisted on carrying a cushion to sit down upon and a parasol to shield her from the sun and rain'.[19] Prejudice against women labourers was intense. When the wife of an Essex cowman went out to hoe turnips her husband declared 'if his wife was to work in the fields, he would stay at home'.[20]

Country Life was the first influential journal to publish propaganda in favour of women in agriculture. As early as September 1914 it was describing the work of Breton peasant women; in January 1915 it was praising the work of women in the North of England, 'a fine sturdy class, who can perform all but the heaviest agricultural tasks as efficiently as men'. Enthusiastic titled ladies used its pages to advertise their schemes for bringing more of their sex back on the land.

Lady Wantage invited 'strong, healthy young women' of eighteen to join her training course. Lady Londonderry formed an agricultural branch of the Women's Legion and received an annual grant of £200 from the Board of Agriculture until the Legion was declared inefficient and closed down. She was persuaded to concentrate on fruit-bottling. Mrs Dawson Scott's Women's Defence Relief Corps made its first appeal for women to prepare themselves for active service in September 1914: 'more than charity, more than knitting was required'. The women of France were the shining example: 'who saved the vintage of 1914? The women! Who was responsible for the lavish supply of vegetables in the great markets in Paris? The women!'[21] But at its peak in the summers of 1916 and 1917 the Corps only placed 500 women on the land. Its belief that three days' training under the supervision of a farmer would be sufficient was wildly optimistic.

Even farmers fortunate enough to have sufficient labour could do nothing about the weather: it was atrocious through the winter of 1915 and the spring of 1916. Frosts and heavy rain meant that less wheat was planted in November. Spring sowing was late because of constant wet weather culminating in the freak blizzard of 28 March. The ground was so sodden that work was impossible; on many farms the previous year's ploughing remained undone and root crops were left in the ground.

The vagaries of the weather were to be frustrating throughout the war years for farmers keen to make profits out of the rapidly rising prices obtained for their produce. In the previous spring (1915) Robert Saunders noted how Sussex farmers 'had a very teasing time. Wheat was 60s. a quarter and of course they wanted to sell, but couldn't thresh [because of the wet]. Mr Fenner had the engine on his ground for seven weeks and not a single day was fit.' But in May 1915 the arrival of rain 'pleased the farmers greatly as the grain badly needed rain and the hay crop is an important matter this year, owing to the stooks being sold to the Cavalry at Maresfield Park.'[22]

Matters were made worse for farmers in the spring of 1916 when conscription was finally introduced. The problem was not just finding labour to work on the land but deciding who out of the labourers left on the land should enlist, who could be exempt. The battle between farmers and the government was complicated by bitter skirmishing between farmers and their employees.

Farmers were exempt. Their sons and their labourers were not. Pamela Horn cites many examples of cases where appeals tribunals used their influence to grant exemptions to farmers' sons at the expense of agricultural labourers. Some farmers 'ostensibly retired from business and announced that their son had taken over the farm'. In Wales, some farmers asked 'land agents to insert their sons' names in tenancy agreements to show that the farm was being run jointly by father and sons.'[23]

The decisions of tribunals were not always on the side of farmers, however, whether sons or labourers were up for appeal. A tribunal in Essex showed itself to be woefully ignorant of farming requirements. The local hurdle-maker for Great Leighs, 'Alix' Alefounder, was called up. Instead of pointing out that Alix was a hopeless victim of asthma, his employer 'enlarged on the fact that he was the only "hurdle maker" in the place, but the helpless idiots on the tribunal did not know what a hurdle was, or how necessary for sheep-penning, and they dismissed the application at once.' Two weeks later the hurdle-maker was returned to his village, medically unfit. Another farmer in the area used the right tactic in keeping his shepherd: 'if he were taken away he must sell his sheep, and then there would be only one flock left in all this parish'. Also the shepherd had four young children, 'if he were taken and killed the country would have a long time to keep them'.

In the novel *Little England*, published in the last year of the war, Sheila Kaye-Smith romanticises the response of her hero Tom

Beatup. He wants to stay on his Sussex farm but fails the appeal tribunal: his father and younger brother can cope. The vicar gives him a lead in how to accept the decision: 'Think of the farms round Ypres, and Dixmond, think of the farms round Rheims and Arras . . . Perhaps every thud you hear means the end of a little farm.' Tom realises 'we're all eighteenth Sussex hereabouts'.[24]

Albert Copps, who was married with two children, enlisted under the Derby Scheme in 1915. When conscription came in he noticed the man in his rural community who had been loudest in urging his fellows 'to go and smash the Hun' managed to avoid fighting by taking a job on the land. The Yorkshire farmers were of course exempt from fighting.

> In quiet moments the vision of myself in the guise of a soldier armed with rifle and bayonet going into battle, gave me some uncomfortable feelings – among them a queer sensation in the pit of the stomach. My farmer friends – safe in their indispensability – did not make it any easier by the smugness of their remarks. I did not fancy myself as a butcher, or being butchered. I could not bring myself to push home the knife to sever the jugular of the squealing pig while my [farmer] father held it by the ears. It was repulsive, and the thought that I might be called upon to stick a man was a nightmare, and I thought that my hesitation might put me in the place of the pig.[25]

In June 1918, over a year after Albert Copps had been wounded at the Battle of Arras, *The Times* was still criticising farmers who were managing to keep their sons at home while agricultural labourers were being taken for military service.

Spring 1916 was the beginning of the build-up to the Somme; more cannon fodder was required by the military. Walter Long (President of the Board of Health and Local Government since May 1915), who had given a patriotic lead to the labourers on and about his Wiltshire estate at the outbreak of war, was now attacking the military authorities for demanding far too much from the land: 'I know in many cases the strain on agriculture has reached very nearly breaking point'.[26] Lord Selborne was attacked in the Commons for not putting up a better fight in defence of farmers. 'The soil was sodden, the spring crops were unsown' and yet, according to Sir Thomas Middleton, 'the recruiting authorities were enlisting their [the farmers'] most active men'.[27] More than a quarter of the men employed on the land before the war had joined the colours.

Some farmers were capitulating over the idea of employing women. J. Herbert Tritton, lord of the manor of Great Leighs, complained to the vicar, Andrew Clark: 'The War Office had taken nine out of thirty-six men from his farms; only old men were left. He must get eight women at once for farm work.' The *Journal of the Board of Agriculture* started its propaganda campaign in favour of women in December 1915. It publicised competitions in which women showed their skills to their male judges, one of whom confessed after an event at Truro, in April 1916:

> some of the work was very well done indeed. The dung-spreading and planting were excellent, and the way in which several of the competitors handled the horses in the harrowing and in the wagons was a surprise to many of the spectators . . . I should like to see some of the men who have been cheaply sneering at the ploughing have a try themselves.[28]

The Milner Committee had recommended the formation of County War Agricultural Committees: part of their work was to organise women's labour and in February 1916, at last with the backing of the government, Women's Farm Labour Committees were established with their own network of district committees and village registrars. Within six months 63 county committees had been formed. Speakers went into the villages, there was house to house canvassing and any woman who registered was given a certificate, 'as truly serving her country as the man who is fighting in the trenches or on the sea'.[29] After thirty days' service she received a bottle-green baize armlet marked with a scarlet crown. *Punch* was quick to comment: 'women who have volunteered to do agricultural work in place of men called to the colours will wear a green armlet, green being selected in preference to red on account of the possibility of cows.' But *Punch* also published a stirring illustration of a woman at the plough, 'Pro Patria. A Tribute to Woman's Work in War-Time'.

The Women's Farm Labour Committees' intention was to encourage village women to return to the land. Of the women who registered most were successful in weeding, fruit and hop picking, the care of poultry, dairy work and gardening. Their wages were a subject of dispute: another battle between the government and workers on the land. The government seemed to be trying to get cheap labour out of patriotic women for the benefit of the farmers. The *Woman Worker* commented in March 1916:

Twelve shillings [a week] is not a proper living wage for a woman; and our masters seem to know this. *The Daily News*, in explaining the government scheme, says 'It is frankly admitted that much of the most necessary work is hard and unpleasant, and by no means extravagantly paid. That is why the appeal is made exclusively to the patriotism of women. There is no question (as in the army itself) of any really adequate reward.' Well, why not? The farmers are doing very well. The price of corn is higher than has ever been known before. Why should women be deprived of 'any really adequate reward'?

Why should women assist in keeping down the miserably low wages of agricultural labourers? . . . no armlets and no 'patriotism' ought to make women work at less than a living wage.

Some women didn't even get twelve shillings. The women who were employed at Lyons Hall Farm, Great Leighs, received only 1s. 6d. a day. They tried to increase their wages when they discovered women on neighbouring farms were receiving 2s. and 2s. 6d. a day. Their employer immediately went to the other farms to negotiate a decrease in the wages of the favoured women labourers. Not surprisingly the women who had been receiving 2s. and more a day put down their pitchforks and refused to work.

Rudyard and Carrie Kipling employed women on their Sussex estate of Bateman's. However, they found themselves caught up in the sexual rivalry between their female labourers and male foreman. One girl was pursued by another into the hall of Bateman's House where Kipling 'found her leaning like Britannia on the pitchfork and howling "Ther dirty woman"'.[30]

Edith Airey, whose father worked on a large country estate, tried work on a dairy farm in Suffolk but found the foreman there was particularly unpleasant to his female labourers. He 'didn't take kindly to having women around and he would sort out most unpleasant jobs for us'. Edith and her sister were sent out into the fields of growing corn to spend all day pulling up docks: 'we didn't see a soul all day . . . so bored . . . up and down the field we went and it was so hot'. In the winter the foreman made them muck-spread. 'We could scarcely lift the fork'[31] and after a few hours they downed tools and left. Instead Edith went off to Brooks Engineering Works in Lowestoft to make shells.

Munitions work was better paid. Near Robert Saunders' village of Fletching in Sussex a munitions works was offering mere boys and girls 30–40s. a week. A family working at the military depot established at Milton, Berkshire, could earn £2–£4 a week: before the war the family could earn only 14s. But even with low wages, dirty and often heavy work, the land still attracted thousands of women. It was, after all, conveniently close for village women: 140,000 volunteered to join the scheme run by the Women's Farm Labour Committees in the spring and summer of 1916, of whom half received certificates and almost as many achieved their green armlets.

As well as attracting village women back to the land, the government was concerned to set up a mobile unit mainly made up of middle-class women, many from towns and cities. This was the Women's National Land Service Corps, the WNLSC, formed in January 1916. Two thousand joined in the first year and, after six weeks' training, were sent out to work, mostly as carters and milkers, although there were some ploughwomen. A group in Evesham, Gloucestershire, working through the summer of 1916, consisted of the daughters of a clergyman, a doctor, a journalist, a lawyer and men in business; there were also ex-teachers, nurses and office-girls. Patriotism was stressed; also making a good impression on the farming communities. However, the young women who arrived at Great Leighs in June 1916 hardly made a good impression on the vicar. Two 'swaggering' women workers:

> they had riding-breeches, like troopers, of a khaki cloth, with brown boots and leggings, and an overall of holland, white, coming to a little

below the knees. Ordinary women's hats. Carrying shortish rattans such as grooms might have. They looked as if they had gone astray, out of a comic opera.

One of the farms used for training the WNLSC was near Fletching. Robert Saunders commented to his son in Canada first on the effects of conscription, then the capitulation of Mr Fenner, one of the staunchest anti-women-on-the-land farmers.

We begin to see the effect of the Groups being called up even in Fletching, first one well known face & then another disappearing. Mr Fenner has been very emphatic over employing 'lady' helpers on his farm, no, he wouldn't etc, now his better half says he has engaged one. You would smile to see them, they wear thick boots, leggings, knee breeches (corduroy), a short smock, and a soft hat. There is a farm at Danehill for training them. The one I saw would have passed for a man anywhere.

The women were the subject of endless jokes in *Punch*. Blanche, again writing to her friend Daphne, explained 'no one need worry any more about agriculture and rotation of crops and all that sort of thing being stopped by the war. *We're* going to see to it. It is positively *enthralling* work! . . . I wish you could see me ploughing, dearest. My ploughman's pinny, big soft hat and leggings are a dream.' Even the cows appreciated the softer touch of 'Miss Wilson' and expressed an interest in fashion:

'She's got nice hands, and her voice is certainly in her favour.'
'What do you think of her hat? Simple, but rather smart, I think.'
'She didn't get that at Mugford's in the village, I know.'

Amy Baker's experiences minding sheep appeared in *Country Life* in May 1916 but would have been better placed in *Punch*. When the sheep in her care stray from their cabbage patch into a more attractive adjoining field she finds herself crawling through the hedge, hatless, her hair loose, giving a passable imitation of a sheepdog. 'It would give me unholy joy to take all the poets who have ever written of sheep and stand them round my cabbage patch to run and bark . . . Think of Mrs Browning and of Christina Rossetti picking up their crinolines.'

Soldiers at the front were composing their own tributes to the fairer sex on the land. The *New Church Times*, formerly the *Wipers Times*, had a piece: 'Lancelot's Letters to Lonely Ladies'.

> I wish we could invite you all to come out here and look round, even in Flanders you would find the country quite charming, in parts . . . Tell me, though, do you REALLY all wear those short skirts and things we see such pretty pictures of in the Illustrated Papers from Home?

One of the most ardent supporters of women on the land was Charles Adeane of Babraham in Cambridgeshire. He was a liberal and advanced landowner, particularly in the war years. He defended the interests of farmers at home, using his position as Lord Lieutenant of the county and as Treasurer (in 1917, President) of the Royal Agricultural Society of England, but he also suggested ways in which farmers could respond more imaginatively to the crisis in food production. He raised money and assistance for the beleaguered farmers of France and Belgium and also for British prisoners of war.

He made many speeches praising the work of women farm labourers, 'indeed agriculture could not be carried on without them'. By July 1916 he employed eighteen on his own estate and found them willing, conscientious and energetic. He tried to persuade farmers to 'put aside all their old bias'; also to pay the women a reasonable wage for their work. 'A woman in a dairy is just as good as a man. Just imagine the man who at a time like the present would not pay the price . . . the farmers [must] bear in mind that men were giving their lives on sea and in the trenches – could they grudge a penny?'[32]

The women got plenty of publicity, they provided material for jokes and had their photographs taken for the illustrated magazines. However, most substitute labour during the war was provided by soldiers, some 45 per cent of the total, although this was not fully mobilised until the spring of 1917. Throughout 1916, farmers could apply to their local Labour Exchanges for assistance: the Labour Exchanges then approached the nearest military camps, supposedly to engage skilled ex-agricultural labourers. In June, with the approach of harvest, farmers applied for over 13,000 soldiers. But the build-up to the Somme offensive was under way: less than 4,000 could be spared. After pressure from the Board of Agriculture, the War Offie was forced to release more men 'if the harvest was not to be lost':[33] between 12 August and 3 October it supplied 16,000. By this time, however, the farmers needed nearer double the number. But every day on the Somme as many thousands were being killed or wounded.

An article in *Country Life* suggested the system was working splendidly, at last the government was doing something 'exceedingly well'. The men 'love agricultural furlough, because it means that in many cases they get back to their own jobs, free from the restraint of military discipline'. This was certainly the idea, but many of the soldiers sent out to farms didn't know one end of a cow from the other. Nearly 1,500 were so useless that 'despite the labour shortage farmers refused to keep them'.[34] The soldiers were also paid generously (unlike the women substitute labourers). The farmers topped up their army pay and they often received as much as their skilled civilian counterparts, worked shorter hours and had clothing provided for free. It is hardly surprising they were called 'state-assisted blacklegs'.[35]

After all the extra help provided by various substitute labourers, the harvest of 1916 was a 'melancholy' affair. Kipling, '*very* busy' on his Sussex estate, called it a 'devil's own job'.[36] Appeals to patriotism were not sufficient to make farmers plough up their grassland. 'Government', they argued, 'could not have any real fear of food shortage or they would themselves have accepted some risks and not left them all for him [the farmer] to face'.[37] At the same time some farmers were doing very well out of the rising prices – in October 1916 prices were 68 per cent above the level of two years before. Lincolnshire farmers, for example, were making vast profits out of potatoes according to *Country Life* magazine: 'one who grows on a very large scale admitted having made £20,000 profit on a thousand acres of potatoes, and regretted the bargain as he had sold the tubers green and did not foresee the immense rise'.

The intensification of the submarine blockade coupled with poor harvests overseas only made matters worse and the government finally intervened. In November milk became the first commodity to have its price controlled. And during the months to follow almost all agricultural products had fixed maximum prices. Also a Wheat Commission was set up in October to take over all dealings in wheat, both home grown and imported.

Charles Adeane rushed to the defence of the farmers who were being accused of profiting from the shortages and high prices. He pleaded for greater contact between the government and the farmers who were not profiteers: 'the man who supplies only one-fifth of the loaf cannot regulate the price'. In December he announced that the Royal Agricultural Society of England was forming a War Emergency Committee. One of its tasks was to give farmers a better public image:

> ... the public did not realize what agriculturalists were doing at the present time. They were practically cultivating the same area of land as before the war with 40 per cent of their best men gone to the front ... There was no question of increasing the area of land under the plough ... If they had taken the advice given by the Board of Agriculture a year ago to plough up the pastures the position to-day would have been very much worse than it was. To keep the land now under the plough in the highest state of cultivation was, he believed, the best way in which they could serve the nation.

But Adeane underestimated just what could be achieved under a new government with a strong interventionist policy and a new President of the Board of Agriculture able to enforce the cultivation of land, to guarantee minimum prices and wages and to make farmers submit to state control.

The Asquith government fell at the end of 1916. Rowland Prothero (later Lord Ernle) was the new President of the Board of Agriculture in Lloyd George's coalition government. His policy was interventionist, not *laissez-faire*: more land could be ploughed up; more food could be grown.

> Do not let us be discouraged by the many circumstances against us. For the nation's sake let us take as our motto for 1917 and 1918 'Back to the 'seventies and better'. We cannot do more. I am sure that farmers will not do less.[38]

[146]

Prothero was given special powers through DORA[39] and established Executive Committees within the County War Agricultural Committees to implement the act: to 'enter on and take possession of any land which in their opinion is not being so cultivated as to increase, as far as practicable, the food supply of the country, and, after entry thereon, do all things necessary or desirable for the cultivation of the land or for adapting it for cultivation'. In January 1917 a Food Production Department was established within the Board of Agriculture. Sir Thomas Middleton was the Deputy Director, his mission to organise the plough-up campaign. In February a Corn Production Bill was introduced in Parliament: when it was passed in August it guaranteed the prices of wheat, oats and potatoes and a minimum wage until after the war. The State was entering the farmyard, impinging on the traditional independence of the farmer. Executive Committees travelled from farm to farm handing out orders, and 'the comments of the farmers do not err on the side of flattery'.[40]

The plough-up campaign began with the usual collision between the demands of the Board of Agriculture and the War Office. When the Food Production Department began its work in January 1917, 'the land was sodden with rain, farm work was in arrears, labour was everywhere deficient, and the outlook for an increase in the area under any tillage crop was a poor one'.[41]

Whereupon the War Office announced that it was going to take 30,000 additional men away from the land. To Prothero it was a 'staggering blow'. The Earl of Derby, Secretary for War, tried to defend his department. He was, after all, trying to win a war. 'I rather resent the insinuation continually made that the War Office has only one idea and that is to get men and to pay no consideration whatever to agriculture or other fields of industry.'[42]

The situation was complicated by the establishment of a Ministry of Food, a more powerful body than the Board of Agriculture (not to become a ministry until 1919). The Board of Agriculture was meant to be representative of farming interests; the Ministry of Food looked after the consumer, which meant controlling prices. Charles Adeane led the attack on the latter which, he claimed, ignored the fact that farming was a business. Prices of some agricultural produce were being fixed below the cost of production, meat in particular.

It is quite clear that the Food Controller has the power utterly to frustrate any attempt to increase the food production of the country. The earth may be scratched, pasture ploughed up and destroyed, but so far as yield is concerned there will be nothing but disappointment unless stock are fed in winter.

In December 1917, looking back over the first year's work of the Board of Agriculture and the Ministry of Food, Adeane was scathing about the 'dual control' which dominated agriculture.

Farmers were doing their best to carry out the instructions of the Food Production Department in regard to the ploughing up of pasture, but what was to prevent the Food Controller from fixing the price of cereals next year at such a price as would result in their endeavour being a loss to themselves? Prices controlled production, and mere cheapness might mean starvation.

Farmers were far from overjoyed by the sort of labour they were offered in the place of their own skilled men to start on the plough-up campaign. Prothero made a speech in Lancashire in February 1917 describing what was on offer now 'the war comes first'. 'You can have women workers, you can make what you can of C3 men, you can have partially disabled soldiers, and you can have German prisoners. Out of this mixed pack you should do your best to get effective work. The business is to get the seed into the ground and to grow it.'[43]

Special Agricultural Companies were formed out of the men physically unfit for active service. They were mostly from the categories C2 or C3 and unfit even for Home Defence. These were to be the Kitcheners of a new agricultural army. But some farmers resented having to train them. Even worse, the new recruits to the land came up for regular medical re-examinations. As they improved in fitness and strength – the result of so much hard work on the land – they could be given a new category and sent off to fight, just as they were beginning to acquire useful skills. Pamela Horn recounts that in 1917 'during the hay and corn harvest . . . the zeal of the medical teams was such that they had to be ordered to cease work because they were disrupting agricultural activities. They were not allowed to recommence their examinations until the end of September, when most harvest had ended.'[44]

The Special Agricultural Companies were joined by members of the Home Defence Force, released on special furlough to help with the spring ploughing of 1917. The usual problem arose: some 24,000 men were made available but only a fraction knew anything about ploughing. Again the military authorities were attacked by the agriculturalists: the result, all skilled soldier-ploughmen still in the country were sent back to the land to help the farmers. Even though these men had to return to their camps in May, before all the ploughing was finished, almost a million extra acres were tilled in 1917.

The German submarine blockade was at its worst in the spring of 1917: passenger ships and merchant ships were being torpedoed indiscriminately, the intention being to starve out the British. Only the adoption of convoys and the use of depth charges gradually diminished the threat. However, supplies of corn in the country were running dangerously low when the government decided to try to plough an extra 2½ million acres in England and Wales to make the 1918 harvest the biggest ever.

The advance plans were made over the early summer of 1917. Ploughing was to begin in the autumn with the farmers requesting the help of 50,000 soldiers to be released on special furlough. Unfortunately for the farmers – and much worse for the soldiers – Passchendaele got in the way. The rain which fell throughout the summer and autumn of 1917 turned the trenches around Ypres into treacherous quagmires. Soldiers were standing up to their waists in water: by the end of the year casualties among the British in the long-drawn-out Passchendaele engagement had reached 300,000. It was hardly surprising that only 35,000 soldiers could be spared for the farmers by Christmas 1917: the rest followed in the spring of 1918.

The farmers were also able to call on a new professional unit of mobile women labourers which had been formed by the coalition government. This was the Women's Land Army, the WLA, which superseded the work of the Women's National Land Service Corps. When the first appeal for recruits was made in March, 30,000 responded: by the time of the 1918 harvest 16,000 were working on the land.

The WLA was paid according to a recognised wage-scale, each recruit was given a month's training, later extended to six weeks, free travel to the place of employment and a free uniform. The uniform was immediately the subject of controversy because it included a pair of breeches, symbol of sexual indecency and depravity and already flaunted by some members of the WNLSC. Instructions as to dress and behaviour were given to each recruit to the WLA: no jewellery, no lace, breeches never to be worn in public unless covered by an overall.

> You are doing a man's work and so you are dressed rather like a man; but remember that just because you wear a smock and breeches you should take care to behave like an English girl who expects chivalry and respect from every one she meets. Noisy or ugly behaviour brings discredit, not only upon yourself but upon the uniform, and the whole Women's Land Army. When people see you pass . . . show them that an English girl who is working for her Country on the land is the best sort of girl.[45]

There were stirring songs, too, just in case 'pluck and patriotism' wore a bit thin after hours of weeding, stone-picking, pulling turnips – this sort of intensive back-breaking labour hadn't changed much since *Tess of the D'Urbervilles*. The WLA could sing these words to the tune of 'British Grenadiers':

> Between the rows of young green corn
>   How gallantly they hoe,
> Blisters and aching backs they scorn,
>   They toil that the seed may grow.
> Oh, of all the Women's Armies, there's none do work so Good,
> As they plough and sow and reap and mow – our Women on the
>   Land.[46]

But even the best sorts of girls still shocked older country folk. A girl arrived in Great Leighs, Essex, towards the end of the war, driving a motor-plough and wearing trousers and a small close-fitting cap. The plough broke down outside Mrs Stokes' cottage. The old lady came out to see what the commotion was about and asked whether the driver was a man or a woman. 'Being told it was a woman, she commented "It isn't decent to come out dressed like that. One never knows what women will do these nowadays. I'm sorry I came out and saw her."'

Members of the WLA were from all sorts of backgrounds. A farmer in Hertfordshire encountered women from tea shops, from domestic service and from behind shop counters. Many women left domestic service for the WLA and found the change a welcome relief. Rosa Freedman received her training at St Augustine's College in Canterbury. 'The work was hard, but after the discipline and confinement of domestic service I found the work liberating and rewarding.'[47] She joined a gang of six girls working for the Wingham Engineering Company. They travelled from farm to farm with a traction engine and a threshing machine. Friendly farmers' wives would supplement their rations with bread and butter or cake. 'One of our landladies would come out to the fields with our tea, in a pot wrapped in a towel, with some lovely thick slices of bread and butter, and she would sit down with us. Her husband was in France.'[48]

Rosa also helped with haymaking near Micheldever in Hampshire and managed to be thrown off a 'demobbed war-horse'. Then she helped to guard a hay dump – fodder for horses in France – near Cambridge. Such dumps were always at risk of being set on fire by spies and had to be guarded day and night. The depot consisted of three old train carriages parked beside the railway line and 'while on duty we would watch the Red Cross trains going through with the wounded, the railway line being free at night'.[49]

Guarding forage dumps was a frequent occupation of the WLA. Girls stationed at a dump in Ringwood in the New Forest were warned to take plenty of warm underclothes, scarves and blankets to survive the winter nights. They were also told by their colonel – who bred golden retrievers – that they could take their dogs too, though not toy breeds. Doris Odlum thought their work at Ringwood a complete waste of time. The dump was quite open and exposed. 'It was therefore somewhat farcical that every week I received a top secret envelope from the War Office with a password for the day which I only communicated to the sergeant and guards actually on duty.'[50] As the soldiers were armed only with truncheons and whistles any attack would have been a walk-over. As it was the hay was finally sent to Italy in February 1918 only to be lost at sea when the ship carrying it was torpedoed.

Throughout the countryside, women from villages, towns and cities were not just experiencing the life of the fields, they were discovering more of their own country, taking on responsibility and even learning to command men. A girl with the Forage Department in Newent, Gloucestershire, relished being saluted by the eight men under her. She was treated with respect wherever she went; 'out all day in all weathers on my motor cycle'.[51] The war changed the attitudes of both men and women towards the concept of women at work. The efforts of women in all sorts of jobs were rewarded when, in February 1918, women over thirty years old received the right to vote. In the early summer of 1918 Lloyd George made a special plea to women to help save the harvest. Instead of its usual jokes about women on the land, *Punch* depicted a buxom loosely clad Ceres wishing a ploughman well with his work: his reply, 'I don't know who you are, ma'am, but it's no good speeding the plough unless we can get the women to do the harvesting.'

In March 1918 Rowland Prothero had addressed members of the WLA of Cambridgeshire after they received badges and stripes from Princess Mary on the green in the centre of Senate House Yard, Cambridge. He praised their patriotism and their professionalism. Others had provided 'the silver bullet and the lead bullet . . . it was up to the agriculturalists to find the food bullet'. 'If the food line breaks at home we rob the gallant dead of the victory they have given their lives to win, and it is up to you to back up the men at the front.'[52]

Not only the women of Britain were helping to provide the 'food bullet'. When Prothero had bluntly told the farmers over a year before what labour was available he had included German prisoners of war. But neither farmers nor the government were enthusiastic about their employment. By the end of the 1916 only a few hundred were employed in timber-felling, helping to supply home-grown pit props to the mining industry. A scheme put to the County War Agricultural Committees in January 1917 was far too restrictive: only 75 prisoners per county could work on the land; they were to be guarded by 35 soldiers; they could only work up to three miles away from the central depots in which they were lodged. Also most rural communities were deeply hostile towards the prisoners. So by April 1917 less than a thousand were employed on the land. A few of these worked near Stanway, the Cotswold home of the Earl and Countess of Wemyss. In the spring of 1917 Mary Wemyss took her weekend guests for a picnic in nearby Hayles Wood where 'we were all interested in seeing the German prisoners'.

At the beginning of 1918, the government lifted the restrictions on the use of German prisoners: three could stay on a farm without a guard; agricultural camps were established throughout the country; migratory gangs of prisoners were organised, to be sent out to wherever they were most needed. Their numbers began to increase, from about 5,000 at the beginning of the year to over 30,000 by the end.

Their contribution to helping with the 1918 harvest was considerable, although not all were efficient agricultural labourers. A farmer in Dunmow, Essex, found his group 'slack and unruly . . . if they are set to work at hoeing, they do as much damage as they can'.[53] The Saxons, Poles and Schleswig-Holsteiners were considered the best labourers: the Prussians the most difficult to handle. Perhaps it was a Prussian who went berserk while working in a gang of eight prisoners near Great Leighs who were 'cutting the border of a field so that the reaping machine might get to work. The farm-foreman in charge had occasion to reprimand one of them. The German seized his bill-hook and slashed off the foreman's head.'

The 'ammunition of the land army', according to *Country Life*, was its agricultural machinery. While the tank was making its first momentous appearance on the western front, the tractor was showing just how indispensable it could be on British farms.

To begin with farmers were reluctant to give up their traditional methods: the tractor was a 'new, untried and rather distrusted implement'. But the army took away their labourers and their horses so they had little choice but to adapt: 10,000 tractors were imported from America during 1917 and 1918 and by the end of the war they were 'eagerly sought after by farmers in every county'. A farmer in Kent was so keen to get the maximum use out of his tractor, and at the same time respond to the government's plough-up campaign, that he ploughed by night. Unfortunately Zeppelins were attracted by the headlights on his tractor and dropped a few bombs on his field. They landed in the untilled soil, giving 'an object lesson as to what can be done by ploughing with explosives'.

The rumbles and puffings and grindings of new machinery filled fields and farmyards all over Britain throughout the last year of the war. Such noises would remain a permanent feature of rural life. The labourers and plough-horses were valiantly serving their country in the ravaged countryside of Belgium and France: those who survived would find their places taken by time-saving and labour-saving machines.

The efforts of men, women and machinery resulted in an increase over the 1917 acreage under plough of 1,989,000 acres. Between 1904 and 1913 Britain's ploughed acreage was 12,916,000. In 1918 it reached 15,700,000, just under the target of three million extra acres. *Country Life* applauded the effort:

> it represents the energy and resolution of the British people and particularly of the British farmers, who, when confronted with the menace that the food supplies would be cut off by submarine warfare, ploughed and harrowed and weeded and sowed until they had more ground under the plough than has ever been before in the records of British husbandry.

Sheila Kaye-Smith portrayed Harry Beatup in *Little England* as the exemplary English farmer. He seems himself and his father as soldiers on the home front: when they go out to sow the newly broken pasture land it is their 'Big Push'.

> These fields that he had prepared, that his plough had torn and his harrow broken, were fields of battle like the fields of France. On them he had fought, for the same reason as Tom had fought the Germans, all the treacheries and assaults of nature, her raiding winds, her storming rains, her undermining rottenness in the soil, her blasting of thunder and choking of heat.[54]

However, in the spring of 1918 not all farmers felt like their fictional representative. In an attempt to introduce justice and equality to conscription, the government, in April, withdrew the old exemptions based upon employment. Farming was included and 30,000 men were immediately called up from the agricultural profession. In the autumn of 1917 the Prime Minister had encouraged the farmers to think of themselves as combatants on the home front. 'Every sack of food you raise is worth ammunition, is worth a gun, to use in this great struggle, and we ask you to come into the fighting line with your food.'[55] Now the farming community felt they had been betrayed, their efforts to plough up extra land would be wasted: who would be left skilled enough to harvest the crops?

But the Germans had launched their final great offensive on the western front on 21 March, breaking through the Fifth British Army and pushing through almost to Amiens. In April and May, while farmers on the home front grumbled about bad weather and diseased crops and their unskilled substitute labourers, the British soldiers on the Ypres sector was pushed back twelve miles and the French were heavily defeated at Chemin des Dames. Rowland Prothero put the situation in perspective in a speech to Parliament. He reminded farmers of their own comfortable billets as compared to the hellish conditions endured by the soldiers:

> ... compare their condition with the condition of the men on the farms, working in their own familiar peaceful surroundings, not risking their lives, their limbs, their eyesight, and their health for all time ... We must remember that what we are asking from the men on the land is as nothing compared with what we are asking from the men whom we send to the front.[56]

On 18 July the Allies, with the assistance of 600,000 American troops, launched their own series of offensive movements. As the Germans were themselves pushed back – the British army stormed the Siegfried line on 29 September – the 'largest harvest of modern times' was being gathered on the home front. Until the very last, rain threatened to ruin crops everywhere but the south and south-east. Sir Thomas Middleton described the closing weeks of his 'Big Push':

> Of all the arduous days in this great adventure of 1918, the closing weeks continued the most arduous for the farmers of the north, the

west, and the midlands. It was only by taking advantage of every favourable hour that they and their men, aided by women, soldiers, prisoners-of-war, tractors, self-binding reapers, and all the resources at the disposal of the Food Production Department, succeeded in saving the crop. The in-gathering of the farmers' corn during fitful intervals in the rain and mist of autumn was a finer feat even than the ploughing and sowing of the great extra area in the sunshine of spring . . . Four-fifths, and more, of the largest harvest of modern times was saved in one of the worst seasons possible, and in face of labour difficulties that it may be hoped will never occur again.[57]

In spite of the weather and the pessimism of farmers and the shortage of skilled labour (the number of men permanently employed in agriculture in January 1918 was 28.7 per cent below the figure at the beginning of the war) the harvest was a success. Wheat had increased in production by 59.3 per cent over pre-war levels. Profits for the farmers were considerable. Robert Saunders found himself 'rather out of place' when he attended a collection being made for a local man leaving Searles estate in August 1918.

The farmers present all began to put their names down for 2gs. There is no doubt farming pays better than it has ever done. Mr Fenner is paying for Ena to live in Lewes to attend the Secondary School, for George to go to the Grammar School at Lewes (Season Ticket), & has just bought them both a new Bicycle, 10gs each.

The fate of British agriculture in the aftermath of the war was very different. In the course of the next decade the value of agricultural output dropped by a half. The system of guaranteed prices introduced in 1917 was abolished in 1921; by 1933 the price of wheat had dropped to its lowest level probably since the sixteenth century. With neither subsidy nor protection, decline and depression were inevitable. During the war, however, farmers and their workforce had tasted victory: they had won their government's fight for food.

We reckoned up calories as we counted rifles or shells; every million represented the food required by one of our people, every billion reduced by some 500,000 tons the demands made on our shipping, and this again, in 1918, meant 100,000 additional American troops on the Western Front.[58]

In Foreign Fields

> I have seen men shattered, dying, dead – all the sad
> tragedy of war . . . [but] this murder of old stone and
> lichened thatches, this shattering of little old churches
> and homesteads brings the tragedy home to me more
> acutely. I think to find an English village like this would
> almost break my heart.[1]
>
> Sergeant Leslie Coulson

THE valley of the Somme and the towns of Ypres, Arras and
Albert are all only about 150 miles from London. Throughout
the First World War people living in Surrey, Sussex and Kent
could clearly hear the guns firing in Flanders and Picardy. When just
under one million pounds of high explosives were detonated simul-
taneously under the Messines Ridge on 7 June 1917, the sound was
heard in London and the light flashes could be seen in Kent. In Sussex,
'the continued pulsation, like the sound of a great propeller on a
Mammoth steamer, seemed never to stop night or day'.[2] As a captain
serving in France with the Cambridgeshire Regiment put it when
writing to his parents: 'England is so absurdly near'.[3]

The London papers reached the trenches only a day late; letters and
parcels took between two and four days. With a few days' leave, an
officer could eat breakfast at the front and dine, the same day, at his
London club. Before returning to France he might enjoy an evening
show in the West End and still be back staring across no-man's-land
the following day. Not only tinned food but fresh – butter, cream,

cheese – could be sent, without deteriorating, to soldiers in the front line. Raymond Asquith, waiting to join in the Battle of the Somme, enjoyed receiving 'cold chicken and a really admirable ham', prepared by Mrs Gould, the cook at Mells Manor House. His sister-in-law's cakes were less successful. 'Cicely has sent me several of those brown ones, which are quite good, but I think rather less than they used to be in Pre-War days, I suspect some economy of material.'[4]

The French countryside over which the British armies trained and fought was not only close in numbers of miles to southern England: the landscape itself looked disconcertingly familiar to many of the soldiers. Siegfried Sassoon was billeted at Montagne in Picardy in November and December 1915.

> Took the Company out at 9 to some arable ground close to the village, which has plenty of woods near it, and small orchards adjoining the houses; one can see miles away over the country all round – rolling ploughlands and dark woods; only a few villages visible, with steeples, as in England. It is a little like parts of East Kent.[5]

Kent was his home county and when some pigeons flew up from a haystack the whistle of their wings reminded him of his own garden at Weirleigh.

Lieutenant Bernard Pitt, a schoolteacher before the war, also recognised the Kent countryside in France when he found himself in 'a hilly wooded region ... with copses full of anemones and delicate periwinkles, and the sapling hazels and willows tasselled and downy with catkins and buds'.[6] To make himself feel completely at home he read Wordsworth's poetry on his country rambles – when he wasn't fighting.

John Masefield first went to France in 1915 as a British Red Cross orderly working with wounded French soldiers at Arc en Barrois, Haute Marne, 'an oolite place with many queer Cotswoldy roofs'.[7] He returned to France in 1916 researching for *The Old Front Line* and again, in 1917, to collect material for *The Battle of the Somme*. The low hills around Verdun and the valley of the Meuse were like Salisbury Plain. The landscape of the Somme was very similar to the gentle chalk downs around Lollingdon Farm, his country home in Berkshire. He explained to his wife 'there are hilly bits to the east of the G.W.R. [Great Western Railway] line just before you come to Cholsey Station (from Reading) which give you a very fair idea of it'.[8] A subaltern in the Royal Warwickshire Regiment thought the sluggish River Somme was more like the Thames above Oxford, further west than Cholsey, 'splitting into numerous channels which flow round osier beds and water meadows and market gardens, between low chalk downs'.[9]

Rudyard Kipling visited the French armies in August 1915. He heard from his son John, whose regiment, the Irish Guards, also went out to France in August and were 'nestling among the downs'[10] in a village similar in size to those in their own Sussex Weald. Kipling was entertained to lunch at a château near Compiègne. The heavily wooded park reminded him of Maresfield, an estate near his country home of Bateman's (and close to the Sussex village of Fletching). But meanwhile, back home, Maresfield Park had itself been invaded by the war machine. It was, according to Robert Saunders, 'being covered with immense huts and stables and a contractor has to make 5 miles of road between the rows of huts'.

Another writer, Ivor Gurney, was fighting in the Ypres Salient in August 1917 when he noticed the cottage roofs were tiled red as in Sussex. And the painter Paul Nash found himself in countryside rather like Sussex in May 1917 when he was serving in the Hampshire Regiment, 'great rolling moorland with a patch of green, rose, brown and other coloured fields'. As a soldier he had the dubious privilege of seeing rather more of the beauties of nature than people safe in England. 'We see all the rarer treasures of nature that so many folk miss by lying in bed. Dawn over the hills, the woods mixtures of mauve, muffled in heavy shadows, while the fields waken into reality when the sun first touches them.'[11]

Heavy snow-falls, severe frosts, heat-waves were all likely to affect the two countries with equal ferocity. The cold snap which Katharine Asquith complained of at Mells arrived in Raymond's trenches a couple of days later. And unusually heavy rainfall in Sussex which Robert Saunders reported to his son in Canada in August 1915 turned the trenches into a treacherous quagmire. A sergeant from Scotland, writing to his parish minister, realised with surprise that the sun he was watching set over a ridge near Cambrai was also setting 'over the peaceful hills of Melford'. While he had spent the day looking out for German snipers, he imagined the minister had been indulging in a day's contemplative fishing. 'I picture you with a heavy basket, winding up your rod and reel by the side of some quiet, moorland loch, listening to the plop of some wily trout that had evaded your most cunning lure.'[12]

Even fishing was not an impossibility for some soldiers, not to mention hunting and shooting, bird's-nesting and gardening. *The Field* had been essential reading for the landed gentry since its founding in 1853. *Country Life* was a more recent publication, founded by Edward Hudson in 1897, but it immediately joined *The Field* in the country houses of the older county families. It was also snapped up by country-lovers rich enough, or who wished they were rich enough, to move into the countryside and buy up part of 'Old England'.

Both magazines were popular among the officer class and found their way to the muddiest trenches and shell-holes, bringing something of the countryside with them. One young subaltern wrote to his father: 'I'm devilish glad to get COUNTRY LIFE and sick when it sometimes gets delayed. The only trouble is that it wears out with the rough handling we all give it.' Subscribers at home could send their still-intact used copies 'by simply handing them over the counter of any Post Office. No label, wrapper or address is needed, and no postage need be paid.' Throughout the war the magazines depicted the traditional life of rural England struggling on as best it could. Soldier-readers confessed it 'a comfort to think that there is a country life for us to get back to, at least for some of us.' *Country Life* in particular also revealed the remarkable abilities of the British army to re-create its favourite rural recreations on the battlefields of France, Belgium, even Mesopotamia and the Middle East.

In December 1914 an officer in the Royal Field Artillery sent a sketch to *Country Life* of his ideal Christmas leave. Entitled 'Going home', it shows the huntsman, hounds at his horse's feet, blowing his horn to mark the end of a day's sport. The previous month the magazine reported 'those at the front are hungry for home news, and not least for the story of their Hunts. The first thing a man seems to do if he gets time off is to snatch a day's sport at home.' But some sort of sport was possible across the Channel. Hounds were sent over to France. Feeding them was no problem: there was no 'lack of flesh for the cauldrons'. The hares often outnumbered the hounds and the battle-scarred terrain, 'ghastly take-offs and landings', proved the downfall of many officers from the most prestigious English hunts.

Shooting game was also popular, for sport and to supplement war rations. Geoffrey Dent, an officer in the 4th Dragoon Guards, pursued hares and partridges on horseback, shot at boar, woodcock, duck and rats and had a go at digging out badgers, all in periods 'on rest' before returning to shoot at the enemy, an equally 'good show'. *The Field* pointed out that any gentleman who excelled in field sports was assured of 'success on the battlefield and in the conduct of those operations which lead to victory in war'. *Punch* also picked up the connection between killing for sport and in war. An officer in a dug-out dreams of the glorious twelfth of August:

> the party moved off in file up the slope of the moor, Sir Percy on his pony in front, then the guests with rifles at the trail, next the bearers and orderlies, and in the rear the ammunition-limbers and regimental baggage. A ration-party would follow later . . . At 10.30 I left my smoking weapon and an empty flask, and at 10.35 went over the top. A little later I brought down no fewer than seven of the enemy with one beautifully timed bomb . . . Meanwhile our bearers were collecting the enemy's dead and finishing off his wounded.

Geoffrey Dent's brother, in the Essex Yeomanry, found shooting a very mucky business 'as it always entails lying on your stomach in a bottomless slough & becoming absolutely caked with mud'. Discovering two pheasants in residence behind his billet he wrote home for a four-penny gin trap 'to circumvent them'.[13] Some officers were fortunate enough to find ex-gamekeepers in the ranks, making it possible to achieve something approaching the professionalism of the pre-war mass slaughtering of game. The gamekeepers also proved rather good soldiers:

> on many big estates more than two-thirds of the staff have exchanged the shot-gun and the traps for the service rifle and the bayonet . . . They are of the right stuff . . . constant practice has rendered their eyesight almost preternaturally keen, and they are able to pick out, on distant slopes and ridges, objects so small in size as to be quite invisible to ordinary observers.[14]

The same could be said of their pre-war enemies, the poachers.

Hunting and shooting were banned in France in 1915. The French government had stopped all sport at the beginning of the war: French officers did not share the English yearnings for the chase. The British forces had to agree with the ally's wishes to stop their sporting activities, particularly when it was pointed out that the country's war-sown harvest was threatened. Also, according to an article in *Country Life*, some unarmed men had been shot at 'in a certain wood where pheasants were numerous, and these shots did not come from sporting guns'. Geoffrey Dent thought the ban 'pretty good rot'. He was more worried about hunting being stopped in England: 'I am afraid everyone will think in terms of food after the war, & we shall probably be as utilitarian & beastly as the French peasants'.[15]

Siegfried Sassoon overcame this reduction in sporting opportunities by pretending he was hunting foxes when he was pursuing Germans through the trenches. 'Eddie,' he wrote to Edward Marsh, who was at the time private secretary to Winston Churchill, 'I chased 40 Boshes out of a trench by Mametz Wood, all by myself. Wasn't that a joyous moment for me? They ran like hell, & I chucked bombs & made hunting noises.'[16]

Gordon Harbord, a close friend of Sassoon's, appears as the character Stephen Colwood in *Memoirs of a Foxhunting Man*. He wrote to Sassoon from France of his desperate yearning to hunt. His horse Priest shared his desire. When

> poking about looking for wagon lines . . . there is just a drizzle falling and the mud in the woods splashes up into mud sparks all over my breeches like it does in Plashett I begin to feel desperate restless. The old Priest loves it too, and after a short dart over a couple of rotten fences if I pull up he stands still & stinks like old times and I know he's listening for railway whistles and trying to construe them into 'hollers'.[17]

When Gordon's 21 days' leave early in 1917 coincided with 22 days of frost (i.e. no hunting), his brother Geoffrey commiserated: 'Most 'eart breaking think ever I heard of. Poor old sod. I wonder you didn't go and dive off London Bridge into the frozen Thames.'[18] Gordon was killed on 14 August 1917. Sassoon wrote 'The Wooden Cross' in his memory:

> . . . I half-believe
> That I shall find you home again on leave,
> As I last saw you, riding down the lane,
> And lost in lowering dusk and drizzling rain,
> Contented with the hunt we'd had, and then
> Sad lest we'd never ride a hunt again.

Meanwhile Geoffrey Harbord was doing his best to keep up hunting where the ban didn't apply. He began in Mesopotamia, buying four couples of hounds, for £8 a couple, from an Indian hunt. He described the terrain in true hunting style:

> . . . the Sinn & Sudan hounds hunt over an area of about 20 square miles in Mesopot. The country consists of about 100% desert & is bounded on one side by the river & the rest by the outpost lines. What wire there is is marked (on the map) & is removed at the beginning of the season.[19]

Moving further east he managed to transport his hounds by barge, 'not looking too fit'. The locals thought him mad to chase jackals and one farmer carried on with his irrigation, reducing the hunting ground to a 'snipe marsh'. But nothing could mitigate the misery of hearing of the reduction of hunts at home. Foxes were actually being shot.

> It makes me terrible miserable sitting in this plague spot and thinking that just to prevent German merchants getting British merchants' trade, half the original foxhunters are dead or crippled and the remainder look like having to drag out a miserable . . . existence, perhaps hunting hares or lambs.[20]

His ambition for a career in soldiering was finished. More than anything he missed the 'smell of ammonia at evening stables'.

When hunting was stopped in France, some of the hounds were left behind. The fortunate ones were adopted as pets by the troops, joining abandoned cats, dogs, doves and pigeons to make the trenches seem a little more like home. One company managed to keep a cow in their trench throughout 1915. Her name was Mary. Every night she was tethered behind a small wood at the back of the trenches to graze, always 'under guard, lest a jealous company in the next trench should be overcome by temptation'.[21] Before dawn she was brought back along a communication trench to the protection of her own dug-out. Raymond Asquith's company made a pet of a sparrow-hawk 'when we were up at Zillebeke; its leg and wing had been broken probably by shrapnel. It lives with my company now and feeds on mice and is very tame and handsome.'[22]

Gardening was perhaps the most bizarre way in which some of the trenches became 'little England'. The *Illustrated London News* thought the phenomenon an expression of the 'home-instinct'. Many of the flowers growing in Flanders and Picardy were common in England. Though no gardener, Raymond Asquith practised his recently acquired knowledge of botany and sent his wife a list of plants flourishing on the Somme as well as in Somerset. An ex-sub-editor of *The Garden* was enthusiastic about the spring show in trenches not far from the front line in 1915. The soldiers used red brick and clinker paths to divide up their plots, 'suggestive of an Italian garden design'. Wild cowslips, celandines and cuckoo-pint were transplanted from the fields and ditches near by, 'yet the roar of heavy guns and the roll of rifle fire are incessant'. One private recalled a trench only 47 yards from the enemy with 'walls lined with basketwork and trellis . . . Bottlenecks and junctions had a homely atmosphere with nasturtiums climbing the trellis.' Behind the lines competitive gardening was popular.

A platoon of A company . . . enclosed a tent in a heart; a border of boxwood marks out the pattern of the heart – the plan is that the crimson of many blossoms shall blend to give a suggestion of passion and loyalty and suffering . . . Primroses and daffodils and narcissi are soon blossoming in plenty. Lilies followed, arums and Solomon's-seal, and then forget-me-nots, pansies and violas.[23]

Punch was quick to point out the craziness of trench-gardening, but at the same time suggested it to be part of British grit. Any nation capable of gardening and fighting at the same time had to win.

The front offered scope for lepidopterists, ornithologists and insect-lovers. *The Garden*'s ex-sub-editor found time between shooting at Germans to crawl along the trenches in search of interesting insect life: 'one point that strikes me as curious when trenching at night [in winter] is the number of glow worms giving off that vivid phosphorescent light which I had always associated with summer time in England'. One second-lieutenant had first heard a nightingale as a schoolboy at Winchester and immediately recognised the song in France, 'infinitely sweet and sad . . . as if the countryside were singing gently to itself'.[24] Another officer wrote to *Country Life* on hearing a little owl, *Athene noctua*. He couldn't help remembering the happy hour he had spent the previous year photographing the same species of owl at her nest in a Kentish orchard. However, when he heard the golden oriole he confessed 'for the first time during the nesting season of 1915' that his interest was 'really wakened'. Ignoring the proximity of the Germans, he struggled up a tree in the surviving wood from where the oriole was singing and succeeded in taking a photograph of the bird's nest. 'And yet the wood is shelled by the enemy every day, several dead cows are rotting in the track through it, and many of the trees are smashed by the explosions . . . And every now and then a rifle bullet will crack into the trees above.' The bird enthusiast encountered a new hazard from the end of 1915: carrying a camera anywhere near the front became a court-martial offence.

Another contributor to *Country Life*, writing about the bird life on the Ypres Salient, was more interested in plunder than innocent observation. He wrote home for his drill and blowpipe and set to work collecting clutches of eggs from the nests of the golden oriole, the nightingale, the garden warbler, the great reed warbler, the swallow and the kingfisher. He looked forward to studying his loot when peace was finally declared. Meanwhile 'with all this tragedy going on it was well to have a hobby to take one's mind off the horrors of war and keep one fresh for work'.

An entry like this in *Country Life* was the sort of material the soldier-journalists of *The Wipers Times* delighted to parody. The British ability to make fun of their national characteristics and to find something to laugh about in the most nightmarish situations flourished in the pages of the newspaper which was printed at the front in erratic bursts throughout the war and with a new name as the company advanced or retreated. Its very appearance made life in France and Belgium more familiar and homely.

The Times still publishes an account of the first cuckoo heard each spring. A fierce correspondence appeared in *The Wipers Times* on the subject of just who heard the cuckoo first; and was it a cuckoo anyway?

Sir, Whilst on my nocturnal rambles along the Menin Road last night, I am prepared to swear that I heard the cuckoo. Surely I am the first to hear it this season.

Sir, In perusing your excellent journal I was particularly impressed with the interest your two correspondents take in 'bird life in the trenches'. Whether the cuckoo who sang, or the cuckoo who heard the aforesaid cuckoo sing are either in existence, is to my mind immaterial. I can emphatically state that I heard the nightingale.

The BEF Times produced a more gruesome parody of articles on gardening which were continuing to appear at home. The thick balls of barbed wire which were so lethal in no-man's-land were known as gooseberries.

'In My Garden'

Where the soil is damp and heavy, an early planting of gooseberries is attended with some risk. This hardy perennial, being a strong grower, will quickly cover an unsightly patch of waste ground. The best crops of this luxurious fruit have been obtained when some support was given by stakes.

One of the greatest ironies of the First World War was the amount of fine writing, painting and music to be created out of so much death and destruction; in many cases to be produced in the midst of the slaughter. Ralph Vaughan Williams worked on his Pastoral Symphony while serving as a private in the trenches in 1916; Ivor Gurney, a private in the 5th Gloucesters, composed songs and poems. Issac Rosenberg, Siegfried Sassoon and Robert Graves composed poems in their dug-outs, often by candle-light, and sent them, scribbled on scraps of paper, to friends in England. Sassoon found 'everything out here . . . asking to be painted or etched: it is wildly picturesque.'[25] Frank Cook, a Royal Engineer, carried his sketch book 'tucked inside my tunic like a breast-plate . . . Filthy and lousy as I was, I managed to keep my sketches intact with all my battle kit.'[26] Paul Nash saw them all engaged in a sort of harvest. 'We are all sent out here to glean – painter, poet, musician, sculptor . . . no one will return empty-handed but bringing his sheaves with him.'[27]

Sassoon's life before the war (he was 28 when he enlisted) had been an extended adolescence, free of responsibilities. With a private income, he lived most of the time at his mother's home in the Weald of Kent, hunting, playing golf and cricket and writing occasional verse. He visited London to order new hunting clothes, to attend the opera and to compare his pastoral lyrics with those of his fellow Georgian poets who included Rupert Brooke, W. H. Davies, John Masefield, John Drinkwater, Wilfrid Gibson and Lascelles Abercrombie. All shared a passion for the English countryside, each identifying with a particular village, valley, range of hills or county. The Old Vicarage at Grantchester was the centre of Brooke's ideal world; the Cotswolds to the south of Birmingham were where Drinkwater encountered 'rosy men, cloth-gaitered, who can tell / The many-minded changes of the year'.[28] Edmund Blunden, who joined the Georgian fraternity early in the war, knew the Kent countryside intimately; Edward Thomas, Georgian essayist and reviewer until the war turned him into a poet, rambled over the southern half of England and Wales.

The Georgians found the perfect harmonious relationship between man and nature in the ordered, productive, rhythmic life of rural England. They chose, or were privileged, to live in cottages and country houses which were part of the landscape, 'homely and friendly-seeming'.[29] They described the working life of the farmer and the recreations pursued by country-dwellers: hunting, fishing, village cricket, gardening. Their ideal green world was unchanging, domestic, intimate, bound by clipped hedges and neat stone-walls, offering views of hills where 'grazing flocks drift on continually'. It was the sort of England Rupert Brooke had in mind when he wrote 'The Soldier', the most famous of English war poems.

If I should die, think only this of me:
That there's some corner of a foreign field
That is for ever England.

The sonnet offered the comforting image of the dead English soldier enriching the soil of the battlefield on which he has fallen, suffusing it with his Englishness. The mood of the poem is gentle and relaxed; death is peaceful. The England which will never die, even in foreign fields, is located in a green and tranquil landscape: a landscape some of the Georgian poets thought worth dying for.

The gorse upon the twilit down,
The English loam so sunset brown,
The bowed pines and the sheep bells' clamour,
The wet, lit lanes and the yellow-hammer,
The orchard and the chaffinch song
Only to the Brave belong.[30]

The French landscape often reminded Sassoon of parts of Sussex and Kent. But more than this, he was sustained mentally and physically by recollections of the England he loved, the 'casual tappings and twinklings of the countryside ... summer evenings after cricket-matches, and sunset above the tall trees, and village-streets in the dusk', hunting, the novels of Thomas Hardy.

I thought of the huntsman walking out in his long white coat with the hounds; of Parson Colwood pulling up weeds in his garden till tea-time; or Captain Huxtable helping his men get in the last load of hay while a shower of rain moved along the blurred Weald below his meadow. It was all for that, I supposed, that I was in the front-line with soaked feet, trench mouth, and feeling short of sleep.[31]

But, in order to preserve and somehow possess the beauties of the English countryside, the 'Brave' were busily engaged in turning France, a 'darling land ... [blessed with] a mellow merciful spirit founded on centuries of beautiful living'[32] into a wasteland of 'mud and swamp and brimming shell-holes'. And over all hung 'the most supernaturally shocking scent of death and corruption that ever breathed o'er Eden'.[33] Country-loving writers and artists such as Sassoon and Blunden were actively engaged in destroying the very way of life which inspired their creativity and which they were willing to sacrifice their lives for. No wonder the experience haunted their writing until their deaths some fifty years after the war.

Blunden clearly realised the horrible irony of the situation. He was perhaps the only poet to emphasise this aspect. He called himself 'a harmless young shepherd in a soldier's coat'.[34] In 'Rural Economy', the war becomes the farmer, planting seeds of iron, carefully feeding them with flesh and blood until the acres bristle a thousandfold.

> Why, even the wood as well as field
> This thoughtful farmer knew
> Could be reduced to plough and tilled,
> And if he planned, he'd do;
> The field and wood, all bone-fed loam
> Shot up a roaring harvest home.

The physical nearness of home, the familiarity of the landscape, the sights, sounds and smells reminiscent of a countryside at peace, were themselves horribly deceptive. The Belgian and French countryside over which the armies fought (a more or less continuous line of entrenchments some 450 miles long) was being reduced to a stinking quagmire of mud and blood; layer upon layer of pulverised bodies. Even today ploughs are still churning up bones and skulls, bits of weaponry and shell cases. Paul Nash called it a 'monstrous land . . . so distorted from its own gentle forms, nothing seems to bear the imprint of God's hand, the whole might be a terrific creation of some malign fiend working a crooked will on the innocent countryside'.[35]

Any momentary comfort offered by the rural surroundings, either behind the lines or at the front, was undermined, mocked, distorted and finally destroyed by the war. A soldier staring across the deceptively green strip of no-man's-land saw what he at first supposed to be a flock of grazing sheep: 'There were hundreds of khaki bodies lying where they had fallen in the September attack on the Hohenzollern and now beyond the reach of friend and foe alike.'[36] Fifty kilometres away from the front, Sassoon imagined for a moment he had found Arcady. 'As I came out of the wood, the ploughmen were driving a big flock of sheep to the farm, silver grey on the dark stubble.' But he could still hear the guns booming: 'Armageddon is still going on'. When he took an evening stroll through the dusky country lanes he heard nightingales singing. Looking up, however, 'the sky winked and glowed with swift flashes of the distant bombardment at Amiens and Albert, and there was a faint rumbling, low and menacing'.[37]

The war lasted four years and three months. The armies caught up in the deadlock of the western front were not absolutely immobile. New trench systems were dug, fresh stretches of countryside were overrun as attempts were made to break through the lines. This meant that soldiers who survived long enough might be withdrawn from one area of devastation, only to take part in the violation of an as yet unspoilt part of rural France.

Before the war the valleys of the Somme and the Ancre close to Thiepval and Grandant were popular holiday resorts. Parisians enjoyed swimming and fishing in the rivers, riding over the gently rolling hills and perhaps indulging in English-style teas at a famous pâtisserie in Thiepval. When one private arrived in Picardy in the spring of 1916, to prepare for the Battle of the Somme, he found its verdant tranquillity overwhelming after the horrors of the Ypres Salient. 'We thought it was lovely country when we got there . . . there were little cottages with gardens and spring flowers coming out. There was a lovely stream near by and the lads used to bathe in it . . . It was so peaceful you just couldn't believe it.'[38]

It is well known exactly what the Battle of the Somme did to the 'lovely country' and to the innocent soldiers of Kitchener's Army, the 'eager, devoted, physical and spiritual élite of the British nation'. On the first day of the battle, 1 July 1916, nearly 20,000 British soldiers were killed; total casualties, both dead and wounded were 50,000. The battle lasted 141 days and by the end the British casualties totalled 415,000. The *British Official History* confessed it was unable to describe the conditions on the Somme by the end of 1916: 'our vocabulary is not adapted to describe such an existence, because it is outside experience for which words are normally required'.

A private in the 9th Royal Sussex Regiment made an attempt. 'The trees were criss-cross, with shattered, splintered limbs, and the stench was awful, and we could hardly put a pick in the ground or shovel but what we would strike a buried body and clothing.'[39] 'The stark and shattered scene: flayed tree stumps, wastes of mud and great pools of water,' reminded an officer in the 6th Battalion Connaught Rangers of 'an ocean floor suddenly exposed and tensed by a crashing re-engulfment'.[40] Another officer wrote home from a different sector, 'perhaps you imagine it as a place of broken trees and ruined houses – as a fact there is nothing – Nothing'.[41]

Leslie Coulson, poet of the English countryside and sergeant in the London Battalion of the Royal Fusiliers, took part in the Somme advance on 1 July. He wrote home:

I have seen men shattered, dying, dead – all the sad tragedy of war ... [but] this murder of old stone and lichened thatches, this shattering of little old churches and homesteads brings the tragedy home to me more acutely. I think to find an English village like this would almost break my heart.[42]

Coulson was killed on 7 October near Lesboeufs, during one of the last advances of the Somme battle. Major Corbett Smith said Coulson died 'that the England he loved might live'. But a poem found on the dead sergeant suggests his pre-war pastoral innocence had been cruelly shattered.

> Who made the Law that men should die in meadows?
> Who spake the word that blood should splash in lanes?
> Who gave it forth that gardens should be bone-yards?
> Who spread the hills with flesh, and blood, and brains?
> Who made the Law?[43]

The war eventually undermined memories of the countryside at home and Brooke's image of the soldier dying with his vision of a green Arcadia still intact. A sergeant-major who had once enjoyed the singing of larks had heard them every morning at stand-to in the trenches: 'those wretched larks made me more sad than almost anything else out here ... Their songs are so closely associated in my mind with peaceful summer days in gardens or pleasant landscapes in Blighty.'[44]

Ivor Gurney clung to the hills and valleys of Gloucestershire, the 'friends' he had left behind. Hearing a cuckoo calling from a nearby shattered wood while cleaning mess tins outside his dug-out, 'what could I think of but Framilode, Minsterworth, Cranham, and the old haunts of home'. But his moment of escape was soured by the very different response of a Welsh soldier standing next to him.

> 'Listen to that damned bird', he said. 'All through that bombardment in the pauses I could hear the infernal silly "Cuckoo, cuckoo" sounding while Owen was lying in my arms covered with blood. How shall I ever listen again.' He broke off, and I became aware of shame at the unholy joy that filled my artist's mind.[45]

When Gurney did have the chance to return to the supposed peace and security of the English countryside he discovered the tentacles of war had the power to stretch far beyond the western front. He was wounded on Good Friday 1917 during the Battle of Arras. From his hospital bed behind the front line he wrote of his dream of life in England after the war.

> O for a garden to dig in, and music and books in a house of one's own, set in a little valley from whose ridges one may see Malverns and the Welsh Hills, the plain of Severn and the Severn Sea; to know oneself free there from the drill-sergeant and the pack . . . One could grow whole and happy there, the mind would lose its sickness and grow strong.[46]

Gurney returned to England at the end of the year, gassed and shell-shocked. But his mind did not grow strong. In March 1918 he began to suffer from hallucinations – he was talking to Beethoven – he threatened suicide and begged to be put in an asylum. There followed four years of mental illness until in September 1922 he was committed to a private asylum for the insane in Gloucester. In December he was moved to a mental hospital at Dartford, Kent, where he remained until his death in 1937. He never saw Gloucestershire again.

Henry Williamson was only seventeen when he enlisted at the outbreak of war; he was in France in time to witness the extraordinary truce with the Germans on Christmas Day 1914. He began to write his tetralogy *The Flax of Dream* in 1918; his bestseller *Tarka the Otter* was published in 1928. Like Gurney, Williamson was unable to forget his experiences in France, particularly on the Somme. 'He was not killed on that battlefield, but he was certainly maimed, crippled and wounded on it.'[47] The war did not lead to his incarceration in a mental asylum, however it affected the way he looked at the countryside. Nature was always to be 'red in tooth and claw'. The violence he had seen in France spilled over into the natural world which featured in his novels and short stories. Always pursuit, pain and death, 'by day and by night great creatures made relentless war on the little mice and voles',[48] and men made war on all living things and their natural environment. Williamson's view of the countryside was overwhelmingly desolate and depressing: the extreme position fostered on the fields of war-torn France.

Visiting the Somme Valley after the fighting had moved on, John Masefield described to his wife what the British army had done to a once-flourishing French farm. He even drew her a sketch:

> we blew the farm & the bricks & the pond & most of the dungyard & all the trees & all the fields to dust & rags & holes, till this is all that can be seen ... corpses, rats, old tins, old weapons, rifles, bombs, legs, boots, skulls, cartridges, bits of wood & tin & iron & stone, parts of rotting bodies & festering heads lie scattered about.[49]

Over half the population of France lived in the countryside at the beginning of the war. This compares with only about a fifth of the population of England and Wales living in rural areas. Over five million of the French were engaged in agriculture: about a million worked on the land in England and Wales. Like the British, however, the French assumed the war would be over in a matter of months and there were no special preparations for agriculture in the event of a lengthy war. Unlike Britain, France had conscription. Even though the harvest was imminent, four million men were immediately called up from off the land – they were stronger and healthier than the urban population. Countrymen who were not fit enough to fight still had to leave the land to work in hospitals and carry out maintenance on the roads and railways.

Women saved the French population from going hungry during the First World War. Many women still worked on the land. Those who had left for better wages and working conditions in the towns were urged to return, first of all to help with the harvest, by a special government plea made on 6 August. Eventually over three million women were employed in agriculture: by the end of the war medals were being awarded to the most efficient women labourers.

This use of women in the fields was markedly different to the situation in Britain, where farmers were reluctant to employ land girls even to feed the chickens. There was 'nothing more shocking . . . than to see women drabbling about in the fields'. Even in 1918, farmers in Hampshire were reported to be willing to employ 'anything that comes along, boys, old men, cripples, mentally deficient'[50] rather than women.

British journals devoted to farming and country life tried to change attitudes with photographs of French and Belgian women performing the most masculine of farming chores. *Country Life*, in September 1915, begged its landowning (male) readers to emulate their allies 'where every man of military age is absent from the fields and the land is cropped right up to the firing line'. An article in the *Essex Times* in March 1916 reminded its female readers that French women were performing every task on the farm, even under shell-fire.

It must not be laid to the door of Englishwomen that because the men have left to fight for them and their children, fewer cows are kept, fewer chickens are reared, fewer potatoes grown and less land cultivated, so that in consequence food becomes ever dearer and dearer.[51]

British soldiers remarked on the bravery and strength of the women. Frank Cook noticed an old woman 'keeping guard over her few grazing cows in the pouring rain and shrapnel bursting overhead while she stood knitting'.[52] A lieutenant in the Royal Engineers commented on their ploughing 'up to a marvellously short distance from the lines . . . only they don't wear breeches and have their photographs in the paper' – a reference[53] to the much publicised but severely limited work of land girls in Blighty.

British soldiers also found themselves helping on French farms and lending horses; so did Belgian refugees, German prisoners of war and imported Spanish labour. The German prisoners were supplied in bodies of thirteen guarded by one sergeant, one corporal and thirteen French soldiers. The farmer had to provide board and lodging including sufficient soap and water for baths; the water in his well was tested for microbes and if dirty he had to pay for its cleaning; sleeping accommodation had to be a foot off the ground with no sign of damp. Not surprisingly the prisoners found themselves considerably better off than the soldiers fighting for France in the trenches.

Occasionally French farmer-soldiers were given leave to help with specific tasks on the fields they were defending. Some were withdrawn from the trenches around Verdun to help with the harvest in the autumn of 1916. The *Illustrated London News* described such a 'harvest of death', publishing photographs of farm workers struggling on with their tasks under shell-fire or alongside soldiers digging trenches. Edward Thomas, staring across no-man's-land from trenches near Arras in March 1917 saw one French farmer ploughing 'right up to crest in view of Hun at Beaurains'.[54]

As soon as the enemy retired from a stretch of countryside, the farmers' families (those exempt from conscription) could return to re-cultivate their land. Old men filled in the shell-holes, boys removed and rolled up the barbed wire entanglements and women began to plough. On the Ypres Salient in June 1915 Geoffrey Dent found the country 'almost painfully fertile, every inch cultivated & all the crops perfect & absolutely clean . . . a lot of flax & sugar beet'.[55] The sub-editor of *The Garden* was also impressed. 'In spite of the shortage of labour . . . their land [is] in remarkably good condition.' His own digging activities made him fully aware of the soil conditions: 'fertile and of great depth, although waterlogged in places owing to the heavy rains. These are points brought home to us very forcibly in our trenching operations'. Rudyard Kipling passed through the village of Gerbervilliers in Alsace in August 1915:

It was the centre of a fight and an occupation and another fight and – it is not . . . ground to powder . . . Again – I am lost for any words. But the undefeated French were coming back and making some sort of life . . . In what had been a farmyard I saw an old man and a great slab-sided deep-chested beast of a girl hauling and tugging at a cart which was to be filled with manure – and the fields about the town were in good shape. The shell-holes still stayed in the pastures – lots of 'em – but in the fields they had been ploughed out. Only the plough avoided the many graves.[56]

Arnold Bennett reported back to *Country Life* the same month from only five miles from the German trenches: 'the whole of the earth seemed to be cultivated and to be yielding bounteously'.

Country Life came up with a scientific reason for such fertility in the war zone: 'when the tide of battle has surged forward, it has been noticed by many correspondents that the earth, as though in haste to conceal the desolating effects, has produced with strange and prodigal abundance'. The explanation:

> chemical fertilisers and munitions come largely from the same source . . . the explosives contain large quantities of nitric acid or nitrates and potash. The unburnt part of these explosives accounts for the extraordinary plant growth . . . By a grim irony, then, the fertilisers which were abstracted from German agriculture to be used in killing the French have had the effect of fertilising the fair fields of France.

Although the fields in the war zone were richly fertilised and women tried valiantly to maintain levels of production, French and Belgian agriculture suffered drastically over the four years of war. Frank Cook gives a clearer picture of typical farmers he encountered in January 1916, 'poor farmers' who were 'stirred to make a little money by providing us with eggs to supplement our rations and even the extra meal in their farmhouses . . . these peasant families were sad and uncommunicative and no wonder. Their own men were away in the French army and only the womenfolk, children and grandparents were left to help out with the farm work.'[57]

By the beginning of 1915 it was estimated that losses in the rural areas of Belgium amounted to £56 million. French losses were estimated to be almost as great. Before the war France was almost totally self-sufficient in corn. By 1917 the labourers who had grown the corn formed 60% of the French army. The same year, the cereal crop gathered was half the amount harvested in 1913. The following year the potato crop had fallen to half and the sugar beet crop to less than a quarter of the 1913 figure.

The Royal Agricultural Society of England was the first body to try to help the allied farmers. A visit from the Société des Agriculteurs de France led to the establishment of the Agricultural Relief of Allies Fund in February 1915. The Earl of Northbrook was chairman and Charles Adeane of Babraham secretary. The Royal Agricultural Society immediately sent out ten reaping machines to help on farms in the Marne and its President, the Duke of Portland, made a direct appeal to British farmers:

> imagine we saw our buildings and crops going up in flames, our servants, and perhaps our families maltreated or killed, and our cattle butchered or driven away by the invader.[58]

But for the defence of their own homeland put up by the Belgians and the French 'our village homes in England might now be as desolate as theirs, and our countryside be as marked as theirs with the graves of its brave defenders'.

In July 1914 Lord Northbrook and Charles Adeane visited some of the worst affected areas of France and Belgium to witness the destruction for themselves and to discover what sort of aid was required. Everywhere Adeane went he saw 'enough to make angels weep'. What if British farmers had been forced to provide the battlefields, 'to suffer all the horrors of invasion and war'?

> Death and destruction and fresh life are in close proximity here. The soldiers' red képis hang on wooden crosses in the fields where they fell, and show like red poppies above the corn . . . At Sommeil . . . the little church was still standing . . . The church was filled with soldiers, some sitting, some kneeling, some standing, all devout. In

front of them a soldier priest was chanting a patriotic hymn, every other verse being sung by the soldiers. The spirit of self-sacrifice was stamped on all their faces. It was magnificent and it was war.

Adeane's report appealed specifically for Southdown rams and Large White boars to be sent to Marne and Meuse. The King responded by sending five shearling rams from his Sandringham flock and by December 1915, live stock, machinery and seeds sent to Champagne and Lorraine were having beneficial effects. Marne and Meuse received similar assistance including 61 rams, 11 boars, 2 goats, 1,800 head of poultry, 20 binders, 40 harrows and 50 ploughs. By the end of the war the fund had distributed £265,000 worth of stock, implements and seeds.

As well as helping the French and Belgian farmers in kind, the fund was of tremendous value in promoting British prestige on the Continent. It showed how real the sympathy of British farmers was towards their allies. Adeane was the driving force behind the fund and immediately the war ended he once again travelled to France to organise the distribution of necessary stock and implements.

But the rape of a once-lovely land was not averted. Edmund Blunden summed up what was done to the French countryside in 'Report on Experience':

> I have seen a green country, useful to the race,
> Knocked silly with guns and mines, its villages vanished,
> Even the last rat and last kestrel banished –
>   God bless us all, this was peculiar grace.

Rupert Brooke's sonnet had promised a peaceful, clean, noble death in foreign fields: the sort of death the war cemeteries along the western front now commemorate with their regular lines of uniform gravestones, immaculately cut lawns, carefully selected shrubs, clipped yews and enclosing walls. His own death could not have come closer to his vision. Charles Lister, who was there at the end, called it a 'perfect death'. Watched over by his closest friends and brother officers, he was carried up the stony slopes of Skyros, the island of Achilles, 'the moon thinly veiled, a man carrying a plain wooden cross, and a lantern leading the way; some other lanterns glimmering, the scent of wild thyme, a dim group of French and English officers, the three volleys: the Last Post.'[59] Now a bronze statue of an idealised naked Brooke looks down over the grave in the olive grove.

Brooke, however, did not die in battle. His optimistic vision was as deceptive as the war cemeteries, whose ordered appearance hides a confusion of graves below the surface, unidentified bits of men. For most soldiers death was neither quick, nor clean, nor peaceful – even though an editorial in *Country Life* claimed the 'red rain of battle' could not be responsible for fertilising the war zone because 'the most common and typical appearance is that of a death which might have been natural save for the small puncture, sometimes accompanied by a slight bleeding and sometimes not, which tells where the fatal bullet has entered'. Paul Nash caught the atmosphere more successfully on returning to record the effects of the war on the French countryside: the landscape was 'one huge grave'.[60] And Robert Saunders, writing to his son in Canada in January 1917 explained 'we have 150,000 graves registered in France, of our fallen who have been buried, but how many more buried in trenches & shell holes, or blown to pieces, no one knows'.

Edward Thomas was able to imagine the probable anonymity of death before he saw any action in France. He wrote 'A Private' in January 1915, six months before he enlisted and two years before he was sent to the front near Arras.

> This ploughman dead in battle slept out of doors
> Many a frozen night, and merrily
> Answered staid drinkers, good bedmen, and all bores:
> 'At Mrs Greenland's Hawthorn Bush', said he,
> 'I slept.' None knew which bush. Above the town,
> Beyond 'The Drover', a hundred spot the down
> In Wiltshire. And where now at last he sleeps
> More sound in France – that, too, he secret keeps.

Thomas's own death was surprisingly clean. He was lighting a clay pipe by his dug-out as the Germans retreated when a last shell exploded close by and stopped his heart: 'There was no wound and his beloved body was not injured . . . He just died standing there in the early morning after the battle.'[61] The pressure of the blast merely creased the contents of his pockets: letters, a notebook and a copy of Shakespeare's Sonnets. Captain Lushington described his funeral to his widow Helen:

> We buried him in a little military cemetery a few hundred yards from the battery . . . As we stood by his grave the sun came out and the guns round seemed to stop firing for a short time. This typified to me what stood out most in your husband's character – the spirit of quiet, sunny, unassuming cheerfulness.[62]

Agny Cemetery, though close to a busy road and approached through allotments, remains a secluded, peaceful spot. A red rose grows out of Thomas's grave.

But Thomas's death was unusual. Isaac Rosenberg did not attempt to give names to the remains of humans left after battle.

> Burnt black by strange decay
> Their sinister faces lie,
> The lid over each eye,
> The grass and coloured clay
> More motion have than they,
> Joined to the great sunk silence.

Rosenberg was killed on All Fools' Day, 1918, somewhere near Fampoux. His body remained unburied for several days as the British and German troops fought over the ground. He was eventually given a temporary grave, together with several other British soldiers, just before the sector was overrun by Germans. The Imperial War Graves Commission believed that they had located this grave in 1926. All the remains were reinterred near by in Balleul Road East Cemetery. A headstone was erected to Rosenberg inscribed 'Artist and Poet'. There is no certainty, however, that his remains rest beneath it. They may be under an adjacent stone; they may not even be in the cemetery.[63]

Rudyard Kipling was informed in October 1915 that his only son John was reported missing. Missing almost certainly meant dead and the *Morning Post* was quick to identify the young soldier with the native land he had died for: 'the boy for whom Puck told immortal tales of the beloved land, for which this supreme sacrifice has now been made'.[64] Caroline Kipling continued to hope her son was alive for the next two years. But John's body was never found. The only eye-witness account – from the fellow Guardsman who had last seen John crying out in agony from a wound in the mouth – was not passed on to his parents.

Raymond Asquith was killed in September 1916 in one of the last advances of the Battle of the Somme. He had sent home descriptions of Maple Copse and Sanctuary Wood – such deceptively pastoral names – which he had entered after the fighting had moved on. Trees and the men who had fought beneath them were reduced to the same putrid hell:

> nothing remained but black stumps of really the most obscene heights and thickness, craters swimming in blood and dirt, rotting and smelling bodies and rats like shadows, fattened for the market moving cunningly and liquorishly among them, limbs and bowels nestling in the hedges.[65]

Seventeen out of the twenty-two officers in his battalion who were in the action in which he fell were also killed or wounded. His brother-in-law Edward Horner was killed in November the following year, not very many miles away at Cambrai. Edward's mother, Frances, had lost her only surviving son as well as a son-in-law. She wrote to her daughter Katharine, Raymond's widow: 'all that is left of our beloveds the vision of a grave in France'.[66] She was fortunate in having graves to visit.

Aftermath:
the countryside at peace

This blessed plot, this earth, this realm, this England.

Shakespeare, *Richard II*
from *Inscriptions Suggested for War Memorials*, 1919

B Y May 1917 there were over 150,000 graves of British soldiers in Belgium and France marked by the Imperial War Graves Commission. The work was begun by Fabian Ware, who took a British Red Cross unit out to France in September 1914. He came to be known as Lord Wargraves: through his initiative, energy and diplomacy, the families of the dead – the Horners and the Asquiths, the Wemysses, the Desboroughs, Helen Thomas among them – would have graves to visit, immaculately laid out and tended in perpetuity.

Locating the graves, tracing the missing, responding to enquiries from relatives on the home front with photographs and information, began early in the war. And when the armies on the western front dug themselves in for the duration, the work became extremely dangerous as well as ghoulish. Newly marked graves and the bodies of the unburied dead could be obliterated for ever under a heavy bombardment. As more and more soldiers died fighting for the same tiny piece of countryside, the problem of where to bury them became increasingly serious. The Canadian Corps who attacked Vimy Ridge in 1917 made sure of their resting places by digging their own graves before the battle. Fabian Ware's registration team helped with the preparations: within twenty-four hours all the graves were occupied, marked and recorded. The more general shortage of land was resolved by Ware's success in negotiating grants of land from the French and Belgian governments, and by the end of the war from Egypt and Greece, to be kept in perpetuity for British cemeteries. The cemeteries were literally designed as little bits of Britain set in foreign fields.

During the war temporary wooden crosses were erected but though modest they made a considerable impact on visitors. William Orpen went out to France as a war artist in 1917 to paint the battlefields. It was summer, over six months after the carnage of the Somme:

> no words could express the beauty of it. The dreary, dismal mud was baked white and pure – dazzling white. White daisies, red poppies and a blue flower, great masses of them, stretched for miles and miles. The sky a pure dark blue, and the whole air, up to a height of about forty feet, thick with white butterflies: your clothes were covered with butterflies. It was like an enchanted land; but in the place of fairies there were thousands of little white crosses, marked 'Unknown British Soldier', for the most part.[1]

Edwin Lutyens, before the war the pre-eminent country house architect, was in France at the same time. He had been approached by Fabian Ware, along with the architect Herbert Baker and Charles Aitken, Director of the National Gallery of British Art at Millbank (later the Tate), to consider the design of the permanent cemeteries and graves to be built after the war was over. Like Orpen, Lutyens was deeply moved by the sight of the battlefields, 'the obliteration of human endeavour, achievement', and the graves: 'Ribbons of little crosses each touching each across a cemetery – set in a wilderness of annuals – and where one sort of flower has grown the effect is charming, easy, and oh so pathetic.'[2] The graves now are scarcely less impressive.

Many of the cemeteries had already been planted with shrubs and flowers. Arthur Hill, the Assistant Director of Kew Gardens, visited 37 cemeteries in 1916 to decide exactly what plants would thrive in the soil. He commented 'the sowing of annuals is of considerable value; they help to brighten places often very barren and desolate; they cheer our men who are constant visitors to our cemeteries and who frequently pass these cemeteries when on the march'.[3] Instead of labouring on English farms, several women chose to go out to the western front as

Yvo Charteris's grave, Sailly le Bourse. Yvo was the youngest son of Hugo and Mary Wemyss. He was killed 17 October 1915. His sister Cynthia Asquith wrote in her diary 'How can one believe it, that it should be the *object* to kill Yvo . . . The sheer pity and horror of it.'

Edward Thomas's grave, Agny Cemetery near Arras. 'As we stood by his grave the sun came out and the guns seemed to stop firing for a short time' (Captain Lushington to Helen Thomas).

Raymond Asquith's grave. Raymond was killed in September 1916 in one of the last advances of the Battle of the Somme.

Firing line in front of Ypres, 1915. Sketch by Frank Cook.

The trenches today, preserved at Beaumont Hamel.

The Somme today, view of Lutyens' Memorial to the missing of the Somme at Thiepval. 'We used to say it could never be reclaimed: that in fifty years it would be the same dreadful morass' (Henry Williamson).

Mary Wemyss at Longniddry,
September 1916, laying the
foundation stone of the first
settlement of the Scottish
Veterans' Garden City
Association.

(*Far left*) Mary
Weymss as a young
girl: 'Mary Wyndham'
by Val Prinsep c.1870.

(*Left*) Mary Wemyss as
a young woman: 'Mary
Lady Elcho' by
Edward Poynter,
c.1886.

An A1 Empire
of A1 MEN

(*Above*) Wemyss Terrace, Longniddry, part of the first settlement of the Scottish Veterans' Garden City Association.

(*Left*) The frontispiece to the Village Centres Council pamphlet.

Stanway House c.1923. Queen Mary, J.M. Barrie, Mary Wemyss, Mary Strickland, Charles Whibley, Simon and Michael Asquith outside the front door.

Stanway grounds July 1929. The 'Ancient Britons scene' in the 'Coming of an', a historical pageant and carnival of seven 'magnificent' episodes held in the grounds of Stanway.

David Charteris at Stanway
August 1912. The eldest son of
Ego and Letty, to become the
12th Earl of Wemyss, and owner
of Gosford and Stanway.

Julian Asquith, 1918. The only
son of Raymond and Katharine
Asquith, to become the 2nd Earl
of Oxford and Asquith and owner
of Mells Manor House.

Aberlady War Memorial. Dedicated by Mary Wemyss on All Saints Day 1919.

Mells village War Memorial. St George, copied from a statue in the chapel of Henry VII in Westminster Abbey.

Edward Horner. Statue by Alfred Munnings for the Horner Memorial, Mells Church St Andrew. 'It was to cost £1000 base and statue and I was so afraid that if I didn't like it I should not know where to put it' (Frances Horner).

Preliminary design for the Horner memorial by Sir Edwin Lutyens.

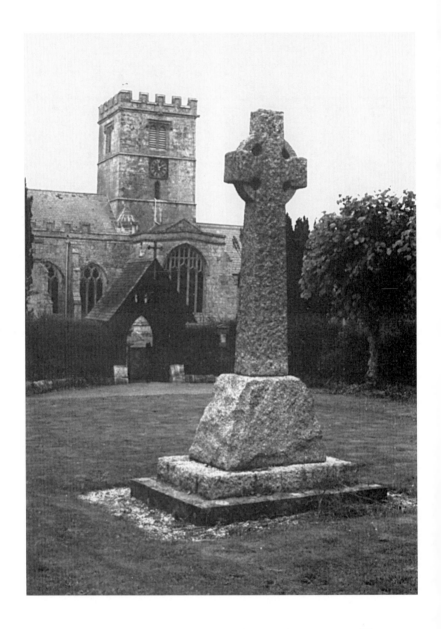

Broad Chalk War Memorial. 'Eighteen out of ninety of our young men did not come back; and now we have their names as nearly imperishable as may be, and much more so than the poor faithful dust strewn in France, or the gentle memories which will last no longer than ourselves' (Maurice Hewlett).

gardeners for the Imperial War Graves Commission. The *Illustrated London News* published a photograph of twenty who were trained at Kew and went out to France in August 1917: the caption to the photograph was predictable: 'some corner of a foreign field that is for ever England'. Rudyard Kipling used the image of the cemetery gardener in his story 'The Gardener'. The heroine, an unmarried mother, goes to France to look for the grave of the son whom she raised as her nephew. The gardener who points out the way to her son's grave is, inevitably, a Christ figure.

The intention of the Imperial War Graves Commission was to use plants in each cemetery native to the countries of the dead soldiers' origins. By 1915 a scheme had been set up to plant maple seeds round Canadian graves in France, and in Gallipoli wattle, an Australian symbol, was planted. When the work on the permanent cemeteries began, daffodils, snowdrops and crocuses were planted for the English; iris, marigolds and cypresses 'sacred and appropriate'[4] for Indian cemeteries; Canadian maples, Tasmanian eucalyptus. West Indian, African and Malayan soldiers were less privileged; the northern climate was too harsh for bougainvillaea.

Ware wanted the design of the cemeteries and of the individual headstones to reflect the non-denominational, democratic spirit engendered in the trenches, with 'no distinction . . . between officer and men lying in the same cemeteries'.[5] If families and friends wished to erect special memorials they should do so in Britain, 'in the homes, villages, etc. of those who had fallen and not in the military cemeteries abroad'.[6] *The Times* supported his position in January 1918:

> in death, all, from General to Private, of whatever race or creed, should receive equal honour under a memorial which should be the common symbol of their comradeship and of the cause for which they died.

The architects, however, could not agree, either on the design of the general monument to be placed in each cemetery, or the design of the headstones. As Baker put it, Lutyens 'would be propelled towards abstract monumental design and I would place more importance on sentiment'.[7] In the end, the Imperial War Graves Commission accepted two general monuments, Lutyens's 'Stone of Remembrance', inscribed with words from Ecclesiasticus chosen by Kipling: 'Their name liveth for evermore', and Reginald Blomfield's 'Cross of Sacrifice'.

The design of the headstones caused more dissent. The Commission decided to have uniform tablet-shaped headstones but with the return of peace their decision became the subject of bitter political and public debate. Lady Frances Cecil, who had lost three sons in the war, led the opposition, supported by A. J. Balfour, demanding the right to erect a cross as an alternative to the tablet-shaped headstone. Balfour even submitted a design for a cruciform stone – Lutyens called it 'extraordinarily ugly'.[8] When the debate came to Parliament in May 1920, H. H. Asquith stood up for the Commission: he was perfectly happy for his son Raymond to have the same tablet-shaped headstone as the others of his regiment who had fallen with him on the Somme. And a letter was read out from Kipling. The body of his son John was never found.

> You see we shall never have any grave to go to. Our boy was missing at Loos. The ground is of course battered and mined past all hope of any trace being recovered. I wish some of the people who are making this trouble realize how more than fortunate they are to have a name on a headstone in a known place.[9]

The graves of half a million men from the British armies would never be located. The other half million received uniform headstones in Portland stone and Hopton local stone, in accordance with the Commission's wishes. By 1923 over 4,000 headstones were shipped to France every week.

As soon as the fighting ceased, visitors poured out to the battlefields to view the destruction and desolation and to locate the graves of family and friends. By 1919 Michelin had produced a fifteen-volume guide to the battlefields, illustrated with photographs. It dwelt on the fertility of the countryside before the war: in the Somme the 'wide straight roads bordered with fine elms', the orchards, the low red-tiled houses, the fields 'once rich and fertile' but now 'like a lunar landscape'.[10] Perhaps Frances Horner carried her Michelin guide book when she picked her way through the mire to find the graves of her son Edward and son-in-law Raymond Asquith in 1919.

> The country was still almost the same as it had been in the war – villages disappeared, and only a signpost pointing to them as if they still existed, the trees all black sticks, holding their leafless limbs up – not a green tree left – and duckboards along the fields and trenches marked with German names – and it was a very grim sight.[11]

When Edward and Raymond were given their permanent headstones, Frances was able to take their temporary wooden crosses back to Mells.

The first cemetery to be completed was at Forceville, designed by Reginald Blomfield and opened in 1920. It was rather like an English country churchyard, 'the most perfect, the noblest, the most classically beautiful memorial that any loving heart or any proud nation could desire to their heroes fallen in a foreign land'.[12] When all the cemeteries and memorials were completed the costs totalled just over £8 million: the Battle of Passchendaele, by comparison, had cost £22 million.

Within only a few years, agriculture flourished again around the war cemeteries; waving fields of corn dotted with red poppies surrounding the clipped yew hedges, immaculate lawns and gleaming headstones. Few survivors of the war had thought that the transformation would be possible. Edmund Blunden recalled 'the idea that these battlefields could themselves ever again become pasturelands, and chateaux with grounds and little lakes and garden-walls, would have appeared sheer fantasy'.[13] The village of Fleury, for example, near Verdun, was completely destroyed during a battle in which a million men were killed. To this day, 'not one stone remains upon another'.[14] However, elm trees possess an unusual ability to propagate and the trees which once grew in Fleury have grown up again from bits of root that lay near the surface of the cratered earth.

Henry Williamson returned to Flanders in 1928. He travelled along the Vlamertinghe Road from Poperinghe to Ypres:

> The fields are beautiful with wind-stroked corn . . . Larks sing in the sky . . . clusters of red-tiled, red-bricked farms and houses . . . We

used to say it could never be reclaimed: that in fifty years it would be the same dreadful morass . . . Now if you would recall 1917 to your memory, you must stay away from this fine agricultural district.[15]

A memorial service was held in Stanway parish church for Ego Charteris, the eldest son of Mary and Hugo Wemyss, on 23 April 1919, three years after he was killed at the Battle of Katia. Sergeant-Major Hyatt bicycled over to Stanway, joining Mary and Hugo for breakfast before the service. The sergeant-major told Mary more of the details of her son's last moments as they walked together through the gardens of the manor house: 'He was wounded in the arm, then in the leg; he was knocked over by the leg wound, but picked himself up and put on a field dressing, saying, "Don't bother about me, go on fighting," and shouting "No surrender boys, no surrender".'[16]

As the Wemysses mourned the loss of their eldest and youngest sons and brooded on the past, their village was beginning to come to life again. The grass was cut on the cricket field. Cynthia Asquith recalled that the 'chief outward and visible sign of a changed world had, indeed, been the cricket field, hitherto so well-trodden and carefully tended, where, through the long slow years of war, the unmown grass rose higher and higher'.[17] Some old players returned, new members joined up and the game was resumed. Mary steeled herself to go and watch. Harry Last, the head keeper on the Stanway estate and a cricketing enthusiast, spoke to her after the first post-war match.

> Ah, I missed seeing that brown head and those long swift legs that swallowed up the ground, the quiet strong voice that kept everyone in his place, and the patience, kindness and tact that considered everyone's feelings.

Last was referring to Ego, captain of the Stanway eleven for year after year. Cynthia added, 'nowhere had my brother Ego . . . seemed more intensely alive than on that cricket field'.[18]

In Mells, Somerset, Percy Long, builder and decorator, whose brother Arthur had been killed in 1915, carefully cleaned the black-out paint off the stained glass windows in the church. He told his children, 'I've been washing the saints' feet.'[19] The vicar, Edward Lear, and his wife started up their theatricals: *Cymbeline* was the first production, performed on the vicarage lawn in the summer of 1919.

Sir John Horner had kept up some shooting throughout the war although his parties grew smaller and smaller. By the autumn of 1918 only the older regulars remained, his son-in-law George Lambton, a vicar and an admiral. Edward was dead and Duff Cooper was serving his country. Shooting at Mells was never just for sport and in the years immediately after the war rabbits were a particular menace to the farmers. Thousands were killed. Sir John blamed their numbers on the 'state in wh. the government left the woods after the war'. In 1924 Richard Hames retired. He had been Sir John's gamekeeper for sixty years. He moved into Mells village to live with his daughters: his son Charles took over and occupied the keeper's lodge at Mells Park. Sir John wrote a tribute to his loyal employee in his gamebook on 21 August: 'there never was such a keeper as Richard Hames, and he was the greatest possible blessing to me ever since 1864 when this book began'.

Throughout the countryside country sports were starting up again. *Country Life* magazine anticipated the desire among its readers to hunt the fox instead of the Hun. In September 1918 it celebrated the return of the Quorn Hunt, even though so many 'who had proved their courage and fearlessness in the hunting fields of our homeland' were now dead. Nevertheless

the fox must live to die in the old-fashioned way, hunted and chased and worried to the end of his time. It is good and comforting to know this, for it means so much to our countryside.

No doubt the fox would have preferred the war to last a little longer.

Some landowners changed sides after the war. Daisy, Countess of Warwick, hostess to H. G. Wells and George Bernard Shaw at her Essex home of Easton Lodge over the weekend just before the outbreak of war, completely altered her opinion about hunting. She was so horrified by the mutilation of troops and horses that she could no longer bear to contemplate taking life for pleasure. Once peace returned her estate at Easton was closed to the local hunt.

She was an exception, however. Across the countryside hunting, shooting, fishing and the increasingly popular game of golf were resumed with gusto by the ruling classes. With the revival of such country sports came the resumption of the country house weekend, so much a feature of the Edwardian era. The visitors' book for Stanway House starts up again in 1921 with a mixture of family and friends.

Hugo and Mary Wemyss continued to move between their Gloucestershire and Scottish estates, also keeping on their house in Cadogan Square. But entertaining on a pre-war scale was no longer possible all the year. Financial constraints forced the family to rent out Stanway and Gosford intermittently throughout the 1920s and 1930s: at one time Gosford was used as a hotel, though run rather idiosyncratically by Hugo and Angela. "The Earl of Wemyss, licensed to retail beer, wines and spirits" appeared over a remote backdoor to comply with the licensing laws.

To begin with, renting out Stanway was a favour to the world-famous and very rich author, J. M. Barrie. Cynthia Asquith had been employed as his secretary since the war – she needed an income as her husband, still suffering from the horrors of the western front, was proving incapable of earning anything like enough to provide for an earl's daughter. When, in 1921, Barrie was left distraught by the sudden death of one of the Llewelyn-Davies boys, Cynthia offered to be hostess for him at her parents' home. For 200 guineas Barrie became lord of the manor for six weeks. As he was earning around £50,000 a year at the time the rent was no burden: but for the Wemysses, 200 guineas could pay for some necessary estate repairs. The arrangement with Barrie continued for twelve summers. After his series of tenancies the artist Thomas Lowinsky sampled the country house life.

Barrie became involved in the life of Stanway village, making friends with Eliza Wedgwood and other close neighbours, but also bringing fresh vitality to the community. Cricket was his favourite sport. In the summer of 1921 he invited the whole of the Australian Test Cricket team from Cheltenham to the village. Four years later he provided Stanway Cricket Club with a new pavilion to replace the old third-class railway carriage. Cynthia was hostess every summer and sometimes Hugo and Mary were guests in their own house. The atmosphere which pervaded Stanway was steeped in nostalgia, perfect for Barrie's maudlin sentimentality. Cynthia found herself unable to distinguish one year from the next and had

> the illusion that the weather was perpetually fine, and that Stanway was an enchanted place . . . always evening – a magic evening in whose lucent atmosphere the house glows apricot-coloured. The elm trees are rimmed with gold; the air is filled with the coo of wood pigeons, the tock of ball on bat, the shouts and laughter of children.[20]

Barrie, writing to Cynthia after the first visit, was moved by the old world charm of the whole experience: 'my feeling, looking back, is that we were all people of to-day, really intruders'.[21]

New life came to Mells village with post-war building activities, though on rather different scales: a new Park House and a row of council houses. Although the Horners had received insurance for the eighteenth-century mansion after it was destroyed by fire in 1917, they had decided not to rebuild. Frances and Sir John had grown used to living in the Elizabethan manor house and did not wish to return to a rebuilt Park House. Sir John was almost 80 years old and there were no sons living to build for. Katharine, Raymond Asquith's widow, would eventually inherit the manor house.

An arrangement for the rebuilding was struck with Reginald McKenna, Asquith's Chancellor in 1915 and married to Frances Horner's niece Pamela Jekyll. For a nominal rent, McKenna would live in the house he built for fifteen years; if he wanted to stay longer the arrangement could be extended; if he wanted to leave the Horners agreed to buy the house from him or sell him the land. McKenna chose Edwin Lutyens to design the house, to be built of fine ashlar stone but retaining the surviving cloistered service court of the old house. McKenna had employed Lutyens on several projects, including his own London house, built before the war, and when he became Chairman of the Midland Bank in 1919, he was able to offer the architect several valuable commissions for banks.

The McKennas moved to Mells in 1925. Two years before, the first council houses to be built in the village were completed. Muriel Horner, one of Sir John's elderly sisters, grudgingly admitted they might 'relieve the congestion' in Mells, 'which I suppose we ought to thank'. Unlike the new Park House, the council houses were built of brick 'because the stone people were so expensive'.

At Clouds, the Wiltshire birthplace of Mary Wemyss, country house life started up again with the return from Salonika in June 1919 of the new owner, Dick Wyndham. There were point-to-points, hunts, balls, redecorating and the successful search for a wife. Unfortunately Dick proved to be better at surviving the trenches of the western front than riding horses, as his young wife Iris noted in the Clouds visitors' book in April 1922:

> *April 12* South & West Wilts Point to Point. Dick ran fifth on Patsy out of fifteen runners in Nomination Race. Olivia [his sister] ran fourth on Saffron out of seven in the Ladies' Race. Pouring wet day.
> *April 21* Poor 'Patsy' broke her leg at the Crawley & Horsham Point to Point. Dick was riding her. This makes the third horse killed at the end of three consecutive seasons. 'Rathnally', 'Timothy Brown', & 'Patsy'.[22]

The resumption of country house life did not consist entirely of entertainment and sport. Iris Wyndham organised the East Knoyle Brownies and raised money for various charities. Older hostesses such as Mary Wemyss and Frances Horner took up their pre-war charities and social work and also became involved in the expansion of the National Federation of Women's Institutes.

The Women's Institute movement in Britain was a direct result of the war. It had first begun in Canada in 1897. The first British Institute was opened in September 1915 in Anglesey under the influence of a Canadian widow who had settled in Wales. Support for the whole concept was widespread and by the beginning of 1917 there were 40 branches in the country; by October 1919 there were over 1,200 branches. The Institutes undoubtedly enhanced the quality of life in villages, both during and after the war. For the first time women could meet together on a regular basis, part of a national association.

Many Institutes concentrated on increasing the supplies of home-grown foods (still their traditional role), but others organised lectures on economics, family planning, education and politics. During the war all the branches provided valuable moral support for mothers and wives anxious about soldiers at the front. One early member commented, 'this is the first organisation I've been able to join in the village . . . everything else is got up by the Church or the Conservatives and I am a Catholic and a Liberal'.[23] Viscountess Barrington, who was involved in the revival of village life during and after the war commented on the role of the Institutes in 1918: they were

> extraordinarily useful in enlarging the women's horizons and brightening their lives, providing valuable instruction in poultry rearing and other agricultural subjects, while prompting many desirable reforms on the conditions of cottage homes and arousing an intelligent interest in the many social questions of the countryside.[24]

The women of Mells held a meeting on 9 December 1920 to start up their branch officially. Frances Horner offered them the building on the village green in which soup had been ladled out to the needy during the war. Throughout the 1920s the Mells Women's Institute was a thriving concern with over fifty members. Frances persuaded her friends to give talks – Lady Muriel Paget on Prussia during and since the war, 'a sad subject' – or to open their houses for visits – Lord Hylton at Ammerdown, the Marquis of Bath at Longleat. Frances realised how much the women of Mells needed a new focus for their energies and resourcefulness, qualities released by the war. During the war

> middle-aged women – yes and old women too – took their places by the side of the young and threw their experiences then their wisdom into the common pit . . . They were greatly needed . . . Then all that ceased, and the outlets in life seem to shrink again and opportunities only to belong to the young . . . I think the Women's Institute movement has come to meet this need for us, and that is why it has gone ahead with such grand strides and is becoming a force in English life.

Mary Wemyss and Eliza Wedgwood started up the North Cotswold group of Women's Institutes soon after the end of the war. Mary was president of the Stanway branch, which had about forty regular members. She spoke at the opening of the Apperly branch (the village where her daughter Mary Strickland had settled) and echoed Frances Horner's sentiments:

> I think the Village Institutes help us to surmount barriers and to make paths of communication – to *canalize our sympathies and energies*. And my friends, since the Great War, we are living in hard, in difficult, in dangerous times.

For many village women the resumption of peace meant redundancy. Their war-time activities ceased with the return of the men. The number of village women permanently engaged in agriculture, for example, had halved by 1921. And the Land Army was finally disbanded after the end of the potato harvest in November 1919. In Little Leighs, Essex, the baker's wife Mrs Mann had been delivering the bread for almost three years since the delivery boy Jimmy Lewin had been called up. But with his return in February 1919 Mrs Mann was out of a job. The Women's Institutes could offer some outlet for thwarted ambition: for a few it offered an entry into the political life of the community through the election of members to parish councils. As women over 30 had the vote from 1918, there was a vital need to stimulate their political awareness and acumen.

> I shall never forget my first visit to the country, to Warwickshire and Oxfordshire, in April 1919. In the early years of the War natural beauty had been to me a forbidden fruit. I was in the Salient during the second battle of Ypres, and the scent of hawthorn and lilac battling with the stink of poison-gas, seemed to underline grimly the indifference of nature to human ills. I remember a June morning, too, in the Chilterns, the beauty of which seemed to me only a savage irony . . . But in that April journey, I recovered the past, and with it hope for the future.
>
> John Buchan, *Memory-Hold-The-Door*[25]

On that April journey Buchan not only recovered the past and hope for the future; he also bought himself a country house, Elsfield Manor, and nineteen acres of land, in the Oxfordshire countryside. The war had left him with an 'intense craving for the country life' and profits from the war-time exploits of Richard Hannay bought him his ideal, the ownership of a piece of the English countryside. Hannay shared the dream with his author. In *Mr Standfast* Hannay walks through the countryside near Oxford: 'I understood what a precious thing this little England was, how old and kindly and comforting, how wholly worth striving for'. His aim was 'to inherit something of this English peace and wrap myself in it'.[26]

Buchan was a successful writer. His taste for country house life dated from the pre-war period when he moved in the circle of the 'Souls'. He was friends with Raymond Asquith at Oxford. But many less well-off citizens who survived the war were also striving for rural peace, for a plot of land to call their own. The 'back to the land' movement of the Edwardian era which had been predominantly middle-class and connected with the idea of rural recreation and appreciation was, in the aftermath of the war, resurfacing among officers and even ordinary soldiers, many of them disabled, who wanted to work the land they had fought for, to raise their families in country villages.

The connection between fighting for England and owning a part of it had been suggested very early in the war. 'Country homes for heroes' was a phrase constantly appearing in newspapers and journals. The Rural League put pressure on the government, its president, Jesse Collings MP, publishing *The Great War: Its Lessons and Its Warnings*, in 1915. Returning soldiers were not going to be content with working as clerks and tradesmen. They were 'accustomed to pick and spade work, digging trenches, etc., and generally to an outdoor life'. Collings interviewed a number of disabled soldiers who confessed they would like to own some land: 'we should be digging our own trenches'.[27] If unable to work the land, some crippled soldiers might be able to take up traditional rural handicrafts, thereby, it was argued, helping to revive rural life.

After the war there must in the nature of things be a large number of wounded soldiers in this country, some of whom will doubtless prefer a quiet country life. If the war has done nothing else, it has shown to all engaged in it the health-giving properties of the open air and whoever has once become impregnated with the spirit of the open air can never be quite happy in town again.[28]

This, of course, was written before the Battles of the Somme and Passchendaele introduced a whole new concept to 'health-giving open air'.

The government set up a committee to consider land settlement for ex-servicemen at the end of 1915 with Sir Harry Verney, a large landowner, in charge. Verney's committee came down strongly in favour of the idea, though it received criticism for supporting tenancies – which it felt offered the smallholder greater financial protection – rather than freehold contracts. In 1916 a Small Holdings (Colonies) Act was passed and another in 1918; also, in 1919, a Land Settlement (Facilities) Act which included a special section applying to cottage holdings. Between the Armistice and 1924, county councils bought and leased a quarter of a million acres. Thousands of men and women applied for holdings (49,000 by 1920) but many were found to be unsuitable as tenants, only half-hearted in their commitment. However, over 14,000 were settled on the land within two years of the end of the war: by 1926 only 15 per cent of all those settled on holdings had actually given them up.

There were several private schemes initiated early in the war – some supported by the government – which combined the desire to assist disabled soldiers and sailors and to improve the quality of country life. Several of these organisations were founded, and achieved charity status but never produced homes for heroes: their ideals were quite dotty. But some still exist today, maintaining country homes for the heroes of later wars.

The Village Centres Council aimed to create 'an A1 Empire of A1 Men' by offering a 'bridge between hospital and civil life'. It purchased an entire village, Enham in Hampshire, before the end of the war, consisting of over 1,000 acres with houses, cottages, farms, a smithy, post office and village hall. Its publicity leaflet announced that a thousand disabled men would be accommodated, trained in rural crafts until ready to join civilian life: 'never again shall the barrel-organ or the paving-stone and the coloured chalks be the portion of the man who has fought and bled and suffered untold mental and physical agonies for our preservation'.[29]

The Women's Scientific Co-Operative Farm for severely disabled soldiers and sailors was a much smaller venture: 65 acres of good arable soil at Sutton Valence in Kent. By 1919 Vanguard Farm was stocked and producing a surplus. Several families had been provided with cottages and the necessary education for running a smallholding. The fund-raising material stressed the health-giving qualities of the site, four hundred feet above sea level, with a beautiful view over the Weald of Kent. The chairwoman of the Co-Operative was Lady Buckmaster.

Viscountess Barrington started up 'Village homes for disabled soldiers and sailors' in Shrivenham, Berkshire. Viscount Barrington was lord of the manor òf Shrivenham as well as a considerable landowner in the counties of Berkshire, Buckinghamshire and Oxfordshire: he built the cottages, his wife wrote the propaganda.

What more fitting memorials could be erected throughout England to the men who have given their lives in their country's cause: what more acceptable provision made for others who have survived but with impaired powers of body and shattered health than these cottage homes, these Village Halls, raised by the concerted effort of all classes of the community, not only in remembrance of those they have loved and lost, but as a means of brightening the lives and improving the social and material conditions of those they have left behind.[30]

Mrs Annabelle Dott, builder, architect and vicar's wife, designed nine five-bedroom houses at Goathland on the Yorkshire moors for 'disabled officers of the public school type and their families'.[31] The Dotts' gift to the nation of the freehold houses plus two acres of land was worth £2,500; Sir Hugh Bell, Lord Lieutenant of the county, gave £1,000 for furniture. The officers and wives were expected to take up village industries such as weaving and basket-making, fruit growing, bee and poultry keeping, even tending a flock of sheep: a long way from their bloody exploits in the war. The *Daily Telegraph* visited the settlement in 1919.

Mrs Dott ... has ever kept the educational – and, indeed, the spiritual – ideal to the fore in this work, and besides the playing field for the youngsters, the opportunities for the practice of art crafts, the steady walks and the beautiful pergola, there is to be the well-head over the central water supply, on which is to be inscribed the names of some of the outstanding actions of the war on sea and land, with the words ... appropriate, indeed, to 'Homes of Honour', as these are to be – 'God gave them a great thing to do and they did it. Te Deum Laudamus'.

One of the better-organised charities to be started during the war concerned with settling disabled soldiers and sailors on the land, which survives to this day, is the Scottish Veterans' Garden City Association. Hugo and Mary Wemyss helped to establish its first settlement at Longniddry, East Lothian. The Association had been the idea of an Edinburgh JP and Hugo became president in August 1915. The following month Hugo offered a site at Longniddry, close to the main railway line between Edinburgh and London, on his Gosford estate. He agreed in July 1916 to remit the annual feu duty for five years.

The committee were keen to revive rural industries and also to emulate the garden cities already established south of the border. A visit was organised to several English garden cities and the ideas gathered were passed on to the architect. By building at Longniddry the committee effectively ended the long decline which had been experienced by the village since the collapse of local weaving early in the nineteenth century and, more recently, the decline in coal mining. A railway station had been opened in 1845 but had failed to revive the community. However, the activities of the Scottish Veterans' Garden City Association brought about a rebirth: in just a few years the village was a thriving community.

On 23 September 1916 Mary Wemyss and Mrs Parker, sister of Lord Kitchener, laid the foundation stones and were presented with silver trowels. The rows of cottages were called Wemyss Terrace and Kitchener Terrace. Anyone giving £250 to the charity could name, but not furnish, a cottage. By the time of the opening ceremony on 29 September 1917 the settlement included Mohawk Valley Cottage USA no. 1 and no. 2 (donations from the Mohawk Valley Garden City

Association of the USA), Colorado Springs Cottage no. 1 and no. 2 (donations from the Caledonian Society of Colorado Springs, USA) and Warrior Cottage (donations from a couple living in London). Many contributions came from bereaved families in memory of husbands, brothers and sons. There were also fund-raising bazaars, which Mary Wemyss helped to organise, held every autumn in Edinburgh. She secretly thought them 'horrid' but one held in October 1918 cost just over £200 to run but raised well over £3,000.

By December 1918 the Longniddry Settlement was selling surplus fruit and jam, pigs and poultry, a sugar beet factory was being erected and many of the tenants were eager to rent smallholdings for themselves after receiving rudimentary agricultural training. A year later there was a village hall for dances, concerts and religious services and a hairdresser's shop. Building the cottages proved a difficult task, however, both during and after the war, as the committee and their employers had to compete with the demands of the military and post-war building schemes. The Ministry of Munitions' demands on wire netting made it difficult for the disabled soldiers and sailors to protect their growing crops from rabbits; timber was difficult to obtain, also manure. But local farmers were happy to plough land for the tenants' fruit farm free of charge.

A typical tenant of the settlement made his successful application for a cottage in March 1918. He was from Peebles, 37 years old with a wife and two sons. He had enlisted in 1915 in the First Garrison Battalion Seaforth Highlanders, but had been discharged in 1917 with chronic gastritis and malaria fever. He was experienced as a jobbing gardener so a considerable asset to the community. Less typical was a tenant, blinded in the war, who walked out of his cottage in 1925, taking refuge with friends in a nearby town. The committee paid him a visit to find out what the matter was with their settlement, and discovered his departure was caused by marital problems: his wife 'was cruel to him'.[32] She received notice to quit.

Hugo continued to be involved with the Association although it was his agent George Connor who attended all the committee meetings. Hugo leased the settlement land for a recreation ground in 1920. Two years later Connor complained that the residents were throwing their rubbish over the high wall into the Gosford estate. But in 1925 it was

Hugo's pheasants which caused havoc, damaging the crops of one of the tenants. The Longniddry Settlement remained the largest of the Association's settlements until the end of the Second World War.

Sir Howard Frank wrote an optimistic article for *Country Life* in May 1915. Things would be different on the land when the war was over.

There has existed for some years a want of confidence on the part of those who owned or were inclined to buy land. I think it will be otherwise when peace is established, and I firmly believe that when that happy day dawns landowners will be able to consider the future with equanimity, safe in the possession of what was formerly re-garded as the first of all gilt-edged investments, and secure in devoting all their energies to the intelligent management of their estates, to the advantage of the State and the community.

F. M. L. Thompson gives rather a different view of the state of the landed interest in the aftermath of the war. 'The apparently stable Edwardian society had in fact resolved upon a social revolution, the liquidation of the landed interest, whose full accomplishment was but deferred by the First World War.'[33]

Landowners were faced with increased taxation – an estate which had paid 9 per cent of its gross rents in income tax, land tax and rates before 1914 might be paying 30 per cent in 1919. Worse still, the Budget of 1919 introduced death duties of 40 per cent on estates valued at £2 million and over. However, rents had remained steady for years, in some cases even falling during the war, and many landowners remained reluctant to raise them sufficiently to cover increased taxes. It was not surprising, therefore, that with the dramatic increases in agricultural land and prices during and immediately after the war, many landowners decided to sell. Those with large estates disposed of outlying parts, 'so liberating capital for more profitable uses';[34] a few gave up the country life entirely.

The sales of land began on a wide scale during the final months of the war; by 1919 there was an avalanche of sales. By the end of the year over a million acres were actually sold. More land was disposed of in 1920, including half the Duke of Rutland's Belvoir estate for £1.5

million. By 1921 a quarter of England had changed hands: some 6–8 million acres. *The Times* commented in May 1920:

> England is changing hands ... Will a profiteer buy it? Will it be turned into a school or an institution? Has the mansion house electric light and modern drainage? ... For the most part the sacrifices are made in silence ... The sons are perhaps lying in far away graves; the daughters secretly mourning some one dearer than a brother, have taken up some definite work away from home, seeking thus to still their aching hearts, and the old people, knowing there is no son or near relative left to keep up the old traditions, or so crippled by necessary taxation that they know the boy will never be able to carry on when they are gone, take the irrevocable step.

For most landowners selling was simple good sense. Few were actually affected by death duties: rather the war had raised the value of their land, the market was 'land-hungry'. Daisy Warwick began to sell off some of her outlying land in September 1918. She had coped with shortage of money during the war by selling off stocks and shares, but in February 1918 a fire had destroyed a large part of Easton Lodge including the Tudor wing, also most of her jewellery and fine clothes and all her correspondence. Daisy had always been something of a rebel in her class – during the war she campaigned against the employment of elementary-school children on the land; also she befriended the German prisoners employed in the fields close to Easton – and although she badly needed money, she refused to raise rents. In 1919, with prices rising even higher, she sold over 5,000 acres in Essex, close to her own home, then more sales followed in Leicestershire including two colliery villages. In all she raised almost a quarter of a million pounds and was able to rebuild the wing of Easton. Most of her property was sold to her sitting tenants. As far as she was concerned, the sooner the estate system collapsed the better: 'founded on something akin to serfdom; the rising tide of democracy has carried it away – unwept, unhonoured and unsung, except by those in whose blood there is something of the flunkey strain'.[35]

Batsford, the Gloucestershire home of Lord Redesdale, came on the market in 1919, together with its surrounding farm land. Although the first Lord Redesdale had died in 1916, only a year after his eldest son and heir was killed, the war itself was not wholly responsible for the sale. David Mitford, second Lord Redesdale, was forced to sell an estate which his father had run for years on hopelessly inefficient lines. Bertie Redesdale had built a brand-new Victorian mansion and taken on vast gardening improvements at a time of low rents and insufficient income. Before the war 'the façade of his existence was imposing, and there was no discernible sign that the structure was not entirely solid'.[36] But by 1919 the heir had no choice but to sell, fortunately for him when prices were high.

Sir John Horner put almost two-thirds of his Mells estate on the market in August 1923 but again his decision was not a direct result of the war. His father had mortgaged the estate in 1865 for £55,000 to make provision for all of his ten children – the land then being entailed to pass directly to the eldest son. Profits from the sale were used to pay off the mortgage: 4,300 acres were sold, including 22 farms, mostly to the sitting tenants. The cost of upkeep of the farms and cottages had been a constant worry to the Horners, who consistently avoided raising rents. Even in 1920, when Sir John had directed his estate office to warn tenants of the possibility of his raising rents, he explained 'he was unwilling to take any definite steps until war conditions had ceased, and it was seen that increased values and costs were likely to permanently remain'.

Unfortunately for Sir John prices did not remain high: in June 1921 the government repealed the Corn Production Act and agricultural prices collapsed. By 1925 the large-scale selling of land practically ceased. Sir John would have done better to put the Mells estate on the market three or four years earlier. More serious for his heirs, he also parted with the mineral rights in 1923. Since then several enormous limestone deposits have been found under some of the farms which were sold. As the family now admit – while listening to the sound of dynamite blasting at the local quarries – ownership of those mineral rights 'could have made us very rich indeed'.

With the collapse in land prices, many country houses began to come on the market and if not sold they were demolished: the landed gentry were giving up and decamping to the city or to dower houses. Some houses could adapt to new functions, serving as schools, hospitals, mental asylums, rather as in the war years when the wounded, the shell-schocked and the convalescent were accommodated in Longleat, Wilton and Clouds. Others limped on without male heirs, until their owners died. Ettie Desborough survived at Taplow House until 1952. Her third son had been killed shortly after the First World War and after her death Taplow was converted into offices: Panshanger, her other country mansion, was demolished. She had clung on to the past, 'a lady of great age, lying half paralysed in a huge empty house, and saying with the heart-rending ghost of a gay smile, "We did have fun, didn't we?" '[37]

Hugo and Mary Wemyss kept Stanway and Gosford but demolished their third country house, Amisfield, in 1923. No one could be found to rent the elegant eighteenth-century house. Tenants had been hard to find even before the war – during the period 1907–14 it was let for ten per cent of the time and empty the rest. The War Office had taken it over in October 1914, paying £500 a year (£300 for the house, £200 for the park). In October 1919 the rent was reduced to £200 a year – less than the Wemysses were to receive from J. M. Barrie for six weeks at Stanway.

The War Office's tenancy agreement ended in December 1920, leaving Hugo and Mary with an empty house, knocked about by the years of army occupation and little possibility of finding tenants. The financial burden seemed too much. Hugo was still paying off death duties from 1914, so the house was offered for sale, but for demolition only. According to the family, 'it was all done in a great hurry with insufficient care and attention'. Ego's widow Letty didn't hear of the demolition. Instead she found out for herself, driving towards Haddington one day. She turned to look at Amisfield and 'to her horror she saw the front wall gaping and sheets of wallpaper flapping from the inside wall.'

Hugo and Mary were no better off for the sale: the trustees of the Wemyss estate received any profits. The individual who gained most from the demolition was Richard Baillie, the 'purchaser demolisher'. 'It is said', according to the descendants, 'that the lead statues on the roof and the (unsuspected) lead sheathing under the road surface of the carriage ramp were in themselves sufficient to recoup all he had paid for the whole building. The rest was found money.'

The warm pink stones of Amisfield soon appeared in buildings in the neighbourhood. Now the Haddington Golf Club House occupies the site of Amisfield: the stables and the walled garden survive, the property of the District Council.

Not only the landed gentry were affected by the fall in agricultural prices. Many of the sitting tenants who had bought up their farms from landlords at inflated prices were faced with bankruptcy. The farmers who started up in the autumn of 1918 were worst off: 'they are indeed fortunate if they only risked their capital on purchasing farming stock at the inflated prices then current and did not also purchase their land under similar conditions'.[38]

Hugo Wemyss's intimate friend Lady Angela Forbes used the profits left over from her Boulogne soldiers' buffets (some £3,000) to organise agricultural training for ex-servicemen on a farm at Brentwood, not far from London: 'practical training for the men who were going to sheath the sword, and hoped to wield the sickle'. Twenty to twenty-five trainees took up market-gardening, dairy and poultry keeping and carpentry. Angela found many of the men woefully over-optimistic about their futures,

'starting on our own' seemed to them the simplest thing in the world. It was an idea that had been fostered by the dream pictures held out in the poultry paper advertisements – 'a thousand pounds a year from three hens' or some such catch phrase.[39]

Her fears for the future of some of the ex-servicemen who took up smallholdings, perhaps as part of the government-promoted schemes, were to be justified. With the collapse in prices, the years after the end of the war proved only the beginning of a financial nightmare, culminating in the depression of the 1930s.

Robert Graves just managed to survive the war. His greatest ambition was to settle in the country with his family, to write and to keep a few animals on a small piece of land. At least he began with few illusions about the financial rewards from living off the land, as he explained to Siegfried Sassoon in November 1918.

I simply *gotter* live in the country & I shall live in the country & what can one do there but read & write & till the kindly fruits of the earth (so that in due time we may enjoy 'em). Of course if you think I'm going to try & run a 300 acre farm you're wrong: if you think even a 150 acre farm you're wrong: I'm not going to make it *pay*. Just enough to keep two-three cows & chickens & keep the family in food. The actual dibs will have to come from the cornucopia (I don't think) of literature.[40]

But when Robert and Nancy Graves settled in Islip near Oxford in 1921 with their four children, the reality of village life was far from their dreams. They disliked the village school – 'formal religion, class snobbery, political prejudice, and mystifying fairy stories of the facts of sex'.[41] Also the village was on the route between the workhouses of Chipping Norton and Oxford. 'Ex-service men were continually coming to the door selling bootlaces and asking for cast-off shirts and socks.'[42] The country was hardly providing 'homes for heroes'.

The Oxfordshire farm labourers who were in employment earned less than Graves. He was receiving 50 shillings a week; the labourers, usually with larger families to support, received only 30 shillings. Pay was as bad, promotion prospects as limited and housing as inferior as before the war. In 1924 the Wheatley Act was passed which offered a special subsidy to local authorities of £12. 10s. per house per annum for forty years in rural areas. However, the financial contribution to the building programme had to come from the rates and 'most rural councillors were reluctant to embark upon a major programme to provide cheap rented accommodation'.[43]

While Robert Graves ranted at the narrowness and superstitious attitudes of the inhabitants of Islip, Rudyard Kipling, from his country house in Sussex, was attacking the post-war newcomers to English villages. He launched an extraordinary campaign in 1919 combining his hatred of Germans with his new hatred of Bolsheviks. He was convinced of the connection between outbreaks of foot and mouth disease and the location of 'Hun prison camps' and wrote to various members of the government to alert them to the threat. To his friend H. A. Gwynne, editor of the *Morning Post*, he wrote pointing out the latest programme of attack undertaken by the Bolsheviks against the bourgeoisie, which included 'the propagation of diseases and other methods of Kultur'.

> It might be worth while to watch people who have come into little villages, whether as cobblers, small tradesmen, and the like, within the past few months, who set up as Socialist or Bolshevik agitators ... I want a better watch kept on queer, talkative Socio-Bolshio strangers in rural districts.[44]

As far as Kipling was concerned, a secret war was now being waged in English villages. No wonder Robert Graves left for Egypt in 1926.

For some countrymen, returning from the army or navy, country life was simply dull after the excitement of war. In Great Leighs in Essex several farm labourers signed up again in the army after only a few weeks back on the land. Returning to farm work was 'like being taken from among a thousand men and put into a coal-hole'.[45] Village life could be dull and ill-paid for the professional class too. Albert Copps returned to his Yorkshire village and to his job as village schoolteacher in January 1919. He had achieved the rank of lieutenant but found himself unable to make ends meet on a teacher's salary of £7 per month less superannuation. In his part of the countryside farm hands were making over £2 a week. Copps took up freelance journalism to supplement his income until his colonel encouraged him to apply to York Technical College for further training. In 1921 he brought his family south: the war had given him the chance to expand his horizons and those of his children, but it also took him away from his Yorkshire village.

> Set into stone their names carved crudely,
> No one passing could help but see
> Thomas Eden, William Bewdley,
> James Llewellyn, and young Ted Lea.
> . . . .
> Nothing is altered; rooks still quarrel
> High in the elms over Bewdley's loft;
> Still the meadows are plagued with sorrel,
> Still the clover springs green and soft.

Evening passes with gentle fingers,
Sunshine fills in the sycamore tree,
And under the leaves the moth light lingers –
But William Bewdley's not there to see.

. . . .

Here where life runs lustily, crudely,
This were heartbreak, to stand and see
Snatched for ever to silence – Bewdley,
Eden, Llewellyn, and young Ted Lea.

(Katherine McIntosh)[46]

Wyke Manor in Worcestershire is one of the few country houses built immediately after the war. It was designed as a memorial to the past rather than a home for the future, built in memory of Lieutenant Hudson, killed at the Battle of Messines in 1917. His tomb rests in an oratory constructed in the north-east corner of the house. Wyke Manor, a fake sixteenth-century yeoman's hall, was meant also to be at the centre of a scheme to help disabled ex-soldiers. Two long rows of almshouses were to be built to provide accommodation. However, only the house was completed. Most of the work available for architects was in the nature of memorials: some simple crosses, few as elaborate memorials as Wyke Manor.

The Great Leighs war memorial was first discussed at a meeting of the Parish Council in September 1919. A public meeting was held; then the War Memorial Committee met at the church and agreed to the suggestion of J. Herbert Tritton, lord of the manor, that a tablet should be erected in the churchyard wall facing the road. As vicar, Andrew Clark was responsible for its erection. He had to have one of the thick pollard elms removed to make space for the tablet, 'very troublesome, because of the tombstones beside it' and it cost him £2. 10s. However, the memorial was finally erected and dedicated in December 1920.

A similar procedure was followed all over the country as village communities met to decide on their preferred memorial. Mary Wemyss dedicated the memorial at Aberlady, the village close to the Gosford estate, on All Saints Day 1919. Hugo had presented the Aberlady Parish Council with a plot of land between the bowling green and the church. This was to be a garden of rest. The South African war memorial, freshly engraved, was moved to the new site, and also an old Venetian well, given to the village by the tenth Earl in memory of his first wife.

George Connor gave the opening speech. 'We have, therefore, on one side of this garden a representation, imaging forth the truth of devotion, bravery, and self-sacrifice. On the other, a representation imaging forth the truth of all that was good and beautiful.' He spoke of Mary Wemyss's special role as a mother who had lost two sons in the war. 'Little wonder that the sons of the women of this country are brave, and that of all words, "mother" is upheld by men as the word most loved and most beautiful.'

Mary placed a laurel wreath on the stone as a crown of remembrance. She then planted a birch tree for remembrance; her grandchildren, David and Martin Charteris, dressed in the uniform of the London Scottish, planted a service tree.

> The service tree is planted as a token, to remind us, that for many a year, we shall all have to render service, in order to make good the evil and the waste caused by the cruel war – not greedy service, not grumbling service, but loving service. Service for love of England and for loyalty for those who died for her.

Mary's daughter Bibs read out Laurence Binyon's poem 'For the Fallen'.

Mary also dedicated the memorial at Gullane close by and made another speech:

> I like to think that when our names are forgotten these names will live in their glory – and will remain as long as this little church remains and even if an earthquake were to destroy the church (or if the Kaiser sent a Zeppelin) their names would not be forgotten. They live in our hearts.

Stanway's memorial inside the parish church was unveiled on 25 April 1920. Eric Gill did the lettering, as he did for the village memorial erected at the crossroads from where the 'men of Stanway' had marched away so many years before. This grander memorial had a statue óf St George and the Dragon by Alexander Fisher (he had taught Mary and her mother Madeline Wyndham to enamel over twenty years before), supported on a plinth made by Sir Philip Stott, architect and lord of the manor of Stanton, the neighbouring village.

Artists, architects and poets – their services were required throughout the decade after the end of the war. At Mells, old friends got to work. The Kensington School of Art was responsible for the memorial inside the church which contained the names of all the fallen from the village. Raymond Asquith's plaque had lettering by Eric Gill and a bronze wreath above it by Lutyens. Lutyens was also responsible for the memorial in the village. The Horners first called a meeting to find out what the village would prefer:

> was it something useful – such as seats, or a village fountain, or a playground or a garden, and they said it was something to look at. Should it be in the churchyard or in the village: they said 'on the road so that passers by might say "look, there is the Mells Memorial"'.

Then Lutyens spent an August weekend in 1919 walking all round the village inspecting possible sites. 'I walked miles Sunday morning with Katharine Asquith to have a preliminary survey. Found a perfect site in the centre of the village, which no one else found, or thought of, and with a little tact and patience it was carried by the villagers with acclamation.' He finished his letter to his wife, 'my weekend was as a spring day, fun and tears. All their young men are killed.'[47]

Frances Horner had a 'long correspondence with Mr Bridges – the poet laureate about the inscription' for the memorial.

> We died in strange lands
> Facing the dark cloud of war
> And this stone is raised to us
> In the land of our delight.

A statue of St George was designed for the top of the column and Frances first tried contemporary sculptors for the work. However, estimates were too high for the village's fund and a copy was made of an early statue in the chapel of Henry VII in Westminster Abbey. In the end the memorial cost over £400, with concrete foundations, base, steps, seat and column all in Portland stone.

The most expensive and elaborate memorial at Mells was private: erected by the Horners to their lost son Edward. Lutyens designed the base; Alfred Munnings the statue of Edward on horseback. Frances's dealings with Munnings began in 1922.

> He started it at once, but he refused to let me see his cast and I got very nervous about it – it was to cost £1,000 base and statue and I was so afraid that if I didn't like it I should not know where to put it.

Eventually Frances visited Munnings in his Sussex studio to quell her fears. Although she liked the finished work she was disappointed in its site. 'I wanted it to go under the tower riding up the Church – but the Church Wardens and the village objected to this – and were altogether rather alarmed at the idea of a horse being put in church.' Fortunately for the Horners they had their own private chapel into which they were just able to squeeze the statue. There it stands, 'the bareheaded saintly young horseman, an Arthurian knight from the pages of Tennyson, riding out on his charger'.[48]

At the same time as she found expression for her private grief and loss, Frances, like Mary Wemyss, was dedicating other memorials in the area, opening fêtes to raise the necessary money. At the village of Orchardleigh she spoke of the importance of all the memorials, and the names contained on them: the men who 'gave us our liberties – they gave us all that makes life fair and desirable – and besides this I think they stirred the nation to a deeper sense of its needs – to a higher standard of service and responsibility.'

The writer Maurice Hewlett attended the dedication of the cross in his Wiltshire village of Broad Chalk:

> Eighteen out of ninety of our young men did not come back; and now we have their names as nearly imperishable as may be, and much more so than the poor faithful dust strewn in France, or the gentle memories which will last no longer than ourselves.[49]

References

Introduction

1 Siegfried Sassoon, *The Weald of Youth* (London, 1942), p. 276.
2 Ibid., p. 278.
3 Rupert Brooke, 'An Unusual Young Man', *Letters from America* (London, 1931), p. 177.
4 Ibid., p. 178.
5 Ibid., pp. 179–180.
6 Helen Thomas, *Time and Again* (Manchester, 1978), p. 95.
7 Edward Thomas, 'This England', *The Last Sheaf* (London, 1928), p. 221.
8 Eleanor Farjeon, *Edward Thomas The Last Four Years* (Oxford, 1979), p. 154.
9 Laurence Housman (ed.), *War Letters of Fallen Englishmen* (London, 1930), p. 68.
10 Ibid., p. 22.
11 Ronald Blythe, *Akenfield* (Harmondsworth, 1972), p. 42.
12 John Masefield, 'August 1914'.
13 Edward Thomas, 'England', *The Last Sheaf*, p. 108.
14 Ibid., p. 109.
15 Paul Fussell, *The Great War and Modern Memory* (Oxford, 1977), p. 155.
16 Ibid., p. 168.
17 Robert Bridges, *The Spirit of Man* (London, 1916), preface.
18 *The Journals of George Sturt 1890–1927*, (ed.) E. D. Mackerness (Cambridge, 1967), Vol. II, p. 702.
19 Meirion and Susie Harries, *The War Artists* (London, 1983), p. 61.
20 John Galsworthy, 'The Islands of the Blessed', *A Sheaf* (London, 1916), pp. 291–2.

21 John Masefield, *St George and the Dragon* (London, 1918), pp. 4–7.
22 Siegfried Sassoon, *Memoirs of an Infantry Officer* (London, 1930), Part Four: Battle, I.
23 A. St John Adcock, *For Remembrance. Soldier Poets who have fallen in the war* (London, 1918), pp. 55–56.
24 Edmund Blunden, 'The Estrangement'.
25 Robert Saunders Papers, Imperial War Museum.
26 Clough Williams-Ellis, *England and the Octopus* (London, 1928), p. 20.

Chapter One

1 Stanway Papers: and see all further references to Stanway, Hugo and Mary Wemyss, Lord Elcho etc.
2 See M. Blunden, *The Countess of Warwick* (London, 1967), p. 245.
3 H. G. Wells, *Mr Britling Sees It Through* (London, 1916), p. 169.
4 Robert Saunders Papers: and see all further references to Fletching and Robert and Elsie Saunders.
5 Quentin Bell, *Virginia Woolf* (London, 1972), Vol. II, p. 20.
6 Rudyard Kipling Papers, University of Sussex.
7 Charles Adeane Papers: and see all further references to Babraham, Charles and Madeline Adeane etc.
8 Paul Nash, *Poet and Painter Being the correspondence between Gordon Bottomley and Paul Nash 1910–1946* (Oxford, 1955).
9 Mells Papers: and see all further references to Mells, Frances and Sir John Horner, Edward Horner etc.
10 See Pamela Horn, *Rural Life in England in the First World War* (Dublin, 1984), pp. 28–9.
11 Andrew Clark, *Echoes of the Great War. The Diary of the Reverend Andrew Clark 1914–1919*, ed. James Munson (Oxford, 1985): and see all further references to Great Leighs, the Rev. Andrew Clark etc.
12 Rudyard Kipling Papers.
13 Frank Palmer Cook Papers.
14 Herbert Asquith, *Moments of Memory* (London, 1937), p. 204.
15 Stanway Papers.
16 *Country Life*, 24.10.14.
17 See Jeanne Mackenzie, *The Children of the Souls* (London, 1986), p. 145.
18 Geoffrey and Arthur Dent Papers, Imperial War Museum.
19 Walter Spradbery Papers, Imperial War Museum.
20 Gordon Bartlett Papers, Imperial War Museum.

21   Ibid.
22   H. G. Wells, *Mr Britling Sees It Through*, p. 250.
23   Mary Cholmondeley, 'Polydore in England', *King Albert's Book* (London, 1914), p. 63.
24   *Country Life*, 28.11.14.
25   Siegfried Sassoon, *Diaries 1915–1918*, ed. Rupert Hart-Davis (London, 1983), p. 164.
26   Rudyard Kipling Papers.
27   Ibid.
28   Kenneth Grahame Papers, Bodleian Library Oxford. Elspeth Grahame to Courtauld Thompson, 29 December 1915; Kenneth Grahame to Austin Purves 18 February 1915.
29   Stanway Papers.
30   Diana Cooper, *The Rainbow Comes and Goes* (London, 1958), p. 137.
31   Robert Saunders Papers.
32   Frank Palmer Cook Papers.
33   Gordon Bartlett Papers.
34   See Cate Haste, *Keep the Home Fires Burning. Propaganda in the First World War* (London, 1977), p. 111.
35   Edward Thomas, 'It's a Long, Long Way', *The Last Sheaf*, p. 140.
36   William Rothenstein, *Men and Memories* (London, 1934), Vol. II, p. 288.

Chapter Two

1   Catherine Abercrombie, 'Memories of a Poet's Wife', *The Listener*, 15.11.56.
2   Robert Frost, *Selected Letters*, ed. Lawrance Thompson (London, 1965), p. 448.
3   Lawrance Thompson, *Robert Frost The Early Years 1874–1915* (New York, 1966), p. 448.
4   Edward Thomas, 'This England', *The Last Sheaf*, p. 216.
5   Eleanor Farjeon, *Edward Thomas The Last Four years*, pp. 94–5.
6   Edward Marsh Papers, Berg Collection, New York Public Library.
7   Robert Frost, *Selected Letters*, p. 131.
8   Ibid.
9   Edward Marsh Papers.
10   Ibid.
11   Ibid.
12   Ibid.

13 Edward Thomas, 'War Poets', *Poetry and Drama* (London, 1914), Vol. II, no. 8, pp. 341–5.
14 Edward Thomas Papers, Dartmouth College Library.
15 John Freeman, 'Happy is England Now'.
16 Christopher Hassall, *Rupert Brooke A Biography* (London, 1964), p. 517.
17 Ivor Gurney, *War Letters*, ed. R. K. R. Thornton (London, 1984), p. 232.
18 Edward Marsh Papers.
19 Ibid.
20 Catherine Abercrombie, 'Memories of a Poet's Wife'.
21 Robert Frost, *Selected Letters*, p. 136.
22 Ibid., p. 142.
23 Lawrance Thompson, *Robert Frost The Early Years*, p. 468.
24 Michael Hurd, *The Ordeal of Ivor Gurney* (Oxford, 1978), p. 63.
25 Edward Marsh Papers.
26 J. E. Gethyn-Jones, *Dymock Down the Ages* (Dymock, 1966), p. 111.
27 A. St John Adcock, *For Remembrance*, p. 162.
28 J. E. Gethyn-Jones, *Dymock, Down the Ages*, p. 86.
29 W. W. Gibson, 'The Question'.
30 Edward Marsh Papers.
31 John Drinkwater, 'The Patriot'.
32 William Rothenstein, *Men and Memories*, pp. 324–5.
33 Edward Thomas, 'Gone, Gone Again'.
34 Edward Thomas, 'The Cherry Trees'.
35 Edward Thomas, Dartmouth Letter Collection.
36 Robert Frost, *Selected Letters*, p. 193.
37 Edward Thomas, 'The Manor Farm' and 'Haymaking'.
38 Edward Thomas, Dartmouth Letter Collection.
39 *Country Life*, 30.10.15.
40 D. H. Lawrence, *Collected Letters*, ed. Harry T. Moore (London, 1962), p. 349.
41 Sandra Jobson Darroch, *Ottoline* (London, 1976), p. 161.
42 David Garnett, 'War Victims Relief', *We Did Not Fight*, ed. Julian Bell (London, 1935), p. 133.
43 Frances Spalding, *Vanessa Bell* (London, 1983), p. 147.
44 David Garnett, *The Flowers of the Forest* (London, 1955), p. 113.
45 Frances Spalding, *Vanessa Bell*, p. 150.
46 Ibid., p. 147.
47 Ibid., p. 151.
48 David Garnett, *The Flowers of the Forest*, p. 116.
49 Quentin Bell, *Virginia Woolf*, Vol. II, p. 32.

50 Frances Spalding, *Vanessa Bell*, p. 156.
51 Ibid., p. 164.
52 David Garnett, *The Flowers of the Forest*, p. 140.
53 *The Guardian*, 27.1.80.
54 David Garnett, *The Flowers of the Forest*, p. 142.
55 Sandra Jobson Darroch, *Ottoline*, p. 214.
56 Leonard Woolf, *An Autobiography* (Oxford, 1980), vol. 2, p. 143.
57 D. H. Lawrence, *Collected Letters*.
58 Harry T. Moore, *The Priest of Love* (Harmondworth, 1976), p. 323.
59 D. H. Lawrence, *Collected Letters*.
60 Harry T. Moore, *The Priest of Love*, p. 359.
61 Meirion and Susie Harries, *The War Artists* (London, 1983), p. 1.
62 Siegfried Sassoon, *Siegfried's Journey* (London, 1945), p. 20.
63 Ibid., p. 7.
64 Ibid., p. 10.
65 Ibid., p. 12.
66 Ibid., p. 12.
67 Ibid., p. 14.
68 Siegfried Sassoon, *Memoirs of an Infantry Officer*, Part Five, III.
69 Ibid., Part Five, IV.
70 Siegfried Sassoon, *Diaries 1915–1918*, p. 167.
71 Siegfried Sassoon, *Memoirs of an Infantry Officer*, Part Ten, IV.
72 Ibid.
73 Anthony Powell, *The Strangers All Are Gone* (London, 1982), Chapter 2.
74 Frank Palmer Cook Papers.
75 Angus Wilson, *The Strange Ride of Rudyard Kipling* (London, 1977), pp. 299–300.
76 Rudyard Kipling Papers.
77 Ibid.
78 Ibid.
79 Ibid.
80 Ibid.
81 Charles Carrington, *Rudyard Kipling His Life and Work* (1st published 1955), Chapter 15.
82 Rudyard Kipling Papers.
83 Dorothy Ponton, *Kipling at Home* (Southend, 1942), pp. 5–7.
84 Rudyard Kipling Papers.
85 Ibid.

Chapter Three

1   Stanway Papers: and see all further references to Stanway, Hugo and Mary Wemyss, Lord Elcho etc.
2   *Country Life*, 25.11.16.
3   Mells Papers: and see all further references to Mells, Frances and Sir John Horner, Edward Horner etc.
4   Gosford Papers.
5   *The Times*, 29.7.14.
6   *Somerset Standard*, 4.12.14.
7   Ibid., 5.3.15.
8   Charles Adeane Papers: and see all further references to Babraham, Charles and Madeline Adeane.
9   Cynthia Asquith, *Diaries 1915–1918* (London, 1968), p. 62.
10 Ibid.
11 Gosford Papers.
12 Cynthia Asquith, Diaries 1915–1918.
13 Miss Letitia Fowler: personal memoir.
14 Cynthia Asquith, *Diaries 1915–1918*.
15 Ibid.
16 Stanway Papers.
17 Cynthia Asquith, *Diaries 1915–1918*.
18 Ibid.
19 John Jolliffe, *Raymond Asquith. Life and Letters* (London, 1980).
20 Miss Pansy Helps: personal memoir.
21 Ibid.
22 F. E. Smith (Lord Birkenhead), 'Edward Horner', reprinted in *Time Remembered* by Frances Horner (London, 1933), p. 370: included in Mells Papers.
23 Cynthia Asquith, *Diaries 1915–1918*.
24 Ibid.
25 Ibid.
26 Ibid.
27 Ibid.

Chapter Four

1   *The Diary of the Reverend Andrew Clark*: and see all further references to Great Leighs, Rev. Andrew Clark etc.

2 Robert Saunders Papers: and see all further references to Fletching, Robert and Elsie Saunders.
3 *Somerset Standard*, 26.3.15; 9.7.15.
4 Miss Lucas Papers, Imperial War Museum.
5 Ibid.
6 Albert Copps Papers.
7 *The Diary of the Reverend Andrew Clark.*
8 Lyn Macdonald, *Somme* (London, 1983), p. 300.
9 *Somerset Standard*, 7.5.15.
10 *The Field*, 19.6.15.
11 Walter Spradbery Papers.
12 *Country Life*, 8.5.15.
13 John Moore, *Portrait of Elmbury* (London, 1945), p. 47.
14 H. G. Wells, *Mr Britling Sees It Through*, p. 248.
15 *The Diary of the Reverend Andrew Clark.*
16 Pamela Horn, *Rural Life in England in the First World War*, p. 192.
17 See Pamela Horn, p. 190.
18 *Somerset Standard*, 28.5.15.
19 Ibid.
20 *The Diary of the Reverend Andrew Clark.*

Chapter Five

1 See Cate Haste, *Keep the Home Fires Burning* (London, 1977), p. 44. Sheila Kaye-Smith, *Little England* (London, 1918), p. 251.
2 *Country Life.*
3 John Moore, *Portrait of Elmbury*, p. 44.
4 A. G. Street, *Farmer's Glory* (London, 1963), p. 35.
5 Pamela Horn, *Rural Life in England in the First World War*, p. 7.
6 Ronald Blythe, *Akenfield*, p. 41.
7 William Rothenstein, *Men and Memories*, Vol. 1, pp. 276–7.
8 T. H. Middleton, *Food Production in War* (Oxford, 1923), p. 2.
9 Ibid., p. 107.
10 See Pamela Horn, *Rural Life in England in the First World War*, p. 4.
11 Ibid., pp. 86–7.
12 Ibid., p. 90.
13 Albert Copps Papers.
14 *The Diary of the Reverend Andrew Clark.*
15 T. H. Middleton, *Food Production in War*, pp. 119–120.

16   See Pamela Horn, *Rural Life in England in the First World War*, pp. 48–9.
17   T. H. Middleton, *Food Production in War*, pp. 137–8.
18   See Pamela Horn, *Rural Life in England in the First World War*, pp. 76–7.
19   *Country Life*, 11.3.16.
20   *The Diary of the Reverend Andrew Clark.*
21   *Country Life*, 5.6.15.
22   Robert Saunders Papers.
23   Pamela Horn, *Rural Life in England in the First World War*, p. 79.
24   Sheila Kaye-Smith, *Little England*, p. 7; p. 33.
25   Albert Copps Papers.
26   See Pamela Horn, *Rural Life in England in the First World War*, p. 78.
27   T. H. Middleton, *Food Production in War*, p. 141.
28   Ibid., p. 143.
29   See Pamela Horn, *Rural Life in England in the First World War*, p. 120.
30   Rudyard Kipling Papers.
31   Edith Airey Papers, Imperial War Museum.
32   Charles Adeane Papers: and see all further references to Babraham, Charles and Madeline Adeane.
33   See Pamela Horn, *Rural Life in England in the First World War*, p. 9.
34   Ibid., p. 97.
35   Ibid.
36   Rudyard Kipling Papers.
37   T. H. Middleton, *Food Production in War*, pp. 156–7.
38   Ibid., p. 165.
39   DORA: Defence of the Realm Consolidation Act, Regulation 2M 'for the issue of Orders relating to ordinating agricultural land'.
40   *Illustrated London News*, 13.10.17. Rudyard Kipling wrote to H. Rider Haggard in February 1918: 'all the Government Departments make us their sport with regulations after regulations. It's a mad world.' *The Record of a Friendship*, ed. Morton Cohen (New Jersey, 1965), p. 97.
41   T. H. Middleton, *Food Production in War*, pp. 181–2.
42   See Pamela Horn, *Rural Life in England in the First World War*, p. 78.
43   *Country Life*, February 1917.
44   Pamela Horn, *Rural Life in England in the First World War*, p. 100.
45   *The Handbook of the W.L.A.*, Papers of Mrs Mazey, Imperial War Museum.
46   Ibid.
47   Rosa Freedman Papers, Imperial War Museum.
48   Ibid.
49   Ibid.

50   Doris Odlum Papers, Imperial War Museum.
51   Douglas Maynard Papers, Imperial War Museum.
52   Charles Adeane Papers.
53   *The Diary of the Reverend Andrew Clark.*
54   Sheila Kaye-Smith, *Little England*, p. 179.
55   T. H. Middleton, *Food Production in War*, pp. 268–9.
56   See Pamela Horn, *Rural Life in England in the First World War*, p. 84.
57   T. H. Middleton, *Food Production in War*, p. 239.
58   Ibid., p. 318.

Chapter Six

1   A. St John Adcock, *For Remembrance*, p. 148.
2   Robert Saunders Papers.
3   Laurence Houseman (ed.), *War Letters of Fallen Englishmen*, p. 22.
4   John Jolliffe, *Raymond Asquith, Life and Letters.*
5   Siegfried Sassoon, *Diaries 1915–1918*, p. 24.
6   Laurence Housman, *War Letters of Fallen Englishmen*, p. 216.
7   John Masefield, *Letters from the Front 1915–1917*, ed. by Peter Vansittart (London, 1984), p. 53.
8   Ibid., p. 204.
9   Charles Edmonds, *A Subaltern's War* (London, 1984), pp. 96–7.
10   Rudyard Kipling Papers.
11   Paul Nash, *Outline an autobiography and other writings* (London, 1949), p. 202.
12   Laurence Housman, *War Letters of Fallen Englishmen*, pp. 98–9.
13   Geoffrey and Arthur Dent Papers.
14   *Country Life*, January 1916.
15   Geoffrey Dent Papers.
16   Edward Marsh Papers.
17   Siegfried Sassoon Papers, Imperial War Museum.
18   Ibid.
19   Ibid.
20   Ibid.
21   *Country Life*, January 1916.
22   John Jolliffe, *Raymond Asquith, Life and Letters.*
23   See Paul Fussell, *The Great War and Modern Memory*, p. 234.
24   Laurence Housman, *War Letters of Fallen Englishmen*, p. 111.
25   Edward Marsh Papers.

26 Frank Palmer Cook Papers.

27 Paul Nash, *Outline*, p. 198.

28 John Drinkwater, 'The Midlands'.

29 Ivor Gurney, *War Letters*, ed. R. K. R. Thornton (London, 1984).

30 E. B. Osborn, *The New Elizabethans. A first selection of the lives of young men who have fallen in the Great War* (London, 1919), p. 5.

31 Siegfried Sassoon, *Memoirs of an Infantry Officer*, Part Four: I.

32 Ivor Gurney, *War Letters*.

33 John Jolliffe, *Raymond Asquith*.

34 Edmund Blunden, *Undertones of War* (London, 1928), p. 266.

35 Paul Nash, *Outline*, pp. 195–6.

36 See Paul Fussell, *The Great War and Modern Memory*, p. 241.

37 Siegfried Sassoon, *Diaries 1915–1918*, p. 26.

38 Lyn Macdonald, *Somme*, p. 27.

39 Malcolm Brown, *Tommy Goes to War*, p. 246.

40 Ibid., p. 247.

41 Laurence Housman, *War Letters of Fallen Englishmen*, p. 68.

42 A. St John Adcock, *For Remembrance*, p. 148.

43 Ibid.

44 Laurence Housman, *War Letters of Fallen Englishmen*, p. 164.

45 Michael Hurd, *The Ordeal of Ivor Gurney* (Oxford, 1978), pp. 72–3.

46 Ibid., p. 98.

47 Brocard Sewell (ed.), *Henry Williamson, the Man, the Writings* (Padstow, 1980), xiii.

48 Henry Williamson, *The Beautiful Years*, *The Flax of Dream* (London, 1936), p. 28.

49 John Masefield, *Letters from the Front*, p. 263.

50 See Pamela Horn, *Rural Life in England in the First World War*, p. 116.

51 Ibid., p. 137.

52 Frank Palmer Cook Papers.

53 Laurence Houseman, *War Letters of Fallen Englishmen*, p. 230.

54 Edward Thomas, *The Diary of Edward Thomas 1 January – 8 April 1917* (Andoversford, 1977), p. 24.

55 Geoffrey Dent Papers.

56 Rudyard Kipling Papers.

57 Frank Palmer Cook Papers.

58 Charles Adeane Papers.

59 C. Hassall, *Edward Marsh* (London, 1959), p. 328.

60 Paul Nash, *Outline*, p. 211.

61 Eleanor Farjeon, *Edward Thomas The Last Four Years*, pp. 263–4.

62 Ibid., p. 264.
63 Joseph Cohen, *Journey to the Trenches, The Life of Isaac Rosenberg 1890–1918* (London, 1975).
64 Rudyard Kipling Papers.
65 John Jolliffe, *Raymond Asquith, Life and Letters*.
66 Mells Papers.

Chapter Seven

1 William Orpen, *An Onlooker in France 1917–1919* (London, 1924), p. 36.
2 Edwin Lutyens, *The Letters of Edwin Lutyens*, ed. by Clayre Percy and Jane Ridley (London, 1985), p. 350.
3 Philip Longworth, *The Unending Vigil* (London, 1985), p. 21.
4 Ibid., p. 74.
5 Ibid., p. 33.
6 Ibid.
7 Ibid., pp. 31–2.
8 Ibid., p. 48.
9 Ibid., p. 52.
10 *Illustrated Michelin Guides to the Battle-Field* (1914–1918), 15 volumes; The Somme (1919), p. 11.
11 Mells Papers: and see all further references to Mells, Frances and Sir John Horner.
12 *The Times*, 2.9.20.
13 Fabian Ware, *The Immortal Heritage* (Cambridge, 1937), introduction, p. 18, by Edmund Blunden.
14 Oliver Rackham, *The History of the Countryside* (London, 1986), p. 233.
15 Henry Williamson, *The Wet Flanders Plain* (London, 1929), pp. 96–7.
16 Stanway Papers: and see all further references to Stanway, Hugo and Mary Wemyss.
17 Cynthia Asquith, *Haply I May Remember* (London, 1950), p. 38.
18 Ibid.
19 Nora Osborne: personal memoir.
20 Cynthia Asquith, *Portrait of Barrie* (London, 1954), p. 149.
21 Ibid.
22 Wyndham family papers.
23 See Pamela Horn, *Rural Life in England in the First World War*, p. 206.
24 Imperial War Museum.
25 John Buchan, *Memory-Hold-the-Door* (London, 1940), pp. 190–1.

26 John Buchan, *Mr Standfast* (London, 1919), Chapter 1.
27 Jesse Collings, *The Great War: Its Lessons and Its Warnings* (London, 1915), pp. 10–11.
28 *Country Life*, 8.5.15.
29 Imperial War Museum.
30 Ibid.
31 Ibid.
32 Scottish Veterans Garden City Association Papers.
33 F. M. L. Thompson, *English Landed Society in the Nineteenth Century* (London, 1963), p. 326.
34 Ibid., p. 329.
35 Daisy Warwick, *Afterthoughts* (London, 1931), p. 241.
36 Jonathan Guinness with Catherine Guinness, *The House of Mitford* (London, 1985), p. 102.
37 See Nicholas Mosley, *Julian Grenfell* (London, 1976), p. 267.
38 Pamela Horn, *Rural Life in England in the First World War*.
39 Angela Forbes, *Memories and Base Details* (London, 1921), pp. 305–6.
40 Siegfried Sassoon Papers, Berg Collection, New York Public Library.
41 Robert Graves, *Goodbye to all That* (London, 1929), Chapter 29.
42 Ibid.
43 Pamela Horn, *Rural Life in England in the First World War*, p. 231.
44 Rudyard Kipling Papers.
45 *The Diary of the Reverend Andrew Clark*.
46 Poem included in Frank Palmer Cook papers.
47 Edwin Lutyens, *The Letters*, p. 372.
48 Anthony Powell, *The Strangers All Are Gone*, Chapter 2.
49 Maurice Hewlett, 'We Commend Our Dead', *Wiltshire Essays* (Oxford, 1921), p. 210.

Bibliography

ABDY, JANE AND CHARLOTTE GERE, *The Souls* (London, 1984).

ABERCROMBIE, CATHERINE, 'Memories of a Poet's Wife', *The Listener*, 15.11.56.

ADCOCK, A. ST JOHN, *For Remembrance. Soldier Poets who have fallen in the war* (London, 1918).

ANDREWS, I. O., *Economic Effects of the War upon Women and Children in Great Britain* (Oxford, 1918).

ASLET, CLIVE, *The Last Country Houses* (London, 1982).

ASQUITH, CYNTHIA, *Haply I May Remember* (London, 1950).

— *Remember and Be Glad* (London, 1952).

— *Portrait of Barrie* (London, 1954).

— *Diaries 1915–1918* (London, 1968).

ASQUITH, HERBERT, *The Volunteer and other poems* (London, 1915).

— *Moments of Memory* (London, 1937).

AUGÉ-LARIBÉ, *L'Agriculture pendant La Guerre* (New Haven, 1925).

BATEMAN, JOHN, *The Great Landowners of Great Britain and Ireland* (London, 1971).

BELL, JULIEN (ed.), *We did not Fight 1914–18. Experiences of War Resisters* (London, 1935).

BELL, QUENTIN, *Virginia Woolf* (London 1971–2), 2 vols.

BLYTHE, RONALD, *Akenfield* (Harmondsworth, 1972).

BLUNDEN, EDMUND, *Undertones of War* (London, 1928).

BLUNDEN, MARGARET, *The Countess of Warwick* (London, 1967).

BOTTOMLEY, GORDON, *Poet and Painter being the correspondence between Gordon Bottomley and Paul Nash 1910–1946*, ed. C. C. Abbott & A. Bertram (Oxford, 1955).

BRIDGES, ROBERT, *The Spirit of Man* (London, 1916).

BROOKE, RUPERT, *Letters from America* (London, 1931).
— *The Poetical Works of Rupert Brooke* (London, 1970).
BROWN, MALCOLM, *Tommy Goes to War* (London, 1978).
BUCHAN, JOHN, *Mr Standfast* (London, 1919).
— *Memory-Hold-the-Door* (London, 1940).
CARRINGTON, CHARLES, *Rudyard Kipling His Life and Work* (Harmondsworth, 1970).
CAUSEY, ANDREW, *Paul Nash* (Oxford, 1980).
CECIL, DAVID, *Max* (London, 1983).
CLARK, ANDREW, *Echoes of the Great War. The Diary of the Reverend Andrew Clark 1914–1919*, ed. James Munson (Oxford, 1985).
COLLINGS, JESSE, *The Great War: Its Lessons and Its Warnings* (London, 1915).
COOPER, DIANA, *The Rainbow Comes and Goes* (London, 1958).
CURL, JAMES STEVENS, *A Celebration of Death* (London, 1980).
DARROCH, SANDRA JOBSON, *Ottoline* (London, 1976).
DEARLE, N. B., *An Economic Chronicle of the Great War for Great Britain and Ireland 1914–1917* (Oxford, 1929).
DRINKWATER, JOHN, *Loyalties* (London, 1919).
— *Seeds of Time* (London, 1921).
— *Patriotism in Literature* (London, 1924).
DUNBAR, JANET, *J. M. Barrie The Man behind the Image* (London, 1970).
EDMONDS, CHARLES, *A Subaltern's War* (London, 1984).
FARJEON, ELEANOR, *Edward Thomas The Last Four Years* (Oxford, 1958).
FIELDING-HALL, H., *The Field of Honour* (London, 1915).
— *For England* (London, 1916).
FISHER, H. A.L., *A History of Europe* (London, 1960), 2 vols.
FORBES, ANGELA, *Memories and Base Details* (London, 1921).
— *Fore and Aft* (London, 1932).
FUSSELL, PAUL, *The Great War and Modern Memory* (Oxford, 1975).
GALSWORTHY, JOHN, *A Sheaf* (London, 1916).
GARNETT, DAVID, *The Golden Echo* (London, 1954).
— *The Flowers of the Forest* (London, 1955).
Georgian Poetry, ed. Edward Marsh (London, 1912–1922), 5 vols.
GETHYN-JONES, REV. J. E., *Dymock Down the Ages* (Dymock, 1966).
GIBSON, WILFRID, *Poems* (London, 1931).
— *Solway Ford and other poems* (London, 1945).
GIROUARD, MARK, *The Return to Camelot. Chivalry and the English Gentleman* (London, 1981).
GRADIDGE, RODERICK, *Dream Houses* (London, 1980).

GRANT, JOY, *Harold Monro and the Poetry Bookshop* (London, 1967).

GRAVES, ROBERT, *Over the Brazier* (London, 1916).

— *Goodbye to all That* (London, 1929).

GREEN, PETER, *Kenneth Grahame 1859–1932 A study of his life, work and times* (London, 1959).

GRENFELL, ETTIE, *Pages from a Family Journal* (Eton, 1916).

GUINNESS, JONATHAN AND CATHERINE GUINNESS, *The House of Mitford* (London, 1985).

GURNEY, IVOR, *War Letters*, ed. R. K. R. Thornton (London, 1984).

— *Collected Poems* (Oxford, 1984).

HARRIES, MEIRION & SUSIE, *The War Artists* (London, 1983).

HASSALL, CHRISTOPHER, *Edward Marsh* (London, 1959).

— *Rupert Brooke* (London, 1963).

HASTE, CATE, *Keep the Home Fires Burning. Propaganda in the First World War* (London, 1977).

HASTINGS, MICHAEL, *The Handsomest Young Man in England. Rupert Brooke* (London, 1960).

HEWLETT, MAURICE, *Wiltshire Essays* (Oxford, 1921).

HOLROYD, MICHAEL, *Lytton Strachey* (London, 1967–8).

HORN, PAMELA, *Rural Life in England in the First World War* (Dublin, 1984).

HORNER, FRANCES, *Time Remembered* (London, 1933).

HOUSMAN, LAURENCE (ed.), *War Letters of Fallen Englishmen* (London, 1930).

HURD, MICHAEL, *The Ordeal of Ivor Gurney* (Oxford, 1978).

HUSSEY, CHRISTOPHER, *The Life of Sir Edwin Lutyens* (London, 1950).

— *Inscriptions suggested for war memorials* (London, 1919).

JACKSON, STANLEY, *The Sassoons* (London, 1968).

JENKINS, ROY, *Asquith* (London, 1978).

JOLLIFFE, JOHN (ed.), *Raymond Asquith Life and Letters* (London, 1980).

KAYE-SMITH, SHEILA, *Little England* (London, 1918).

— *King Albert's Book* (London, 1914).

KIPLING, RUDYARD, *Something of Myself* (London, 1937).

— *The English in England* (New York, 1963).

— *The Record of a Friendship* (New Jersey, 1965).

LAMBERT, ANGELA, *Unquiet Souls* (London, 1984).

LAWRENCE, D. H., *Women in Love* (Harmondsworth, 1961).

— *Lady Chatterley's Lover* (Harmondsworth, 1961).

— *Collected Letters*, ed. Harry T. Moore (London, 1962), 2 vols.

LETTS, W. M., *Hallow-e'en and poems of the war* (London, 1916).

LIDDIARD, JEAN, *Isaac Rosenberg: the Half Used Life* (London, 1975).

LONGWORTH, PHILIP, *The Unending Vigil* (London, 1985).

LUTYENS, EDWIN, *The Letters of Edwin Lutyens to his wife Lady Emily*, ed. Clayre Percy & Jane Ridley (London, 1985).

LUTYENS, EDWIN, *The Work of the English architect Sir Edwin Lutyens* (London, 1981).

MACDONALD, LYN, *Somme* (London, 1983).

MACKENZIE, JEANNE, *The Children of the Souls. A tragedy of the First World War* (London, 1986).

MARSH, JAN, *Edward Thomas A Poet for his Country* (London, 1978).

MARWICK, ARTHUR, *The Deluge British Society and the First World War* (London, 1965).

MASEFIELD, JOHN, *Gallipoli* (London, 1916).

— *St George and the Dragon* (London, 1918).

— *Collected Poems* (London, 1934).

— *Letters from the Front 1915–1917*, ed. Peter Vansittart (London, 1984).

MICHELIN, *Illustrated Michelin Guides to the Battle-Field* (1914–1918) (1919), 15 vols.

MIDDLETON, T. H., *Food Production in War* (Oxford, 1923).

MITCHELL, DAVID, *Women on the Warpath. The story of the women of the First World War* (London, 1968).

MONTGOMERY, J. K., *The Maintenance of the Agricultural Labour Supply in England and Wales during the War* (Rome, 1922).

MOORE, HARRY T., *The Priest of Love* (Harmondsworth, 1976).

MOORE, JOHN, *Portrait of Elmbury* (London, 1945).

MOSLEY, NICHOLAS, *Julian Grenfell* (New York, 1976).

NASH, PAUL, *Outline: An autobiography and other writings* (London, 1949).

ORPEN, WILLIAM, *An Onlooker in France 1917–1919* (London, 1924).

OSBORN, E. B., *The New Elizabethans. A first selection of the lives of young men who have fallen in the Great War* (London, 1919).

PLAYNE, Caroline, *Society at War 1914–1916* (London, 1931).

PONTON, DOROTHY, *Kipling at Home* (Southern, 1942).

POUND, REGINALD, *The Lost Generation* (London, 1964).

POWELL, ANTHONY, *The Strangers All Are Gone* (London, 1982).

PUNCH, *Mr Punch's History of the Great War* (London, 1919).

RACKHAM, OLIVER, *The History of the Countryside* (London, 1986).

REILLY, CATHERINE (ed.), *Scars upon my Heart* (London, 1981).

ROSS, ROBERT H., *The Georgian Revolt* (London, 1967).

ROTHENSTEIN, WILLIAM, *Men and Memories 1872–1922* (London, 1934), 2 vols.

RUSSELL, BERTRAND, *The Autobiography of Bertrand Russell* (London, 1968), vol. 2, 1914–1944.

SANDERS & TAYLOR, *British Propaganda during the First World War* (London, 1982).

SASSOON, SIEGFRIED, *Memoirs of a Foxhunting Man* (London, 1928).

— *Memoirs of an Infantry Officer* (London, 1930).

— *Sherston's Progress* (London, 1936).

— *The Old Century and Seven More Years* (London, 1938).

— *The Weald of Youth* (London, 1942).

— *Siegfried's Journey* (London, 1945).

— *Collected Poems* (London, 1947).

— *Diaries 1915–1918*, ed. Rupert Hart-Davis (London, 1983).

SEWELL, BROCARD (ed.), *Henry Williamson, the Man, the Writings* (Padstow, 1980).

SEYMOUR-SMITH, MARTIN, *Robert Graves: His Life and Work* (London, 1982).

SMITH, JANET ADAM, *John Buchan* (London, 1965).

SPALDING, FRANCES, *Vanessa Bell* (London, 1983).

STAMP, GAVIN, *Silent Cities* (London, 1977).

STEVENSON, JOHN, *British Society 1914–1945* (Harmondsworth, 1984).

STONE, GILBERT (ed.), *Women War Workers* (London, 1917).

STREET, A. G., *Farmer's Glory* (Oxford, 1983).

STURT, GEORGE, *The Journals of George Sturt 1890–1927*, ed. E. D. Mackerness (Cambridge, 1967), 2 vols.

SYKES, CHRISTOPHER, *Nancy* (London, 1972).

TAYLOR, A. J. P., *The First World War* (Harmondsworth, 1966).

— *English History 1914–1945* (Harmondsworth, 1970).

TERRAINE, JOHN, *Impacts of War 1914 and 1918* (London, 1970).

— *The First World War 1914–18* (London, 1984).

THOMAS, EDWARD, *The Last Sheaf* (London, 1928).

— *Collected Poems* (London, 1969).

— *The Diary of Edward Thomas 1 January–8 April 1917* (Andoversfor 1977).

THOMAS, HELEN, *As It Was and World without End* (London, 1972).

— *Time and Again*, ed. Myfanwy Thomas (Manchester, 1978).

THOMPSON, F. M. L., *English Landed Society in the Nineteenth Century* (London, 1980).

TUCHMANN, BARBARA, *August 1914* (London, 1962).

TURNER, E. S., *Dear Old Blighty* (London, 1980).

VANSITTART, PETER (ed.), *Voices from the Great War* (Harmondsworth, 1983).

VELLACOTT, JO, *Bertrand Russell and the Pacifists in the First World War* (Brighton, 1980).

VENN, J. A., *The Foundations of Agricultural Economics* (London, 1933).

WARE, FABIAN, *The Immortal Heritage* (Cambridge, 1937).

WARWICK, DAISY, *A Woman and the war* (London, 1916).
— *Afterthoughts* (London, 1931).
WATERSON, MERLIN (ed.), *The Country House Remembered* (London, 1985).
WELLS, H. G., *Mr Britling Sees It Through* (London, 1916).
WEMYSS, MARY COUNTESS OF, *Family Record* (London, 1932).
WEST, ANTHONY, H. G. WELLS, *Aspects of Life* (London, 1984).
Whitaker's Peerage, Baronetage, Knightage and Companionage (London, 1920).
WILLIAMS-ELLIS, CLOUGH, *England and the Octopus* (London, 1928).
WILLIAMSON, HENRY, *Tarka the Otter* (London, 1927).
— *The Wet Flanders Plain* (London, 1929).
— *The Beautiful years, The Flax of Dream* (London, 1936).
WILSON, ANGUS, *The Strange Ride of Rudyard Kipling* (London, 1979).
WOLH, ROBERT, *The Generation of 1914* (London, 1980).
WOOLF, LEONARD, *An Autobiography* (Oxford, 1980), 2 vols.
WOOLF, VIRGINIA, *The Diary of Virginia Woolf*, ed. Anne Olivier Bell (Harmondsworth, 1979), vol. I, 1915–1919.

Index

Abercrombie, Catherine, 47, 49, 50, 51, 53
Abercrombie, Lascelles, 12, 47, 48, 49, 50,
   51–3, 57, 67, 168; 'Ryton Firs', 53
Aberlady (East Lothian), 76, 79, 93, 104;
   village school, 80; war memorial, 207–8
Adeane, Charles, 23–4, 27, 28, 29, 32, 42,
   46, 86, 103, 144, 146, 147–8, 178
Adeane, Helena, 42, 103
Adeane, Madeline, 40, 90, 95
Adeane, Pamela, 35, 89, 102, 103
Adeane, Robert, 24
Agny cemetery, Thomas's grave in, 181
agricultural camps (for PoWs), 153
agricultural machinery, 19, 153–4
agricultural training for ex-servicemen, 204
Agricultural Relief of Allies Fund, 178–9
air raids, Zeppelin, 43, 61, 112–15, 120,
   153–4
Airey, Edith, 142
Aisne, Battle of the (1914), 41, 77
Aitken, Charles, 184
Alcock, Alfred, 95
Alcock, Mrs, schoolmistress, 90
Alefounder, 'Alix', hurdle-maker, 138
Allen, Revd, 88
Allingham, Helen, 16
Amesbury Abbey, 18
Amisfield (Wemyss Scottish mansion), 79;
   Army occupation of, 81–2, 203;
   demolition of (1923), 203–4
Ammerdown, 193
Apperly Women's Institute, 194
anthologies of poems and stories, 15, 50
Antrobus, Sir Edmund, 18
Armistice Day (11 Nov. 1918), 103–4, 129
Arras, 158, 176, 180; Battle of (1917), 17,
   59, 139, 173

Asheham village, 22
Ashurst Wood, 'Bramblehurst', 111–12
Asquith, H. H., Prime Minister, 25, 28, 38,
   46, 95, 109, 122, 146, 186
Asquith, Herbert ('Beb'), 25, 29–30, 78,
   87, 90–1, 102; '1916', 90–1; The
   Volunteer, 90; 'The Western Line,
   Flanders 1915', 76
Asquith, Mrs Herbert (née Cynthia
   Charteris), 25, 78, 87, 88, 89, 90–1, 92,
   94, 100, 101–2, 188, 190–1
Asquith, John, 90, 100
Asquith, Katharine, 100, 102, 160, 182,
   191, 209
Asquith, Michael, 90
Asquith, Raymond, 25, 26, 32, 41, 94–5,
   98, 100, 103, 159, 160, 165, 182, 186,
   187, 195, 209
Astor family, 37
Australian soldiers, 118; graves of, 185

Baber, Mr, chauffeur, 108
Babraham Hall (Cambs.), 23, 24, 28, 32,
   46, 86, 89, 90, 103, 144
'back to the land' movement, 49, 195
Baddeley, St Clair, 78
Bailleul convent hospital, Edward Horner
   in, 86
Baillie, Richard, 203
Baker, Amy, 143–4
Baker, Herbert, 184, 185
Baldwin, Stanley, 72
Balfour, Arthur, 26, 38, 81, 186
Balleul Road East Cemetery, 181
Barrie, J. M., 36, 190–1, 203
Barrington, Viscount and Viscountess, 193,
   197

Bartlett, Captain Gordon, 33, 44
Bateman's (Sussex), Kipling's estate, 28,
    39, 40, 73–5, 141, 145, 160
Bates, Captain, 125–6
Bates, Sir Edward, 82
Bates, Gilbert Thompson, 82, 96–7, 98
Bath, Marquis of, 36, 193
Batsford (Glos.), 201–2
Baumann, Fräulein, 32
Beauchamp, Lord, 46, 53
Bedford Square (No. 44), Morrell home, 59
The BEF Times, 167
Belgian refugees, 33–6, 83, 102, 176
Belgian soldiers, wounded, 36
Belgium, 170; agriculture, 177–8, 179; *see
    also* Western Front
Bell, Clive, 59, 60, 64, 66, 67
Bell, Sir Hugh, 197
Bell, Quentin, 63–4
Bell, Vanessa, 59, 60–4, 74
Bellingham, Joseph and Tom, 109
Bellingham, Mrs Joe, 109
Belton House, 33
Belvoir estate, 200
Bennett, Arnold, 177
Bentinck, Lord Henry, 23–4
Beyart, Mr and Mrs, 35
Blackwell, Major, 134
Blewbury (Bucks.), 40
Blomfield, Reginald, 187; 'Cross of
    Sacrifice', 186
Bloomsbury Group, 59–66, 67–8, 70, 74
Blumenfeld, R. D., 22
Blunden, Edmund, 18, 168, 170, 187;
    'Report on Experience', 179; 'Rural
    Economy', 170
Blunt, Wilfrid Scawen, 100–1
Blythe, Ronald, 14, 132
Blything Tribunal, 62
Board of Agriculture, 130, 137, 146; Food
    Production Department, 147–8, 156
Bonham-Carter, Violet, 95
Borton, Colonel and Mrs, 36
Bottomley, Gordon, 52
Boulogne, death of Julian Grenfell in, 86–7
Braintree, 128; air raids on, 112–13, 114
Brassey, Lord and Lady, 37, 69
bread rationing, 122–3
Bridges, Robert, 209; *The Spirit of Man*
    (anthology), 15
British Army: camps and billets, 29–30,
    31–2, 115–18, 127; casualties, 41–2, 95,
    101–2, 123, 124–9, 149, 171–2;

conscription, 23, 59, 61, 109, 126,
    138–9, 154–5; country houses made
    available to, 32–3, 79, 81–2, 115–17;
    disease and accidents, 31; equipment and
    clothing, 29; farm work by soldiers, 136,
    144–5, 149, 174; letters home, 42–3,
    111–12, 126–7; recruitment/enlistment,
    23–33, 38, 109–10, 132, 134–5, 136,
    139, 140; requisitioning of horses for, 43,
    133, 134; Territorials, 23–4, 31; Western
    Front, 158–74
British Army Units:
    Argyll and Sutherland Highlanders, 81
    Army Service Corps, 54, 118
    Artists' Rifles, 13, 57, 58
    Cambridgeshire Regiment, 14, 24, 158
    Coldstream Guards, 41, 116, 125; 2nd
        Battalion, 40
    6th Connaught Rangers, 172
    4th Dragoon Guards, 162
    3rd East Anglian Field Ambulance, 32, 118
    East Surrey Regiment, 28, 111
    Essex Regiment, 32, 33, 125, 128, 162
    Fifth Army, 155
    Foreign Service Battalion, 29
    Gloucestershire Yeomanry, 26, 81, 84,
        85, 92, 94
    3rd Gloucesters, 33
    5th Gloucesters, 167
    1st Grenadier Guards, 87
    Hampshire Regiment, 160
    15th Hussars, 25
    Irish Guards, 75, 160; 2nd Battalion, 72
    London Scottish, 208
    King's Royal Rifle Corps, 83, 87
    9th Lancers, 40
    16th Lancers, 110
    London Regiment Scottish Rifles, 14th
        Company, 45
    Lothians and Border Horse, 81
    Lowland Brigade, artillery section, 115
    10th Middlesex Regiment, 23
    North Somerset Yeomanry, 25, 26, 32,
        115, 125
    Royal Engineers, 29, 168, 175
    Royal Field Artillery, 13, 30, 126, 161
    Royal Fusiliers, London Battalion, 172
    Royal Horse Guards, 25
    Royal Marines Light Infantry, 125
    9th Royal Sussex Regiment, 171–2
    Royal Warwickshire Regiment, 160
    Seaforth Highlanders, First Garrison
        Battalion, 199

Shropshire Light Infantry, 30
1st Somerset Light Infantry, 39
4th Somerset Territorials, 35, 125
Sussex Yeomanry, 11
2nd Wiltshire Regiment, 42
Broad Chalk memorial, 210
Brooke, Rupert, 12, 13, 15, 17, 47, 49, 50, 51–2, 54, 55, 78, 168; death of, 50, 51, 179–80; *1914 and Other Poems*, 52; 'The Old Vicarage, Grantchester', 16, 168; 'The Soldier', 51, 168–9, 172, 179; 'An Unusual Young Man', 12; war sonnets, 15, 51
Brown, Major William, 114
Brownlow, Lord, 33
Buchan, John, 194–5; *Memory-Hold-The-Door*, 194; *Mr Standfast*, 195; *The Thirty-Nine Steps*, 45, 118
Buckmaster, Lady, 197
Burford (Cotswolds), 68–9
Burghley House, near Stamford, 32–3
Burne-Jones, Edward, 100
Burne-Jones, Philip, 90

Cadogan Square (No. 62), Wemyss' London home, 79, 190
Canadian Corps, 183
Canadian Red Cross, 37
Canadian soldiers, 116–17; graves, 185
Carrington, Dora, 59
Carver, Lieut., 13, 17
Castle Combe, 105–6
casualties, 41–2, 95, 101–2, 114, 122, 124–9, 149, 171–2; *see also* war graves
Cecil family, 32, 33
Cecil, Lady Frances, 186
Cecil, Lord Hugh, 33
censorship, 110–11, 112
Chapelwood Manor (Sussex), 37, 69–70
Charleston (Sussex), 63–4
Charteris, Bibs, 88, 89, 90, 92, 93, 208
Charteris, Cynthia *see* Asquith, Mrs Herbert
Charteris, David, 90, 91, 92, 94, 95, 208
Charteris, Ego, Lord Elcho, 25, 26, 77, 80, 81, 84–5, 91, 92, 93–5, 100, 188
Charteris, Evan, 90, 91
Charteris, Guy, 30, 92, 93, 95
Charteris, Letty (*née* Manners), 77, 88, 94, 203
Charteris, Martin, 90, 94, 208
Charteris, Mary *see* Strickland, Mary

Charteris, Yvo, 25, 26, 41, 77, 83–4, 87–8, 90, 91, 92, 93
Chaucer, Geoffrey, 57
Chelmsford, 113, 120
Chemin des Dames, French defeated at (1918), 155
Cheveney (Kent), 36
Cholmondeley, Mary, 34
Christmas: presents for the troops, 40; at Stanway, 46, 90–1; Tewkesbury Fair, 131
Christmas Day truce with Germans (1914), 174
Churchill, Winston, 23, 163
Churchward, Squire, 43
Clark, Revd Andrew, vicar of Great Leighs, 41, 106, 107, 110, 113–14, 116, 119, 120, 122, 123, 124–5, 126–7, 140, 207
Cliveden (Bucks.), 37
Clouds (Wilts.), 41, 77, 85–6, 89, 93, 203; chapel, 85; post-war, 192; as wartime convalescent home, 89–90
coal mining, 24, 107–8, 125, 198
Cobbett, William, 57
Coleridge, Samuel Taylor, 49
Collings, Jesse, *The Great War*, 195–6
Compleat Angler, 15
Conder, Charles, 60
Connor, George, 79–80, 81, 92, 199, 208
conscription, 23, 59, 61, 106, 109, 126, 138–9, 154–5; appeals tribunal, 61, 62, 138, 139; in France, 174–5
Contalmaison, Battle of (1916), 111–12
convalescent homes, country houses used as, 36–7, 89–90
Cook, Frank, 22–3, 29, 71, 168, 175, 177
Cookson, Mrs Agnes, 82–3
Cooper, Alfred Duff, 21, 26, 97, 189
Copps, Albert, 113, 134, 139, 206
Corn Production Act (1917), 147
Corn Production Act, repeal of (1921), 203
'corrupt coterie', 25
Coulson, Sgt Leslie, 158, 172
country houses/estates, 49, 77–104, 132, 195; Army accommodated in, 32–3, 79, 81–2, 115–17; converted into convalescent homes or hospitals, 36–7, 80, 81, 89–90, 124; death duties, 42, 79–80, 86, 200, 201; financial problems, 79–81, 97, 200, 202; post-war, 189–92, 195, 196, 207; refugees housed in, 34–6, 80; renting out, 82–3, 96–7, 200, 202;

country houses/estates – *cont.*
  sale of, 18, 200–4; weekend entertaining, 190
Country Life, 23, 24–5, 31, 37, 38, 43–4, 46, 49, 58, 78, 92, 109–10, 121, 122, 127–8, 132, 137, 143, 145, 153, 154, 161, 163, 166, 175, 177, 180, 189, 200
County War Agriculture Committees, 140, 152; Executive Committees, 147
Craiglockhart War Hospital, Edinburgh, 70
Crowborough camp, Sussex, 29, 31
Crypt House Press (Glos.), 51
Cushat, Revd, 38

Daily Express, 22, 28, 71
Daily Mail, 44, 111
Daily News, 141
Daily Telegraph, 39, 197–8; 'Lansdowne Letter', 71
Davies, George Llewelyn, 36
Davies, W. H., 12, 49–50, 168
death duties, 18, 42, 79–80, 86, 200, 201
Death Duties (Killed in War) Act (1914), 86
De La Mare, Walter, 51–2, 67
Dent, Arthur, 32
Dent, Geoffrey, 32, 162, 163, 176
Derby, Earl of, 147
Desborough, Ettie Grenfell, Lady, 39, 86–7, 203
Desborough, Lord, 86
Didbrook (Cotswolds), 21, 76, 90
disabled servicemen, 18, 124, 195; settlement schemes for, 196–200, 207
DORA (Defence of the Realm Consolidation Act), 147
Dott, Mrs Annabelle, 197–8
Drinkwater, John, 12, 47, 49, 51, 55–6, 168
Duchess of Connaught's Canadian Red Cross Hospital, 37
Dudfield, Benjamin and Bruce, 92
Duncombe Park (Yorks.), 33
Dymock village, 54–5

East Knoyle, 90; Wyndham family plot in cemetery, 85
East Knoyle Brownies, 192
Easton Glebe, 22
Easton Lodge and Park (Essex), 22, 33, 34, 189, 201
The Egoist, 'Song: In Wartime', 50
Elsfield Manor (Oxon.), 194–5
Enham (Hants.), 196–7
Ewebank, Florence, 61

Far Oakridge (Glos.), 45, 55, 56
Farjeon, Eleanor, 12, 13, 48, 57
farm labourers, 18, 130, 205, 206; Army recruitment of, 131, 132, 134–5, 136, 138–9, 140; conscientious objectors work as, 62, 63; German PoWs work as, 152–3; soldiers granted furlough to work as, 136, 144–5, 149; Special Agricultural Companies, 148–9; wages and living conditions, 131–3; women, 136–7, 140–4, 148, 149–52, 175–6, 194
Farmer, Mr and Mrs, of Ledington, 48
farming/agriculture, 19, 107, 108, 115, 130–57, 194; and conscription, 138–9, 154–5; damage and losses caused by Army, 133–4; food production, 130–57; in France, 174–9; harvesting, 24–5, 37, 49, 69, 113, 118, 133, 136, 145, 148–9, 152, 153, 155–6; mechanisation, 19, 153–4; Milner Committee, 134–5, 140; plough-up campaign, 17, 133, 147, 148–9, 153–4; post-war fall in prices, 202, 204; price controls, 146, 147–8; requisitioning of horses for Army, 43–4, 133, 134; *see also* food; land
Feilden, Col. Henry Wemyss, 39–40, 73
Fenner, Mr, of Fletching, 43, 138, 143, 156
Feversham, Earl of, 33
The Field, 86, 105–6, 161, 162
Fisher, Alexander, 209
Fitch, Private Arthur, 125
Fitch, Private Dick, 125
Fitch, Mrs Sophie, 125
Fitch, Walter, 125
Fletching (Sussex), 22, 30, 40, 106, 107, 108, 109, 110, 112, 117, 142; casualties, 127, 128–9; entertainment for war-wounded, 124; VTC, 121; women farm workers, 143
Fleury (France), 187
food, 192; imports, 131, 136, 149; price control, 146, 147–8; production of, 130–57; profiteering, 122–4, 145, 146; rationing/shortages, 95–6, 122–4, 134, 145; rising prices, 43, 92, 122, 137, 145; *see also* farming
Forbes, Lady Angela, 87, 90, 100, 204
Forbes, Flavia, 90
Forceville war cemetery, 187
Formidable, HMS, 125
Fowler, Letitia, 89–90
France: devastation of countryside, 169–72, 174, 178, 180, 187; farming in, 174–9;

hunting and shooting banned in (1915), 163, 164; women workers, 175–6; *see also* Western Front

Frank, Sir Howard, 200

Freedman, Rosa, 151

Freeman, John, 50–1

Frost, Elinor, 47–8, 53

Frost, Robert, 12, 24, 45, 47, 48, 49, 50, 53, 57, 72

Fry, Roger, 60

'The Gallows' (home of Abercrombies), 47, 50, 51, 52, 53–4

Galsworthy, John, 16

The Garden, 165, 166, 176

gardening: in the trenches, 161, 165, 167; in war cemeteries, 184–5

Garnett, David ('Bunny'), 59, 60–4

Garsington Manor (Oxon.), 59–60, 64–5, 67–8, 70

Gatcombe House (Isle of Wight), 36

Gell, Hon. Mrs, 84

Georgian Poetry (ed. Marsh), 15, 49, 50–1, 132

Georgian poets, 12, 15, 47–59, 67, 78, 168

Gerbervilliers (Alsace), 176–7

German prisoners of war employed as farm workers, 48, 152–3, 176, 201

German submarine blockade, 134, 136, 145, 149

Gertler, Mark, 59, 60, 66

Gibson, Geraldine, 54

Gibson, Wilfrid, 12, 45, 47, 48, 49–50, 51–2, 53–5, 57, 168; 'The Golden Room', 47; 'war' poems, 54–5

Gill, Eric, 208, 209

Gladstone, Viscountess, 33

Glenconner, Lord, 95

Goathland settlement for disabled officers (Yorks.), 197–8

Gore, Charles, Bishop of Oxford, 64

Gosford House and estate, 77, 79, 80, 82, 87, 88, 91, 93, 95, 101, 104, 190, 198, 199, 203

Graham, William, 97

Grahame, Elspeth, 40

Grahame, Kenneth, 40

Grant, Duncan, 59, 60–4, 66

Graves, Nancy, 205

Graves, Robert, 56, 70, 204–5, 206

Gray, Cecil, 66

Gray, Thomas, 16

Great Leighs (Essex), 27–8, 34–5, 41, 106,

107, 110, 134–5, 140, 153, 206; air raids, 112–14; casualties, 124–5, 126–7, 128; conscription, 138; Lyons Hall, 27–8, 107, 115–16; memorial services, 124–5; special constables, 119–20; war memorial, 207; women farm workers, 140, 141, 142–3, 150–1

Grenfell, Billy, 26, 87

Grenfell, Ettie *see* Desborough Lady

Grenfell, Julian, 26, 86–7; 'Into Battle', 25

Green, J. L., 25

Grover, Mr, butcher of Fletching, 109, 127

Gullane war memorial, 208

Gurney, Ivor, 52, 53–4, 160, 167, 173, 174

Gwynne, H. A. ('Taffy'), 22, 205

Habgood, Captain, 111

Haggard, Rider, 23

Haldane, Lord, 25, 38

Hames, Charles, 189

Hames, Richard, gamekeeper, 98, 102–3, 189

Hames, Wyndham, 102–3

The Happy Warrior, 84

Harbord, Geoffrey, 163, 164

Harbord, Gordon, 163–4

Hardy, Thomas, 57, 68, 169

Hatfield House, 33

Helps, Dr George Crawford, 108, 123

Helps, Pansy, 35–6, 41

Herbert, Nan, 36

Hewlett, Maurice, 210

Hill, Arthur, 184

Horn, Pamela, 134, 138, 148

Horner family, 77, 79, 82, 96–100, 107, 109, 191, 209, 210

Horner, Cicely, 99

Horner, Edward, 25, 26, 31–2, 35, 38, 77, 78, 86, 87, 97, 98–9, 100, 103, 125, 182, 187, 189, 210

Horner, Frances (Lady) (*née* Graham), 25, 35, 38, 39, 77, 82, 87, 96, 97, 99–100, 102–3, 123, 126, 182, 186–7, 191, 192, 193, 209, 210

Horner, George, 109

Horner, Sir John, 25, 82–3, 98, 99, 100, 189, 191, 202

Horner, Muriel, 109, 191–2

horses, 118; requisitioning of, 43–4, 133, 134

hospitals: cottage, 124; country houses converted into, 36, 37, 80, 124; VAD, 124; Winchcombe, 88–9, 90, 91, 93, 100, 101–2

Hudson, Edward, 161
Hudson, Lieut., 207
hunting and shooting, 17, 37, 161–4; post-war, 189–90, 192
Huxley, Aldous, 59
Hyatt, Sgt-Major, 188
Hylton, Lady, 39
Hylton, Lord, 34, 38, 193

Illustrated London News, 165, 176, 185
Imperial War Graves Commission, 75, 181, 183, 185–6
Inge, Dean, 51
invasion scares, 22, 44
Islip (Oxon.), 205

Jekyll, Gertrude, 49
Jekyll, Pamela *see* McKenna
John, Augustus, 60

Katia, Battle of (1916), 93, 94, 101, 188
Kaye-Smith, Sheila, *Little England*, 130, 138–9, 154
Kensington School of Art, 209
Kessingland Grange (Norfolk), 23
Kilmersdon (Somerset), 36; Rifle Association, 38–9
Kipling, Carrie, 73, 141, 182
Kipling, Elsie, 39, 73
Kipling, John, 71, 72, 73, 74, 160, 181–2, 186
Kipling, Rudyard, 23, 28, 39–40, 71–5, 141, 145, 160, 176–7, 181–2, 186, 205–6; 'The Gardener', 185; 'If', 73; 'Mary Postgate', 71–2; 'My Boy Jack', 72
Kitchener, Field-Marshal Lord, 24, 25, 28, 29, 171, 198
Knafferton (East Yorks.), 113
knitting and sewing garments for the troops, 37, 38, 39, 41, 92
Knole Park (Kent), 33

Lacey, Francis, 108
Lamb, Henry, 60
Lambton, George, 189
land: changing ownership of, 18; death duties, 42, 79–80, 86, 200, 201; land holdings for ex-servicemen, 18, 195–6; post-war sales of, 18, 200–2; settlement schemes for disabled servicemen, 196–200; taxation, 200; Underdeveloped Land Duty, 79; wartime requisitioning of, 17, 115, 133–4; *see also* farming

Land Settlement (Facilities) Act (1919), 196
Last, Harry, Stanway head keeper, 96, 188
Lawrence, D. H., 59, 60, 65–6, 72; *Lady Chatterley's Lover*, 66; *The Rainbow*, 66, 91; *Women in Love*, 66
Lawrence, Frieda, 59, 60, 66
Lear, Revd Edward and Mrs, 109, 125, 188–9
Ledwidge, Francis, 17
letters home from the front, 42–3, 111–12, 126–7
Lewis, Wyndham, 66
Light, Bert, 40
Lister, Charles, 26, 179–80
Little Easton, 22
Little Iddens, 47–8
Little Leighs (Essex), 194
Lloyd George, David, 135, 146, 152
Lollingdon Farm (Berkshire), 159
Londonderry, Lady, 137
Long, Captain Arthur, 125–6
Long, Percy, 114, 188
Long, Walter, 27, 28, 139
Longleat, 36, 193, 203
Longniddry Settlement (East Lothian), 198–200
Lonsdale, Earl of, 27, 28
Loos, Battle of, 15, 87, 186
Lowinsky, Thomas, 190
Lucas, Lord, 36
Lucases, Misses, of 'Bramblehurst', Ashurst Wood, 111–12
Lugard, Lady, 33
Lushington, Captain, 181
Lusitania, 85
Lutyens, Edwin, 49, 184, 185, 186, 191; Mells war memorials, 209, 210; 'Stone of Remembrance', 186
Lyons Hall, Great Leighs (Essex), 27–8, 107, 134; army camp at, 115–16
Lyons Hall Farm, 135, 141
Lyttleton, Alfred, 81
Lyttleton, Hon. Mrs Alfred, 33

McInnes, Angela (later Angela Thirkell), 100
McIntosh, Katherine, 206–7
McKenna, Pamela (*née* Jekyll), 191
McKenna, Reginald, 191
Mainwood, Lily, 109
Manchester Guardian, 49
Mann, Mrs, baker's wife of Little Leighs, 194

Manners, Lord and Lady (of Avon Tyrrel), 41
Manners, Lady Diana, 25, 32, 41, 94
Manners, John, 41
Manners, Letty *see* Charteris
Manners, Lady Marjorie, 25
Manners, Lady Violet, 25
Mansfield, Katharine, 59
Maresfield Park army camp, 29, 116–17, 138, 160
Marsh, Edward, 16, 49, 50, 52, 54, 163; *Georgian Poetry* edited by, 15, 49, 50–1
Mary, Princess, 152
Maryon-Willson family of Searles, 108
Masefield, John, 14, 16, 159, 168; *The Battle of the Somme*, 159; *The Old Front Line*, 159
Mediterranean Expeditionary Force, 111
Mells (Somerset), 25, 78–9, 82, 86, 95, 96–100, 102–3, 105, 107–9, 125–6, 160, 188–9, 191–2; amateur theatricals, 109, 125, 189; coal mining, 107–8, 125; Manor House, 38, 78–9, 82–3, 98, 109, 159, 191; memorial service, 125–6; new council houses, 191–2; sale of estate, 202; village, 35–6, 41, 43, 78–9, 107–9, 114, 123, 125–6, 188–9; war casualties, 125–6; war memorials, 209–10; Women's Institute, 96, 193
Mells Park (Somerset), 82, 96–7, 102, 125, 189; destroyed by fire (1917), 97–100, 191; rebuilding of, 191, 192
memorial services, 42, 46, 77, 88, 94, 95, 101, 124–6, 127, 188
Messines Ridge, Battle of (1917), 112, 158, 207
Micheldever (Hants.), haymaking near, 151
Michelin Guide to the Battlefields, 186
Middleton, Sir Thomas, 133, 140, 147, 155–6
milk, price control of, 145–6
Milner Committee, 134–5, 140
Milton, John, 16
Milton military depot (Berkshire), 142
Ministry of Food, 147–8
Mitchell, Colin, 'Autumn in England', 54–5
Mitchell, William, 40
Monro, Harold, 49, 51, 57; 'Carrion', 51
Montagu, Edwin, 109
Moore, John, 119, 131
Morning Post, 22
Morrell, Lady Ottoline, 23, 59, 60, 62, 64, 65–6, 68, 74
Morrell, Philip, 59, 60, 64, 65, 67, 74

Morris, William, 16
munitions work, 142
Munnings, Sir Alfred, 210
Munster, Prince, 116
Murry, John Middleton, 59

Nash, John, 24
Nash, Paul, 24, 160, 168, 170, 180
National Agricultural Labourers' and Rural Workers' Union, 132
National Federation of Women's Institutes, 192–4
National Trust, 77
New Church Times, 144
New Numbers, 15, 51, 55, 78
New Statesman, 12
Newent Forage Department (Glos.), 152
Northborough (Lincs.), 118
Northbrook, Earl of, 178
Norton, Harry, 62
Norton St Philips (Somerset), 126

Odlum, Doris, 151
'The Old Nailshop' (Herefordshire), 12, 47, 49, 52, 54
Omega Workshop, 60, 61
Orchardleigh, 210
Orpen, William, 184
Oxford Book of English Verse, 15

pacifists/conscientious objectors, Bloomsbury, 59–66, 67–8, 70
Paget, Lady Muriel, 193
Panshanger, 203
Parker, Mrs, 198
Parliamentary Recruiting Committee, 28
Passchendaele, Battle of, 149, 187, 196
patriotism, 11–16, 25, 55–6, 57, 59, 67, 77, 105–7, 133, 142, 145, 152
pets, Army, 164–5
Pitt, Lieut. Bernard, 159
Poetry Bookshop, Bloomsbury, 49, 51
Ponton, Dorothy, 74
Portland, Duke of, 178
Powell, Anthony, 71
Poyntz House, Mells, 35
Prew, James and Mrs, 35
profiteering, 122–4, 145, 146
Prothero, Rowland (later Lord Ernle), 130, 146–7, 148, 152, 155
Public Schools' Camp, 29
Punch, 34, 38, 121–2, 132, 135, 140, 143, 152, 162, 165; 'Our Village', 106

Quaker War Victims' Relief Fund, 60
Quiller-Couch, Arthur, 15
Quorn Hunt, 189

rationing, 95–6, 122
Rauceby Hall (Leics.), 36
Redesdale, first Lord (Bertie), 202
Redesdale, David Mitford, second Lord, 201–2
refugees, Belgian, 33–6, 80, 83, 102, 176
Ribblesdale, Lord, 43
Ringwood forage dump, 151
Roberts, Field-Marshal Earl, 84
Romsey (Hants.), 118
Rosenberg, Isaac, 181
Ross, Robbie, 68
Rothenstein, William, 16, 45–6, 53, 55, 72, 133
Rothschild, Lord, 27, 28
Royal Agricultural Society, 24, 178; War Emergency Committee, 146
Royal Literary Fund, 49
Royal Navy: Grand Fleet, 23
Rural League, 195
Russell, Bertrand, 59, 60, 64, 68, 70
Rutland, Duchess of, 25
Rutland, Duke of, 200

St Albans, 30–1
St James's Place (No. 23), Wemyss' London house, 79
Salisbury Plain, 29–30
Sassoon, Siegfried, 11, 12, 13, 17, 18, 31, 37, 43, 67–71, 104, 159, 163, 167–8, 169, 170, 171, 204; 'Does It Matter', 89; Memoirs of a Foxhunting Man, 71, 163; 'The Wooden Cross', 164
Saunders, Elsie, 40, 43
Saunders, Roberts, 18, 22, 28–9, 30, 37–8, 40, 46, 106, 108, 110, 112, 116–17, 121, 123, 127, 128–9, 137–8, 142, 143, 156, 160, 180
Saunders, Ron, 28, 112
Saunders, Wally, 23
Saunders, William, 29, 112
Scott, Mrs Dawson, 137
Scottish Veterans' Garden City Association, 198–200
Searles (Sussex), 108, 109, 121, 156
Seely, Sir Charles, 36
Seely, Jack, 36
Selborne, Lord, 130, 133, 136, 139
Shakespeare, William, 57

Shaw, George Bernard, 22, 189
Sheffield Park (Sussex), 108, 109, 121
shelling by German cruisers, 43
Shove, Fredegond, 64
Shove, Gerald, 64–5
Shrivenham (Berkshire), village homes for disabled soldiers and sailors in, 197
Sittingbourne camp, 29
Small Holdings (Colonies) Acts (1916/1918), 196
Smith, Major Corbett, 172
Smith, F. E. (Lord Birkenhead), 100
Soames family of Sheffield Park, 108
Somerset Standard, 42, 105, 110, 125
Somme (river/valley), 158, 160, 165, 171, 174; Battle of the, 67, 68, 69, 92, 94–5, 111, 112, 117, 130, 139, 145, 159, 171–2, 174, 182, 184, 186, 196
'Souls' (aristocratic coterie), 39, 195
Special Agricultural Companies, 148–9
special constables, 118, 119–20; night patrols, 120
spies and spy scares, 44–6, 66, 118–19
The Spirit of Man (anthology), 15
Spradbery, Walter, 32
Stanley, Venetia, 109
Stanton village, 76, 88–9, 91, 209
Stanway Cricket Club, 188, 190
Stanway House and estate (Glos.), 21, 26–7, 35, 37, 76–81, 83, 84, 88, 89, 90–4, 95, 100, 101–2, 103, 153, 203; Christmas at, 46, 90–1; food rationing, 25–6; renting out, 190–1; weekend entertaining, 190
Stanway parish church, 78–9, 80; memorial services, 42, 46, 77, 88, 94, 95, 101, 188; war memorial, 208
Stanway village, 76, 78–9, 80, 188, 190; war memorials, 208–9; Women's Institute, 193–4
Stevenson, William John, 109
Stewart, Patrick Shaw, 26
Stoddart, Thomas, 115–16
Stott, Sir Philip, 209
Stracey, Lytton, 59, 60, 62, 67
Stratford, Minnie, 35
Street, A. G., Farmer's Glory, 131
Strickland, Mary (née Charteris), 88, 101, 194
Strickland, Tom, 88, 100
Sturt, George, 15–16
Sunday Pictorial, 90
Sutherland, Duke of, 36

Sutton Valence (Kent), Vanguard Farm, 197
Syms, Private Charles, 111–12

Taplow Court (Bucks.), 39, 87, 203
taxation, landowners', 200
Tearle, Godfrey, 134
Tennant, Bim, 95
Tennant, Edward, 26
Tennant, Jack, 87
Tennant, Mark, 87
Territorial Army, 23–4; East End of London company, 31
Tester, Wally, 18
Tewkesbury, 119; Christmas Fair, 131
Thomas, Edward, 12, 13, 14–15, 16, 17, 24, 45, 47, 48, 50, 53, 56–9, 168, 176; 'As the Team's Head-Brass', 56–7; death of, 59, 180–1; 'Haymaking', 57–8; 'Lob', 58–9; 'The Manor Farm', 57–8; 'A Private', 180; rural essays, 49; *This England* anthology, 57
Thomas, Helen, 12–13, 47, 181
Thombs, Alfred, 96, 101
Thompson, F. M. L., 200
Thornycroft, Hamo, 68–9
Thynne, Ladies Kathleen and Emma, 36
The Times, 51, 68, 70, 94, 98–9, 100, 139, 185, 201
Toddington, 21
Tomsett, Private Arthur, 111
Townsend, James, 42, 46
tractors, 153–4
Tritton family of Lyons Hall, 116, 125, 134–5
Tritton, Captain Alan, 41, 116, 125
Tritton, Joseph Herbert, 27–8, 107, 140, 207
Tritton, Mrs, 116

VAD hospitals, 124; Winchcombe, 88–9, 90, 91, 93, 100, 101–2
Van de Werve family, 35
Vaughan Williams, Ralph, 'Pastoral Symphony', 167
Verdun, 159, 176, 187; Battle of, 91
Verney, Sir Harry, 196
Village Centres Council, 196–7
Vimy Ridge, Battle of (1917), 183
Volunteer Home Defence (VTC), 120–2; Home Defence on Special furlough (agricultural), 149

wages: farm labourers', 131, 133, 205; guaranteed minimum, 146; munition workers', 142; women's, 141, 142, 150
Wantage, Lady, 137
war graves/cemeteries, 75, 179, 180–1, 182, 183–7; monuments and headstones, 185–6, 187
war industrial centres, bombing of, 112–15
war memorials, 76, 126, 128–9, 185–6, 187, 207–10
War Refugees Committee, 33, 36
war work, voluntary, 37–41, 61, 77, 88, 92, 96, 123
Ward, Charles Henry, 126–7
Ware, Sir Fabian, 75, 183–4
Warwick, Daisy, Countess of, 22, 33, 34, 43, 189, 201
Weald of Kent, 11, 18, 168, 197
Webb, Philip, 85
Wedgwood, Eliza, 88–9, 190, 193
Weirleigh, Sassoon's country home, 11, 69, 70, 159
Wells, H. G., 22, 34, 120, 189; *Mr Britling Sees It Through*, 120
Wemyss, Francis Charteris, tenth Earl of, 79, 80, 208
Wemyss, Grace, Dowager Countess of, 88, 90, 92
Wemyss, Hugo Charteris, eleventh Earl of, 26–7, 37, 79–82, 82, 87, 88, 90, 91, 93, 94, 96, 157, 188, 190, 198, 199–200, 203, 207
Wemyss, Mary Countess of, 21, 25, 26–7, 35, 37, 39, 41, 42, 46, 76–104 *passim*, 153, 188, 190, 192, 193–4, 198–9, 203, 207–8, 209
West Wittering (Sussex) 60
Western Front, 158–74; devastation of countryside, 169–72, 174, 178, 180, 187; familiarity of landscape, 159–60, 169, 170; insect and bird life, 166–7, 172–3; hunting and shooting game, 161–3; nearness of England to, 158–9, 170; pets, 164–5; post-war visits to, 186–8; trench-gardening, 165, 167; war graves, 75, 179, 180–1, 182, 183–7
Weston, Joseph, 109
Wheat Commission, 146
Wheatley Act (1924), 205
Williams-Ellis, Clough, 18–19
Williamson, Henry, 174, 187–8; *The Flax of Dream*, 174; *Tarka the Otter*, 174
Wilson, Woodrow, 73

Wilton, 203
Winchcombe VAD Hospital, 88–9, 90, 91, 93, 100, 101–2
Winchcombe parish church, 83
Wingham Engineering Company, 151
The Wipers Times, 166–7
Wissett Lodge (Suffolk), 61–2
Woman Worker, 141
women: farm workers, 136–7, 140–4, 148, 149–52, 175; French farm workers, 175–6; gardeners in war cemeteries, 184–5; munition workers, 142
Women's Defence Relief Corps, 137
Women's Farm Labour Committees, 140–1, 142
Women's Institutes, 96, 117, 123, 192–4
Women's Land Army (WLA), 149–52
Women's Legion, agricultural branch, 137
Women's National Land Service Corps (WNLSC), 142–3, 149
Women's Scientific Co-operative Farm, 197
Woolf, Leonard, 62, 65

Woolf, Virginia, 22, 61, 62–3, 65; *Night and Day*, 62
Wordsworth, William, 15, 16, 49, 159
Wrest Park (Beds.), 36
Wright, Louis Percy, 128
Wright, Louis Walter, 128
Wyke Manor (Worcs.), 207
Wyndham family, 77, 85–6, 96
Wyndham, Edwina, 89
Wyndham, George, 41, 84, 85
Wyndham, George Hereman, 85
Wyndham, Mrs George (Sibell Grosvenor), 85
Wyndham, Guy, 84, 85, 89
Wyndham, Iris, 192
Wyndham, Madeline, 41, 85, 89, 209
Wyndham, Olivia, 89, 90, 192
Wyndham, Percy ('Perf'), 26, 41, 77, 85, 86
Wyndham, Richard, 85–6, 89, 192

Ypres Salient, 82, 149, 155, 158, 160, 166, 171, 176, 194

Zeppelin raids, 43, 61, 112–15, 120, 153–4